W9-BKI-322

God—Mystery—Diversity

Books by Gordon D. Kaufman

Relativism, Knowledge and Faith (1960)
The Context of Decision (1961)
Systematic Theology: A Historicist Perspective (1968, 1978)
God the Problem (1975)
An Essay on Theological Method (1975, 1979, 1995)
Nonresistance and Responsibility, and Other Mennonite Essays (1979)
The Theological Imagination: Constructing the Concept of God (1981)
Theology for a Nuclear Age (1985)
In Face of Mystery: A Constructive Theology (1993)

God

Christian Theology in a Pluralistic World

Mystery

Gordon D. Kaufman

Diversity

Fortress Press / Minneapolis

GOD—MYSTERY—DIVERSITY
Christian Theology in a Pluralistic World

Copyright © 1996 Augsburg Fortress. All rights reserved. Except for brief quotations in critical articles or reviews, no part of this book may be reproduced in any manner without prior written permission from the publisher. Write: Permissions, Augsburg Fortress, 426 S. Fifth St., Minneapolis, MN 55440.

Biblical quotations, unless otherwise noted, are from the New Revised Standard Version Bible, copyright © 1989 by the Division of Christian Education of the National Council of the Churches of Christ in the United States of America. Used by permission.

Cover design: Cheryl Watson, Graphiculture
Text design: David Lott
Author photo: © Bradford F. Herzog

Library of Congress Cataloging-in-Publication Data

Kaufman, Gordon D.
    God, mystery, diversity : Christian theology in a pluralistic
  world / Gordon D. Kaufman.
        p.   cm.
    Includes bibliographical references and index.
    ISBN 0-8006-2959-0 (alk. paper)
    1. Theology, Doctrinal. 2. Theology—Methodology.
  3. Christianity and culture. 4. Christianity and other religions.
  5. Religious pluralism—Christianity. I. Title.
  BT75.2.K37 1996
  230—dc20   95-25882
                                                            CIP

The paper used in this publication meets the minimum requirements of American National Standard for Information Sciences—Permanence of Paper for Printed Library Materials, ANSI Z329.4-1984.

Manufactured in the U.S.A.   AF 1-2959

00   99   98   97   96   1   2   3   4   5   6   7   8   9   10

Contents

Part Four: Religious Truth as Pluralistic

In memory of Karolyn

MYSTERY, UNDERSTANDING, DIVERSITY

Our attempts to understand human existence and the world
are made against a background of uncomprehended Mystery.

Attempts to understand
    employ inventions of pictures or patterns or stories,
        of orderings and unifyings
    that hold together the infinity of particularities,
        the infinity of complexities.

Attempts to understand are made possible by the prior attempts
        to understand of countless earlier generations —
    their creation of languages and other forms of symbolization;
    their development of complex modes of thinking and reflection;
    their establishment of communities and institutions that
        support and enhance a rich social and cultural life.

Understanding is always some particular person's
        or group's achievement,
    and from other vantage points may seem
        inadequate, incomplete, misleading, prejudiced;
    when we are compelled to accept such understandings
        against our will,
    they become repressive, oppressive.

Our attempts to understand human existence and the world
        can be liberating
    only if we understand and accept these limitations
        of all our attempts to understand,
    only as we learn to live in community with
        those who seem to us so alien.

Preface

In 1975 the first edition of my *Essay on Theological Method*—in which I argued that Christian theology is, and always has been, an activity of "imaginative construction" by persons and communities attempting to set out a comprehensive and coherent picture of humanity in the world under God—was published. In the following academic year (1976–77) I served as a visiting professor at the United Theological College in Bangalore, India. This gave me an opportunity to test, for the first time in a nonwestern setting, the conception of theology that I had sketched in that small book. The openness and freedom to move in new directions encouraged by the notion of imaginative construction proved liberating for many of my students at the college, who had felt bound to highly westernized versions of Christian faith. It also freed me, in my contacts with representatives of nonwestern religious traditions, from the burden of attempting always to defend traditional Christian dogma. I was led instead to listen and learn from these others with whom I was in dialogue and to consider the implications their views might have for reformulation of the Christian message in ways more suited to the Indian sociocultural and religious world. The conception of theology, and the way to do theology, to which I had become increasingly committed in the previous four or five years showed itself pertinent not only to the situation of Christianity in the West: it also seemed to help Indian Christians in their attempts to contextualize their own faiths more adequately. Moreover, it opened doors to stimulating and creative conversation with representatives of non-Christian religious (and secular) communities.

During this stay in India I wrote two articles dealing with some of these matters, publishing them both under Indian auspices. Revised versions of these essays were later included in my book, *The Theological Imagination: Constructing the Concept of God*;[1] and, with further revision and updating, they now appear as Chapters 1 and 2 in this book. These essays represent my first attempts to come to terms publicly with some of the issues raised, for Christian faith and theology, by our growing consciousness today of the significance of the radically pluralistic character of human sociocultural and religious existence. The original version of much of what appears here as Chapter 3 was written in Japan in 1983 as a lecture to be presented to audiences of Christians, Buddhists, and others interested in interreligious dialogue; this lecture set out, for the first time in public, my approach to the question of interreligious dialogue. I have continued to reflect on and write essays and lectures on these matters over the years, and I have also participated rather continuously in interreligious dialogue groups—Buddhist/Christian and Jewish/Christian/Muslim—during the past decade. As a result of this attention to our human religiously plural situation, I have become convinced of the importance to Christian faith and theology of the existence of a wide range of religious traditions around the globe, and I have gradually tried to articulate this growing sensibility in articles and lectures in quite diverse places.

This book brings together a sampling of some of these materials in what I believe is a fairly coherent statement about the place and tasks of Christian theology in today's culturally and religiously plural world. Many of the articles collected here have been previously published in an earlier form. These have all been revised (some drastically) to conform more adequately to my present theological understanding, and to enable them to fit together into a coherent theological statement. At some points, however, the differences between my present views and those I held while writing some of the earlier articles (dating back to the '70s) are substantial, making it difficult to update the earlier text. In such cases I have let the main lines of the original text stand and have indicated in footnotes the respects in which these formulations do not represent adequately the theological position I now hold. I have given the dates of original publication (or of writing, in the case of previously unpublished materials) in footnotes on the first page of each chapter, making it easy to ascertain just when the ideas in that chapter were initially worked out.

Chapters 4, 6, and 7—which sketch the core of the reconstruction of Christian theology demanded (in my view) by our present experience and understanding of religious pluralism—are based on the Nathaniel W. Taylor Lectures given at Yale Divinity School in October, 1995. I am grateful to Dean Thomas Ogletree and the Divinity faculty for the invitation to deliver these lectures (thus providing me with the opportunity to think through these ideas in this way), and for the warm hospitality extended to me and my wife on the occasion of their delivery at Yale. The basic theological standpoint expressed in those lectures—and in this volume as a whole—has been worked out in a much fuller way in my recent book, *In Face of Mystery: A Constructive Theology*;[2] and many of the ideas found here are based upon arguments developed more fully there. In this book, however, I have focused the entire discussion on the implications this basic theological standpoint has for our understanding of religious and cultural diversity. In so doing I have also sought to show the significant impact my growing appreciation of the significance of non-Christian religious traditions has had on my own theological thinking.

The issues raised by religious pluralism for Christian theology are being increasingly discussed today, and a number of important ways of thinking about these questions have been proposed. In this book I have, for the most part, not attempted to take up these various positions, but have concentrated on articulating a stance somewhat different from any currently on the table, one which (I think) deserves wider circulation and discussion. I hope this volume will prove to be a significant contribution to this important ongoing conversation.

The Introduction and Part One of this book set the stage for what follows by sketching the conception of Christian theology with which I work and the implications of the present widespread consciousness of religious and cultural pluralism for theology and its tasks. In Part Two, then, we turn to some central Christian themes—the understanding of human existence (Chapters 4–5), the concept of God (Chapter 6), and the interpretation of Christ (Chapter 7). Reconstructions of each of these are proposed, in light of theological questions raised by the fact of human diversity as well as by the enormous social, political, and economic problems we all face, as we seek to live together on our rapidly shrinking planet. Part Three is based on some sets of papers and comments prepared for or presented in dialogue with Buddhist scholars on different occasions. It gives, I hope, some sense of the sort of concrete issues Christian theologians face as they move into direct encounter with articulate representatives of other faiths and shows also how this sort of dialogue can stimulate surprisingly novel theological reflection (for example, in the chapter on "God and Emptiness"). Part Four brings the book to conclusion with some wider reflections on what I call a "pluralistic" or "dialogical" conception of religious truth, a way of thinking about truth that responds, in my view, to the new possibilities opened for us by our contemporary experience of human diversity in an ever more intraconnected and intradependent world.

Although it is Christian *theology*—Christian thinking, in our pluralistic world, about the symbols of faith—with which we are primarily concerned in this book, I want to make it clear that I regard what is written here as itself an expression of Christian faith. In the Preface to *In Face of Mystery* I attempted, under four headings, to give some sense of the faith and piety that inform my theological reflection; and it may be well to conclude this Preface by mentioning these again:

(a) my deep sense of the ultimate mystery of life; (b) my feeling of profound gratitude for the gift of humanness and the great diversity which it manifests; (c) my belief (with this diversity especially in mind) in the continuing importance of the central Christian moral demand that we love and care for not only our neighbors but even our enemies; and (d) my conviction (closely connected with this last point) that the principal Christian symbols continue to provide a significant resource for the orientation of human life.[3]

This present book, like that earlier one, I regard as an expression of my piety toward that ultimate mystery which we all confront. In the course of many aeons of time there has emerged out of this mystery a tension or movement in the world toward humanization, even humaneness; and this can only call forth from us humans our deep gratitude and profound respect. We really do not know just what this all means, however, for when we seek understanding of these matters, we find ourselves up against the very limits of our knowledge—the ultimate mystery of things. In my opinion it is of great importance, in this situation, that we affirm strongly the radically pluralistic character of our human existence, and that we learn to appreciate sympathetically the many different religious (and secular) faith-perspectives in and by means of which we humans, in the course of our long journey on planet Earth, have sought to gain understanding of ourselves and to find our proper places in the world.

Christian faith and the Christian symbol-system are one family of these faith-perspectives. In this book I seek to think through and to sketch briefly what seems to me required of this family today: we need to work out, and commit ourselves to, a Christian stance fully appreciative of the religiously and culturally pluralized world within which we live. To do so, we need to search our traditions for whatever resources they may offer to illuminate this situation, thus helping to provide orientation as we seek to live appropriately within it. But we also need to go beyond this, moving forward with whatever reconception and reconstruction of Christian symbols and praxis are demanded of us today. I have sought to make suggestions here on these several fronts. In doing so, I have tried to keep in mind, and I hope my readers will as well, that such attempts at theological retrieval and construction should never make claims to finality. They are rather, at best, serious proposals made in face of the ultimate mystery that confronts us all.

In preparing this text for publication, as well as in countless other ways, I have received much help from Maggie Stanley, the Theology Department secretary at Harvard Divinity School; I want to make clear my deep gratitude for the things she does for me. I am also indebted to Michael West, my editor at Fortress Press, for thoughtful suggestions about the organization of the materials in this volume, for his careful editing of the text, and for the many ways he helped to facilitate a comfortable relationship with the Press. Alan Revering prepared the indexes, and to him also sincere thanks are due.

Introduction

The Vocation of Theology

How should Christian theology be done today? Can it be regarded as a calling to a special task in the world, a *vocation*? If so, what sort of vocation is this? Is it a vocation that, because of the sufficiency of its own resources, is quite properly led to ignore or turn away from unfamiliar religious and cultural traditions? Or does theology have an internal dynamism driving it to open itself to ever wider circles of human life and meaning? Four somewhat different ways to explore these questions suggest themselves: a historical approach; that of the study of religion; of philosophy; and then, finally, an approach through what seems directly implied by the term *theology* itself. Let us consider these in turn.

I

One might argue that the question of what theology is—and thus the question of what kind of vocation theology might be—can best be answered historically. *Theology*, after all, is a word in the English language, and it can be understood only in that historical context; and the vocation of Christian theology (as I suggest we consider it here) is an activity or calling that developed in western culture, in the context of western religious and educational institutions and intellectual disciplines. The subject matters with which this theology deals, the problems it faces, the methods it has devised—all of these emerged in western history. Realities of the sort with which we are here concerned, it can be argued, have no other being or meaning than that found in their history. To understand what this word means, then, and to grasp what sort of vocation theology might be, what

This chapter is a revised version of a lecture, "Theology as a Public Vocation," originally published in *The Vocation of the Theologian*, ed. T. W. Jennings, Jr. (Philadelphia: Fortress Press, 1985), 49–66. Though my concern in this chapter is principally with the vocation of specifically Christian theology, the term "theology" is also frequently used here in a more generalized sense. Used with permission.

sort of intellectual discipline is involved here, we should begin historically, attempting to see what these *have been* in the past. We must engage in studies of theological language, theological ideas, theological problems and methods, to answer our question about theology as a vocation; and these will enable us to see what theology has been in the past, and thus, presumably, what it is.[1]

A strictly historical investigation of theology, however, is not really sufficient for our purposes here. For it can tell us only what theology has been, how it has developed; it cannot tell us either what theology is now, or what it might be, or should become, in the future. And these questions are just as important for ascertaining the nature and possibilities of theology as historical questions. Indeed, if we are asking about theology as a vocation that one might choose to enter, they are more important. Our investigation of theology must, thus, extend beyond the mere gathering of historical knowledge. What sort of further moves should be made?

The relatively new discipline of religion studies may suggest itself as helpful here. Christian theology (as suggested above) is often understood as a (largely) western mode of religious reflection. Perhaps if we break out of the parochialness (of our western religious traditions) to a consideration of human religiousness generally, taking note of the place that reflection has had in other traditions, we will be in a better position to understand not only what theology has been but what it might now become. There is much to commend this approach to our question. As we shall see at many points in this book, the role in human life played by religious symbolism, and by critical reflection on and development of that symbolism, throws important light on the basic human significance of theological reflection; and thus on the role that theology can play in human affairs.

But religion studies, like historical studies, are fundamentally descriptive in character. They can tell us much about the place that intellectual reflection has had in the various religious traditions, thus bringing to light uses and meanings of theology that we might otherwise overlook; but they have no way of moving beyond this descriptive work to the development of criteria and standards for refining and reforming theological reflection. Religion studies, no more than history, can present us with a new vision—or even just a proposal—of what theology might be, or should become, in the future. To the extent they attempt to do that—to the extent they attempt to provide us with a normative understanding of "thinking about God" (*theo-logy*)—they must make critical and systematic assessments of the meaning(s) of the symbol "God," assessments that do not reduce this meaning to something prescribed by some general theory of symbolism. That is, they must engage directly in something quite close to what is ordinarily regarded as theological analysis and reflection. As we shall see, this symbol makes extraordinarily universal and comprehensive claims for itself, defying reduction to or subsumption under any alien or independent analytical scheme or intellectual categories.

This comes out most clearly, perhaps, if we turn to philosophy, to see whether that most comprehensive of human intellectual disciplines may not provide the best standpoint from which to define the proper place and role of theology. For our purposes here it does not matter whether we understand philosophy in the classical sense of metaphysics, as dealing with the question of reality as such; or in the more modern sense, as a second-order critical discipline reflecting on the claims to knowledge of the other sciences, defining their proper arenas, their methods and their limits, and clarifying their interrelations with each other; or in that most contemporary way, as critically examining the various "language games" in which human beings are engaged, ascertaining the rules of each such game and determining how it is properly played. In each of these cases, philosophy seems to present a kind of overview or perspective—whether on reality as a whole or on human life and some of its activities—which should enable us to assign theology its proper place and role. And with that in mind, we might be able to say something about the vocation of theology.

I do not want in any way to disparage the importance of such philosophical inquiries and overviews. Certainly, to the extent that theology wants to claim that God is *real*, it must take metaphysical inquiries into what this sort of contention means and involves quite seriously. And to the extent that the theologian claims to *know* something about God, he or she must attend carefully to the epistemologists' studies about what can properly count as knowledge, how various knowledges are gained, what their possibilities are and what their limits, how they can be distinguished from mere subjective opinions or beliefs. Further, inasmuch as theologies are, after all, *talk*—talk about God (as well as other subjects)—theologians do well to listen carefully to what linguistic philosophers have to say about the "grammars" of our languages. There is a great deal to be learned from philosophy about what theology is or can be, and thus about the proper tasks of theology and the methods that theologians employ. And this will certainly bear on the sort of vocation that theology can be and how that vocation can best be carried out.

But a finally authoritative answer to our question cannot be found here either. Although philosophy has a certain legitimate superintendency over other human disciplines and activities, it would be a mistake to grant it ultimate authority over theology. At most, we can allow that theology and philosophy stand in a kind of dialectical relation to each other. Philosophers' questions about the nature of reality as such and about the possibilities and the limits of human knowledge and language certainly bear significantly on theological work. But the central concern of theologians will be rather different from that of philosophers: theology—as the word itself suggests and as historical researches would confirm—seeks to attend directly to our thinking about *God*, our speaking of (and to) *God*. That is, the inquiries of theologians are directed toward that ultimate point of reference in terms of which all else—all reality, all knowing, all speaking, all experiencing, indeed all philosophy!—is to be understood. In attempting to speak and think of God, theologians seek to articulate that in terms of which everything else without exception must be grasped to be understood rightly.

In western religious traditions God has been conceived as "the creator of the heavens and the earth," "the lord of history," "the ground of being," "the source of all that is," "the absolute, unconditioned reality," "that than which nothing greater can be conceived," "the Alpha and the Omega." These are very diverse modes of expression with quite distinct meanings, but in one respect they are all different ways of making essentially the same point: that in using the word "God" we intend to refer to that behind or beyond which we cannot go in any experience, thought, or act of imagination. We mean that which circumscribes and limits all else, that which relativizes every other reality (including especially, of course, us humans and our thinking), that which is, therefore, the ultimate point of reference in terms of which everything must be understood if it is to be understood rightly. If then, theology—disciplined thinking about God—is to be true to itself and its subject matter, it will have to be in and through its exploration of that very subject matter (the question of *God*) that it finally comes to understand itself; not in terms that other disciplines such as philosophy or history or religion studies might assign to it. Since what we mean by God, what we can say about God, has always been the special task central to the work of theology, since the significance of our talk about God and the possibilities and the limits of that talk are issues that virtually define theology, it seems clear that the most straightforward way to ascertain the kind of vocation theology is would be to enter directly into theological work itself.

Theology (like philosophy) is a *reflexive* activity. Unlike disciplines such as chemistry or sociology or history of music, which study objects other than themselves, theology and philosophy (in studying their objects) must develop theories of themselves as well as of their objects, since they are themselves included among the objects they are trying to understand. Any philosophical theory of reality or of knowledge that does not or cannot explain what sort of reality philosophy itself is, and what sort of knowledge it attains, is obviously deficient. Every adequate philosophy must include a theory of itself. Similarly theology: any interpretation of that ultimate point of reference in terms of which all else is to be understood, which does not include an explanation or interpretation of theology itself in terms of that point of reference, is clearly deficient. Theology, like philosophy, must include a theory of itself in connection with its theory of God. And, by the same token, philosophy and theology will each include theories of the other; they are, thus, dialectically related to each other. Each can throw light on the other, but neither dares abdicate to the other its responsibility of self-direction and self-definition. Each must understand itself as having a significant autonomy and freedom in relation to all other disciplines.

But what do any of us know about the ultimate point of reference in terms of which everything is to be understood? that which grounds this vast universe and gives us thus a more profound understanding of it? Doubtless there are ancient myths both in and out of the Bible that speak of such matters, but can thoughtful persons today even venture so much as an opinion on such things? Theology attempts to deal with a subject matter that seems in principle inaccessible to us, in principle unknowable. Philosophy at least, even in its most pretentious forms, attempts only to deal with things in so far as we can know them; theology, however, attempts to speak of, to grasp rationally, a transcendent or ultimate point of reference. Surely human beings should confine themselves to more modest vocations.

II

However difficult, even impossible, the theological task might seem, it is one that should not be put aside. We are beings who cannot but seek to understand and to know, and this not just because of the pleasure or the joy we gain through these activities: we are beings who must *act*, agents who must make decisions and take actions that affect ourselves and others—this day, this week, the next few years, possibly for a lifetime and more. There is no way we can avoid deciding, avoid acting, avoid taking responsibility. We are, as Jean-Paul Sartre has said, "condemned to be free." But we are able to decide and to act only if we know something about our own powers and potentialities, about what we are able to do in this particular situation. Moreover, we are able to make decisions only if we have the capacity to imagine different possible actions that we might perform; only if we can envisage the consequences of each such act with some reliability; and only if we have criteria enabling us to assess the several possibilities available to us, so we can choose which to actualize. In short, only if we have a considerable knowledge of the world and of the possibilities open to us in the world, and knowledge about ourselves and our potentialities—as well as knowledge of those others roundabout us with whom we are interacting—will it be possible for us to decide and act at all. Knowledge is not a dispensable luxury for us humans, even if we are completely illiterate and among the humblest of the humble. Some sense of the world, of the human place and human possibilities within the world, and of our own position in all of this, is needed by each of us.

For the most part, it has been in and through the human imagination's creation of religious myths and traditions that pictures of the world, and stories of the human place and task within that world, have been produced, gradually becoming promulgated throughout whole societies over many generations. These pictures and stories have been many and various in human history, and we cannot begin to examine them here. I want to point out, however, that such pictures and stories are indispensable to human beings because of our need for orientation in life. Apart from them, human action, and the taking of responsibility for our action and our lives, would be impossible. I am not claiming that these pictures or stories are accurate, that human beings in their various religious traditions have come to know the *truth* about the world and about themselves. I am saying, rather, that these imaginative constructions are indispensable to human beings. We must have a worldview, a conceptual scheme, within which to order all of the "blooming, buzzing confusion" of life (as William James called it), or we will not be able to live and act at all. Our great religious traditions have provided us with such world-pictures.

With this perspective, which the historical and the sociological study of religion brings us, we can see more clearly the role and task—and the human significance—of theology, with its concern for an ultimate point of reference in terms of which all else can be understood. Christian theology is a discipline in which attempts are made to grasp and to understand and to set forth a picture of the world and of human life that has *God* as its focal center, and which seeks, thus, to see and understand all else in relation to God and God's activity. The vocation of theology, thus, like reflection in other religious traditions, seeks to serve the human need to find orientation in the world and in life. Not simply immediate or proximate orientation for this present moment of experience or this particular small decision—such orientation might be provided by pop psychology, by prejudice, or simply by the regularities of custom or habit. Rather, Christian theology is concerned with that underlying human task of finding orientation for the long haul, for life as a whole, orientation for one's children and one's children's children, for one's whole society, indeed for all of humanity. Is orientation of that order and magnitude available to us? How can claims about it be assessed and by what criteria criticized? How can they be transformed for greater adequacy? These are questions to which all religious traditions address themselves (at least implicitly), issues that the intellectual reflection and the search for understanding within those traditions have pursued. Although in earlier periods of western history philosophy also sought to address these questions, today it is preeminently theology that continues to concern itself with them; and it is to these issues, therefore, that one must be prepared to give oneself if one takes up theology as a vocation.

For those in Jewish, Christian, and Muslim traditions the question about human orientation in life is framed largely in terms of what H. Richard Niebuhr has called "radical monotheism."[2] For this perspective meaning and value and being are not diffused into several different foci, into a variety of gods or powers. Rather, they are all focused in one central point—God—which is taken as the ultimate point of reference for understanding everything: every value, every experience, every desire, every act of imagination. In a monotheistic world-picture everything is brought together into a single ultimate order and thus does not lie under threat of disintegration into unrelated multiplicities and finally chaos.[3] By "God" is meant that—whatever it might be—which holds together in a significant unity all of this multiplicity and richness of experience and reality; God is that from which it all ultimately came and to which it all must go. But God has been more than simply the Alpha and Omega of life. In these traditions God is seen as a fundamentally moral reality, one characterized by justice and goodness, mercy and truth, as well as by the power to create and to destroy. So human moral existence also, and our pursuits of value and truth and meaning, are to be understood as grounded in God and oriented properly only in relation to God. Through encouraging us to focus attention on the ultimate unified grounding of all dimensions of existence and all creatures of the world, monotheistic heritages enable women and men to see life "steadily and whole" (to use again the words of William James). It is the special vocation of theology, working with its great symbol "God," to specify what this can mean for our times, our lives, our problems today. That is, it is theology's task to consider how "God" is to be understood today, and what it is to understand ourselves as "under God."

If Christian theology is centrally concerned with the question of God, as I am contending here, and if that concern means that theologians must make themselves responsible ultimately to God, then the major error or aberration or confusion into which they may fall is idolatry, giving primary attention and loyalty to objectives and goals and values other than or less than God. Several idolatries are especially tempting to those working in

theology today. Serving the church, for example, is undoubtedly of importance to Christian theologians. But this must never become theology's driving motivation: that would be putting an idol in the place where only God
can rightly be. The needs of the nation or one's ethnic group, major social
problems—racism, sexism, classism, poverty, injustice, and the like—may
quite properly engage the interests and energies of theologians. But none
may become all-consuming. The interests of the university in, for example,
the impartial pursuit of truth, the values expressed in literature and the
arts, in history and philosophy and the sciences, are all worthy and significant concerns of theologians today. But these interests and demands that
arise in the university setting of much theological work also must not be
allowed to divert theologians from their central responsibility: to deal seriously and critically with the question of God. The principal standard of
judgment with which theological work should be pursued is not the question of truth and falsity, or good and evil, or right and wrong, or beauty
and ugliness, however important each of these contrasts may be: it is the
one implicit in the conceptual distinction of God from the idols, a standard
that takes up into itself all these others, illuminating the place of each in
human life and yet relativizing them all in light of that which is ultimate.

Since the central criterion of judgment for theologians is that ultimate
point of reference in terms of which all else is to be understood, theology
is—at least potentially—critical theory par excellence.[4] Theologians must
not allow themselves to be diverted from that fundamental task and
responsibility. Failing to be fully critical, including especially failing to be
fully self-critical—that is, critical of all their own concepts and symbols,
their procedures, objectives, traditions, critical of the institutions and the
social structures that support them—is disastrous for the theological enterprise and can make it into a dangerously destructive activity. To take up
the task of reflecting critically on God and the idols, then, and to understand how that reflection applies not only to our world and our society but
also to ourselves and all our concerns, is to begin thinking theologically. To
undertake this as one's life work is to accept theology as one's vocation.

III

It would be a mistake to suppose that the question of God—of the ultimate point of reference—can be dealt with completely abstractly. One
always begins such reflection with a concrete and particular conception of
God, a conception mediated by a particular tradition of religious life and
thought. It is because the conception presented by tradition has been
found meaningful and nourishing in some significant way that the symbol

of God first grasps one as worthy of attention and respect, and even of the devotion of a lifetime. It is out of and on the basis of one's Baptist or Presbyterian past, one's Christian or Jewish or Muslim experience, or perhaps on the basis of wider cultural or philosophical reflection and literature that calls attention to theological issues, that one first comes to think about the question of God at all and is impressed with its import and urgency. And so we are, first of all, Christian or Jewish or Muslim theologians, Roman Catholic or Orthodox, Protestant or humanist theologians, attempting to understand who or what God is in the light of those traditions which have formed us.

There is, however, a dialectical tension between the tradition that has formed us, giving us our conception of God, and the *ultimacy* of this point of reference, of which tradition has made us aware. Theologians seek to dig ever deeper into what tradition has given them, in order better to understand the God mediated through it. But at the same time, they may—in light of the claims of that God to which tradition presents itself as responding—become increasingly sensitive to the faults and failures of this tradition itself. Although Christian theologians must drink deeply from the Bible and the best of biblical scholarship, and from the many great Christian writers of past and present, they must simultaneously learn, thus, to take up a critical stance over against all of these in the name of that very God of whom these also had attempted to speak. An outstanding example in recent years of the way in which the Christian tradition continues to nourish such criticism of itself, and its most sacred documents and concepts, is to be found in the growing consciousness—responding to feminist critiques—that it is theologically intolerable to continue to employ, almost exclusively, male gender language and images of God in Christian worship, reflection, and speech. That such radical criticism of the tradition, reaching all the way back to its biblical roots, can appear and be taken seriously, is one of the most encouraging signs of the continuing vitality of theological reflection in our time. Christian consciousness of the significance of the diverse forms of human religiousness around the globe has been undergoing similar radical transformation in recent decades. It is this changing self-understanding of Christian faith, in face of today's religious and cultural pluralism, that provides the central theme of this book.

Theologians cannot properly do their work without continuous nourishment from the theological traditions they have inherited; and they must, thus, regularly attend to ongoing scholarship in biblical studies and the history of Christianity. But their responsibilities today also require significant encounter and dialogue with representatives of other religious and secular perspectives, and attention to historical and comparative studies of religion and culture—as well as to insights and concepts made available by the social and natural sciences, history, and philosophy. It is the God of all the universe ("the creator of the heavens and the earth") that theology is seeking to understand and to interpret; and this cannot be done without some grasp of the way in which the world as a whole, and humankind within this world, are understood in the best knowledges available to us. Today, if one is to take up theology as a vocation, one must have an interest in the whole wide range of human experience, knowledge, and imagination—in its full religious and cultural diversity—and one must be prepared to bring this all into relationship with that ultimate point of reference that we call God. As we do this, we must regularly remind ourselves of another matter: modern poets, philosophers, psychologists, literary and social critics have much to teach us about the *self*-deception and ideological self-justification to which the human spirit so often falls prey in its intellectual and other activities. These insights, also, must be incorporated into the self-critical self-consciousness of the theologian who, with such grandiose concerns, can easily slip into exceedingly destructive idolatries. In the vocation of theology there must be an openness to new insight and new understanding from any and every perspective. There is no room for parochial preference for one's own tradition or community or one's own familiar values and ways of thinking. All must be approached, examined, and assessed critically, with an eye to that ultimate point of reference, God, in terms of which each nuance and each idiosyncrasy can be seen in proper perspective.

Theology understood in this way, it should be clear, is an almost impossible task; and no one can claim to be, in the proper sense of the word, a theologian. Nevertheless, orientation for human life remains as indispensable today as it ever has been, however difficult it may be to obtain or define. The repeated and persistent shipwrecks to which our all-too-human idolatries inevitably bring us make careful theological reflection and study urgent. It is important, therefore, to continue seeking to order our world, and our lives within this world, in relationship to that ultimate point of reference (whatever it might be) in terms of which every reality finds its proper place. Our idolatrous anthropocentrism has brought us to near-destruction of the ecological web that sustains life on this planet. Our idolatrous ethnocentrisms and egocentrisms lead to terrible disasters in human life and culture in many places around the globe.

I have said that the theologian's ultimate responsibility is to God and that secondarily, therefore, the theologian has a special responsibility to the traditions out of which "God-talk" emerged and which have nourished it. But these very responsibilities, we can now see, also imply our accountability to all of humankind, to the rest of life on planet Earth, indeed to planet

Earth itself. And all of this together makes it urgent that theologians take much more seriously than we often have in the past the many other religious, cultural, social, and intellectual traditions of humankind. To take up theology as a vocation is to commit oneself to assuming these wide-ranging responsibilities as one's lifework.

IV

Very little has been said in this introductory chapter about the distinctiveness of *Christian* theology. However, I hope it will be clear from what I have said about the significance of tradition that this is not because I regard this as unimportant or because I do not think of myself as primarily a Christian theologian. For Christian faith Christ is regarded as significantly revelatory of that ultimate point of reference to which all else must be oriented, God; and Christian theology, thus, has always concerned itself with the nature, work, and significance of Christ. In this christocentric emphasis, however, Christ should not displace God in the order of theological thinking and valuing. There can be Christ-idolatries, Christolatries and Jesusolatries, as well as other sorts. And the Christian churches have often been guilty of these, particularly in their metaphysical interpretations of the person of Christ and in their not-infrequent claims that outside the sphere of Christ there is no salvation. Jews and Muslims have long insisted that notions of these sorts represent a perverse falling away from and compromise of faith in the one true God. And both Muslims and Jews have suffered (and continue to suffer) much at the hands of Christians, partly because of the fanatical and idolatrous uses to which our Christ symbolism has all too easily lent itself. Today, conscious as we are of the horrors of the Holocaust, we must be especially careful about how we develop our christologies. Our thinking about Christ, if it is to be properly *theological*, must subserve our thinking about God—or it will itself become one more perverse and idolatrous human intellectual activity. Theology is first and foremost "thinking about God," not "thinking about Christ."[5]

I hope it is obvious that the question of misplaced commitments and loyalties in human affairs—what I have discussed here under the rubric of idolatry—is no passing or temporary phenomenon. It is a continuously recurring problem in human life everywhere. The issue, thus, of God and the idols—of those affections and commitments which are fulfilling and redemptive, and those which are corrupting, diseased, and destructive—is still with us and likely to remain with us as long as human communities and individuals are anything like they now are. So the central human issue that generates the problematic to which theology addresses itself is likely to have—unhappily—a bright future ahead.

Does this mean that there will be, far into the future, a vocation for *theologians*—for those who attempt to address this issue with the aid of the symbol "God," bequeathed to us in the West largely by the Judeo-Christian tradition? Doubtless that depends on many factors—sociological, economic, religious, moral, intellectual. In short, it depends on the kinds of societies and cultures, the kinds of human beings, that we become. In this time of great cultural and religious confusion, and of rapidly accelerating social change in directions previously unknown in human history, no one is in a position to prophesy with conviction on this issue. I will venture to say, however, that if theologians do succeed in addressing themselves persistently and with insight to the issue of God and the idols, they will be performing an important service for ongoing human self-understanding, whatever may be the social and cultural and religious developments in the future.

In this chapter I have set out one particular way of conceiving theology as a vocation, largely ignoring other approaches (however valuable they may be). One's vocation becomes truly theological, I have argued, only when and as the issue of God and the idols becomes central to one's work. In this book I shall attempt, with this conception of theology in mind, to articulate an understanding of the growing conviction among Christians that the thoroughly pluralized character of human religious and cultural life must today be interpreted in a much more positive way than has ordinarily been done in the past.

Part One

Christian Theology and Religious Pluralism

For Christian faith, as we noted in the Introduction, the central focus of human life, the ultimate point of reference in terms of which all human existence is to be ordered—all devotion, activity, and reflection—is *God*. The major concern, therefore, that should guide Christian theology is the proper understanding and interpretation of the symbol "God." In this book we are especially interested in exploring how the widespread consciousness today of the significance of religious and cultural pluralism bears on Christian thinking and faith. Hence, in Part One we turn immediately to consider how the understanding of theology will be affected, if we regard this pluralism as a principal characteristic of the context within which theological reflection must now be carried on.

Chapter 1 begins to sort out these issues by noting briefly some of the ways non-Christian religions have been understood theologically, and by taking up the bearing which worldwide historical processes of modernization during recent centuries have on our attempts to think about these matters today. The initial version of this chapter was written in Bangalore, India, during my first extended period out of the West, a time in which I was forced to reflect—in the context of a society in which only a small percentage of the people regarded themselves as Christian—on the meaning of Christian faith in today's wider world. It explores, under those circumstances, my attempt to make judgments about what is central in Christian faith, what more peripheral; and suggests that a "criterion of humanization" is important for assessing various features of today's living religions. Since in many respects I continue to work along the lines first laid down in this article, it poses some major questions to which we will return frequently in the rest of this book. I am deeply indebted to two books by the Indian theologian M. M. Thomas, *Man and the Universe of Faiths* (Bangalore: Christian Institute for the Study of Religion and Society, 1975), and *Salvation and Humanisation* (Madras: Christian Literature Society,

15

1971) for some of the fundamental insights without which the position set forth in this chapter could not have been developed.

The original version of what is here presented as Chapter 2 was also written in Bangalore and was presented to a theological colloquium there in the spring of 1976. It was my attempt to state briefly and cogently how my understanding of theological method (to which I had fairly recently come) as essentially an activity of "imaginative construction" opened up important new possibilities for Christian reflection and Christian life in ("non-Christian") cultures such as India's. With some revisions bringing the articulation of these ideas more clearly into line with my present thinking, it still represents one of the clearest short statements of my views on how theology should be done today, particularly in view of the religiously and culturally pluralized world of which we are becoming increasingly conscious.

Chapters 1 and 2, although originally written in a context in which I was being forced to recognize the parochial character of many of my prior theological assumptions, represent only the starting-point of my attempt to come to terms with the wider issues with which today's religious and cultural pluralism confront Christian faith and theology. My thinking about those matters crystallized further during the next few years, and especially during my next sabbatical (1983–84). In the fall term of that year, my wife and I lived in Kyoto, Japan, for several months, and I was much engaged in discussion and dialogue with Buddhists. I lectured on several occasions under both Buddhist and Christian auspices and published some of the ideas on which I had been working in an article entitled "The Historicity of Religions and the Importance of Religious Dialogue" (*Buddhist-Christian Studies* 4 [1984]: 5–15). This article was later expanded into a larger essay on "Religious Diversity, Historical Consciousness, and Christian Theology," of which the present Chapter 3 is a revised version. This chapter, bringing Part One to a conclusion, states concisely the way in which (in my view) Christian theology must be reconceived and relativized today, in light of our modern/postmodern understanding of human existence as thoroughly historical and our awareness of the significance of its religiously and culturally pluralistic character.

Chapter 1

Christian Theology and the Modernization of the Religions

From the very beginning Christians were so impressed by the power and significance of salvation through Jesus Christ that they were led to make highly exclusivistic claims:

> There is salvation in no one else [than Jesus Christ], for there is no other name under heaven given among mortals by which we must be saved.
>
> (Acts 4:12)
>
> No one knows the Father except the Son and anyone to whom the Son chooses to reveal him.
>
> (Matt. 11:27)
>
> I am the way, and the truth, and the life. No one comes to the Father, except through me.
>
> (John 14:6)

The implication was that saving truth was known to Christians alone, and the church was not long in drawing the conclusion that "outside the church there is no salvation" (Cyprian). The problem of the "righteous pagan" has always been recognized in the churches, of course, but such individuals have usually been understood more as exceptions that proved the general rule. The possibility that other religions, communions, or traditions have access to saving truth was hardly given serious consideration through most of Christian history. Even Judaism, from whom Christians received both their fundamental understanding of God and also their first scriptures, was believed to have forfeited its special place in God's economy through rejecting God's Messiah. In Christian faith alone was genuine salvation for humans to be found.

Through much of their history the churches have been able to maintain variations of this exclusivistic position, and Christian theologies have con-

First published in *Bangalore Theological Review* 8 (1976): 81–118; reprinted in *The Theological Imagination: Constructing the Concept of God* (Philadelphia: Westminster Press, 1981). Used with permission.

fidently regarded themselves as resting on the absolutely secure foundation of God's special revelation, a foundation unavailable to any other religious traditions. But during the past two centuries a steadily increasing pressure from the other great world religions has been felt by Christian theologians. As nonwestern cultures became better known, and it was discovered that profound conceptions of human life were harbored within very different religious traditions, it no longer seemed plausible to regard other religions as totally and completely in error. How, then, was their truth to be understood? How could the finality of salvation through Christ, and of Christian truth, be preserved if it were admitted that other religious orientations knowing nothing of Christ nevertheless knew a significant salvation and truth?

A number of approaches to this question have been suggested, none of them entirely satisfactory. Perhaps the most widely accepted view—with origins going back at least to the second century, and variations formulated by such leading and diverse modern figures as G. W. F. Hegel and F. D. E. Schleiermacher, Karl Barth and Karl Rahner—is the contention that final religious truth lies only within Christian faith, but approximations to or preparations for that truth are found in varying degrees in other religions. This has the advantage of saving the absoluteness or finality of Christian claims while at the same time acknowledging a certain validity to other religious perspectives. But it is an intrinsically unstable position. Exposure to the subtlety and sophistication of religious life and reflection in, for example, Hinduism, Buddhism, or Judaism, makes very pressing the question whether the Christian claim to ultimate superiority over others is not simply special pleading. Moreover, when one examines carefully the interpretation of human life and its fulfillment provided in these other traditions, it becomes increasingly difficult to understand in what sense they really are approximations to the Christian position. Instead they appear to express significantly different conceptions of the human condition and its salvation, conceptions which, in their profoundest formulations, seem to be alternatives to Christian faith more than direct preparations for it.

Perceptions of this sort often lead to some version of religious relativism, such as that formulated (fairly late in his life) by Ernst Troeltsch. According to Troeltsch, the great religions each express the profound and lasting insights into human life and its meaning that have come to light in a particular cultural tradition. Each, therefore, is appropriate to its own culture, but none can claim finality (or even significant relevance) for all of humankind. Christianity, thus, expresses and communicates that truth which is ultimate and saving for westerners; but it has no right, any longer, to claim that it is the mediator of religious truth for all humanity. We live in a culturally plural world, and only a diversity of religious orientations can be fully appropriate to that fact.

This solution to the problem has not proved much more satisfactory than the other. Not only did it deny the proud claims of Christian faith: it went so far as to despair of bringing the diverse truth-claims of the various great religious traditions into significant interconnection with each other. It thus raised pressing questions about whether religions could any longer legitimately claim that *truth* was that with which they were most fundamentally concerned. Thus, relativistic acid ate away at one of the deepest and most precious religious contentions, and in this way further weakened the authority of the religions in what was already a rising tide of secularism and skepticism.

Is there not some way to acknowledge the cultural relativity of each religious tradition but still maintain that in and through the great religions ultimate truth of some sort is to be found? Could one not hold that each of the religions represents partial and relative insight into the ultimate reality and truth for which all are reaching but which none successfully or adequately formulates? A third position maintains that each of the great religions in its own way is attempting to express and cultivate a sense or idea (or experience) of "transcendence" or the "absolute," the "infinite" or "God." Hence, rejecting the exclusivistic and imperialistic claims of each, we can and must learn from them all. On this view, religious relativism does not prove the falsity of the religious enterprise, as skeptical secularists often claim. Rather, it demonstrates the real magnificence and profundity of the religious quest for an ultimate that always finally eludes us. Humanity is deeply religious in its very nature, and it is in religious fulfillment that true human fulfillment lies. Although this position seems to have its roots in Hinduism, especially as articulated by such writers as Vivekananda and Radhakrishnan, it appears to be increasingly appealing to Christian writers, particularly those, like W. C. Smith and John Hick, who are especially concerned about the rising tide of secularism in the modern world. This position, of course, implicitly gives up all claims to the finality or definitiveness of specifically Christian faith.

All these positions, it seems to me, suffer from a common defect: they attempt to resolve an essentially *historical* issue—the problem of properly understanding the claims and tensions and interrelations of various religious faiths with each other—in static or structural, instead of dynamic, terms. In so doing they implicitly presuppose that history has already come to its end, at least with respect to the relation of the various religious faiths to each other; and that it is possible, therefore, to see *now in the present* what the proper and permanent structure of those relationships is.

Whether the claim is that Christian faith is the realization or fulfillment of that to which the other religions are only approximations, or that each religion is to be understood as essentially a ·function of and thus relative to a particular culture, or that human beings are essentially religious in nature and all religion, therefore, is reaching for a transcendent reality which ultimately eludes each tradition, the approach is the same: each of these theories presents us with an interpretation that claims (at least implicitly) to lay bare the permanent and essential structure of human religiousness, and possibly of human nature. But if human existence is a thoroughly historical reality,[1] and religion, like human nature itself, emerges only gradually in history and changes continuously in history, it is a mistake to look for any such permanent structural solution to the question of the relations of the various religions to each other. Rather, our attempts at understanding here—whether philosophical or theological, secular or religious—should themselves be historical in character, in keeping with the reality and the problems we are seeking to grasp. That is, we should see the tensions and the interrelations of the various religions (including, of course, Christianity) as an ongoing historical development—a process in which the issues are not always the same and the relationships not always constant—a development that has come to a certain focus in the modern period and that can be expected to move in new directions in the future.

Our task is to understand as well as we can the present direction and nature of this movement into the future. As with any massive historical development, the attempt to understand what is going on in the present involves some idea of the direction(s) in which the movement is going, and thus some conjecture about the future of the whole process. Understanding of present historical realities is always, in this sense, predictive or prophetic in character, and it is a mistake to think that purely empirical or phenomenological description of them is either possible or sufficient. If it is true that the great religious traditions are historical realities, and that their encounter and struggle with each other is thus to be understood in historical terms, it is surely a mistake in principle to interpret this encounter largely in a static-structural way (as in all the approaches mentioned above). Rather, we must attempt to grasp the dynamic of the historical movement of these faiths; and if we are attempting to develop a theology of religious pluralism, we shall have to try to understand and interpret that movement theologically.

I

What constitutes a theological interpretation of a historical movement? How is a theological interpretation to be distinguished from some other sort of interpretation, say a philosophical, or simply a historical, interpretation? Is there any justification for going beyond strictly historical analysis and conjecture to a theological interpretation of the matter?

One answer to these questions might be that it is for a specific group of persons, for example Christians, that a theological interpretation of something is prepared: it is an interpretation of the pertinent facts in terms of basic Christian beliefs. The purpose of theological interpretation, thus, would be to show what the facts under consideration mean from a Christian point of view, as well as how Christian beliefs are illuminated by those facts. Since many people have Christian commitments, theology's service would be to help make intelligible to such persons the present historical encounter of the great religions.

This conception of theology and its purposes is certainly not to be despised, but it has serious limitations. In the first place, it makes theology into a parochial discipline, an activity of interest largely to Christians. Any claims of theology to be dealing with matters of wider human concern or with general human truth seem to be implicitly given up, and this cuts the intellectual nerve that gives life to the theological enterprise. Second, to regard theology as largely an exposition of the beliefs of Christians (or some other particular group), and the application of those beliefs to a special set of problems or a particular situation, is to assume that the beliefs of religious groups are relatively fixed and stable, that they are readily ascertainable, and, above all, that they are not themselves to be subjected to critical appraisal and reconstruction but are simply to be accepted as the proper basis for "theological interpretation." Certainly it is possible to proceed in this fashion, but doing so only further compromises the intellectual integrity of theology.

However important it may be for religious groups like the Christian churches to engage in interpretive and indoctrinative work of the sort I have just been describing, this is not the conception of theology with which I wish to approach the present encounter of the great religions. It is, I believe, an approach that the present movement of religious history is rendering out of date and misconceived. For it seems to take for granted that religious groupings are fairly stable and easily definable and that they hold to static and fixed bodies of belief which can be readily ascertained. But none of these assumptions is true at the present time, certainly not for the Christian churches. If anything is clear, it is that there is little agreement about what Christian faith involves today and what constitutes proper Christian belief. It might be possible—however difficult—to come to some agreement (through careful historical study) on what defined the several major branches of Christianity in the past, at least in some periods of the past; but almost all such patterns and conceptions are under strong attack in one quarter or another today. Of course, it is always possible to regard some practices and beliefs out of the past as "normatively Christian," and to insist that any deviation from these is a movement away from faith—and religiously conservative parties make just such claims—but all such contentions are in the last analysis arbitrary preferences. Who is to decide what is the "classical" or "normative" form of Christian faith or the Christian church? Why should any particular decision of that sort be acknowledged as authoritative and binding? If anything characterizes the present situation, it is the breakdown of all such claims about Christian faith and the Christian churches. Even in Roman Catholicism, which has gone the furthest among the churches in specifying how the church and its faith are to be definitively ascertained and defined, the authority of the magisterium seems to be seriously damaged, and Catholic priests and laity everywhere are "making up their own minds" about what they believe and what they shall do.

Conservatives may still wish to maintain that it is possible and necessary to give an authoritative and binding definition of Christian beliefs and praxis, and that theologians should proceed on that basis, but such positions express a kind of romanticism about how things used to be. History has moved Christian faith beyond that sort of possibility, willy-nilly, and theologies alert to their own historical situatedness can no longer proceed easily on such assumptions. Theologians can no longer take it for granted that there is a fixed body of beliefs simply to be interpreted and explained. On the contrary, a major task for theologians today is to ascertain just which beliefs and concepts inherited from tradition are still viable, and to determine in what ways they should be reconstructed so they will continue to serve human intellectual and religious needs. To do their work properly in today's world, theologians must ascertain what is in fact going on in that world, must see what directions the history of the churches and the history of religious reflection are moving, and must seek to make their work relevant to and appropriate for that movement. Theology can no longer look simply to authoritative or normative decisions or situations in the past for its principal guidance. It must orient itself toward that future into which we are (quite rapidly) moving, a future which is open and indeterminate in many respects.

From what standpoint should such theological interpretation of the present encounters and movements of the world's religions be undertaken? If everything is in question, where do we gain a footing? As I have already suggested, this will depend more on our conjectures about what is going to happen in the future than our suppositions about what has proved immoveable in the past. Of course all our notions about the future are rooted in experience and wisdom gained in the past. So it would be foolish to attempt to cut ourselves completely loose from that past out of which we have come. Rather, we must guess, as well as we can, what trends and tendencies in the present historical turbulence are a clue to the future, and attempt to develop a theological position that will make sense of and take account of the significance of those developments.

When making a journey through difficult and uncharted territories, one attempts to travel light, taking along only essentials that will be needed on the journey. What are the theological essentials? What theological concepts or doctrines have such usefulness and importance to our movement into an open and unknown future that—in the light of our present understanding of things—we dare not leave them behind?

Agreement is not to be expected, of course, with respect to questions of this sort, and here I can only give my own assessment of our situation in the hope that it will be illuminating also for others. Humans everywhere, I think, are becoming increasingly uncertain about the future into which we all are seemingly being propelled with greater and greater rapidity. And women and men everywhere are beginning to wonder whether we will be able much longer to maintain the hope that eventually a relatively humane world will be created. We are worried about contamination of the environment which sustains our lives; we are concerned about the terrible human misery in which large portions of humanity must presently live; we are haunted by the specter of mass starvation if population growth cannot be satisfactorily controlled; we wonder whether the basic necessities for a decent human life can be attained for the larger part of humanity without such a rigidly planned social and economic order as to destroy individual rights and liberties; we fear that the clash of ideologies in the world today—or even just a kind of unseemly accident or happenstance—might lead to a nuclear holocaust of enormous destructiveness; we sympathize with the desires of oppressed and underprivileged people of all sorts and descriptions to gain new freedoms, to take full responsibility for themselves and their lives, and to become genuinely self-determining, and yet we who enjoy these privileges fear the massive social, political, and economic revolutions that such changes must inevitably bring. In many parts of the world today there appears to be a passion to reconstruct the present order into one more truly humane. This is, I think, one of the great aspirations of our time—underlying much of the unrest in our world—whether we are Americans or members of the so-called third world, Christians or Buddhists, adherents to western-style democracy or advocates of a carefully planned social order. How shall we build a new and more humane world for all the peoples of the world?

With this focus and aspiration as a point of departure, let us consider the function of theological beliefs and conceptions. What role or task do, or can, such beliefs have in the search for a better human order? Do some theological concepts or doctrines have such usefulness or importance for our movement into an open and unknown future that we dare not leave them behind? Can the worldwide struggle for a more humane society provide us with a criterion for doing theological work today?

Before trying to answer these questions, let me make explicit what is involved in this way of addressing the theological task. This approach takes for granted that religious believing and theological analysis and reflection are *human* activities, engaged in for human purposes. This may seem obvious enough when so baldly stated, but in the past it has not sufficiently guided the self-understanding of theologians as they went about their work. For the better part of its history Christian theology has understood itself to be presenting the *truth* about God and humanity and the world, whatever might be the uses of that truth. No doubt it was taken for granted that this truth had important—indeed indispensable—uses for humans: it was the truth about our actual human nature and our ultimate human destiny; it was the truth indispensable to our eternal salvation. Without question the truth with which theology was concerned had an ultimate utility and significance. Yet this traditional understanding of theology has significantly different implications than my proposal that theological beliefs and reflection should serve our aspirations for a new and more humane order. The difference can be put this way: instead of making traditional theological claims about some *extraworldly* or ultimate "salvation" the principal criterion of what we should believe and practice in this world, I am suggesting that what is necessary or required to build a humane order *in this world* should be made the central criterion both for assessing our theological beliefs and for determining the character of the theological task. Theology is done by living human beings in this present world, and it should serve their lives and aspirations. Only such a theology can be justified in the present human crisis and massive human striving. To the extent, then, that theology serves and facilitates our further humanization, it has an important task in the present juncture of history; to the extent that it distracts us from this massive effort for a more humane order—for example, by talk of another world and of other realities that are more important than addressing the issues faced in our present worldwide historical crises—theological beliefs and theological reflection distract us from the very problems that we should be attempting to address.

Such a humanistic and this-worldly criterion for theological work will seem much too nearsighted and restrictive to many. If theologians give up their longer view of what is happening to humanity—a view that takes into account and is focused by our eternal destiny—have we not lost the ultimate lodestar for guiding our reflection on what we should do here and now? Are we not left in the flux and turmoil of conflicting relativities in which there is no ultimately guiding beacon? That is indeed the case. But is not that precisely our actual present situation? Is it not just this ultimate uncertainty about the place and meaning of human existence on planet Earth to which the breakdown of all authoritative conceptions and norms, which we earlier noted, testifies? In the past, church and Bible and tradition enjoyed a special authority for Christian belief and theology because they were assumed to hold within themselves, in some sense or in some way, the ultimate truth for the salvation of all humankind. The deterioration of this authority and normativeness in Christian beliefs and institutions, however, signals a growing doubt regarding these claims about what is of ultimate importance to humanity, and a growing conviction that we ought to order our lives in terms of the actual problems that face us here and now in this world, rather than in terms of some alleged otherworldly destiny.

It is certainly possible to deplore this widespread change of orientation in human consciousness, and it is possible to refuse to accept it as a basis for theological work, to insist that Christian theology must remain oriented, as it was in the past, on a relatively stable structure of beliefs and in the service of an institution believed to be divinely ordained. But such an orientation on, and definition in terms of, the past, we have already rejected for our purposes here. Theology must be done in terms of the awareness that that past is slipping away and we are rapidly moving into a new and quite different future. For such a theology the old benchmarks are gone— or are rapidly disappearing—and it becomes necessary to steer our course in terms of such insights and understanding of human needs and values as we can discern and formulate here and now. This is a fearful and frightening task, but there seems no other course open to us, if we forthrightly acknowledge what is happening in ourselves and our world. The central problem facing the present generation is the construction of a genuinely humane order—lest we destroy ourselves completely. If theological reflection is to be justifiable in this crisis, it must contribute to this work. Today the only theology that we can afford is one that makes a significant contribution to our humanization. A theology, however, that has important contributions to make to our further humanization is well worth attention.

II

We cannot explore in this chapter the full reaches of Christian theology, or the Christian system of symbols, to see where and in what respects they can contribute to the present task of humanization. (Some of these matters will be taken up later, especially in Part Two.) For now we must confine ourselves to the two central symbols of the Christian tradition, "God" and "Christ," and what can be said about these here must be quite brief. These two symbols are especially relevant for our consideration of the relation of Christianity to other religious traditions because together they express both the intention of universality in Christian faith (God) and also the particularity or distinctiveness that sets Christianity apart from other religious orientations (Jesus Christ). If we discover that these two symbols imply themes and emphases that can contribute in important ways to the further humanization of our world, we will be beginning to discern a stance and task for Christian faith and Christian theology appropriate to our growing recognition today of the significance of religious pluralism.

Let us begin with "God." "God" is the highest and most universal of the Christian symbols, and important aspects of the significance of "Christ" are derivative from and dependent upon "God." It was because traditional Christian faith believed that "in Christ *God* was reconciling the world to himself" (2 Cor. 5:19), and that Christ was *God's* definitive revelation, that Christ came to have the centrality he has had in Christianity.* Hence, if we are to understand the meaning and importance of Christ, we shall first have to get clear what is meant by "God." This involves us immediately in the most problematical and difficult issues with which the contemporary mind confronts the Christian tradition. "God-talk" has become highly questionable for many today, including Christian believers and theologians; and some have argued that it can and should be dropped as excess outmoded baggage. That question, however, is not something that should be decided simply on the basis of our intuitions: according to the criterion we are employing here, our assessment of the continuing significance and relevance of the symbol "God" should depend on the degree and the way(s) in which it can contribute to the present struggle for further humanization.

What, now, is meant by "God"? God is said to be the creator of the heavens and the earth and the lord of history, the foundation or source of all that is, the Alpha and the Omega, "that than which nothing greater can be conceived" (Anselm). God is said to be the only proper object of supreme adoration and devotion, the one whose service is perfect freedom, the one who has created us humans and who also works to rescue us from

---

* It should be observed here that much of this section takes over traditional Christian mythic language about God and Christ in (what I now regard as) a too simplistic and undialectical way. Although this way of introducing these matters is useful, it will need to be qualified later on. For a more nuanced articulation of some of the points discussed here, see chaps. 6–7, below. Further discussion can also be found in chaps. 5–7 and 25–27 of *In Face of Mystery*.

the evils of our present existence. Only through giving ourselves to God and to the service of God, we are told, is human salvation—that is, genuine human fulfillment—possible. What can all this mean? Is this all largely mythology, which we may find entrancing if we have a poetic or romantic turn of mind, or is there a significance in this symbol that is important for our contemporary life and struggles?

Certainly some of what is being claimed here is intelligible enough. We are reminded that unless we live in accord with that on which our human existence is grounded, we shall destroy ourselves. To think we can do anything we please, that we can make ourselves into whatever we will, is foolhardy. There are limits set for us and our enterprises that we must honor and respect if a truly humane existence on this earth is to be possible. In this emphasis, that we are ultimately responsible not merely to ourselves but to orders and structures that sustain us and that we violate at our peril, the ancient theological tradition was formulating fundamental human wisdom that modern ecology is rediscovering. But the ancient tradition had an important advantage over more recent secular formulations. It did not need to rest its case for ordering human life beyond itself exclusively on an appeal to rational self-interest: it portrayed a reality of such supreme goodness and beauty and glory that humans would be drawn to give themselves to it without reservation. The image of a loving and forgiving God, one who is both our creator (the source of our humanity) and our redeemer (the fulfiller of our humanity), and who personally cares for us and sacrifices much for our sakes, is able to evoke a kind of gratitude and devotion that breaks the circle of self-centeredness and opens the self to wider moral and humane demands upon it, directing it toward a life characterized by a similar love and self-giving, a life that can help build a new humanity. Since God is believed to be not only the creator of all but one who also wills salvation—fulfillment—for all, true devotion to God requires breaking down the walls that separate and segregate selves and communities, and opening ourselves to that universal community which encompasses all and provides for the fulfillment of all.

I do not claim, of course, that the symbol "God" has in fact always functioned this way in the past: we all know too well the perversions to which it has been subject, making possible very gross forms of inhumanity in inquisitions and torture chambers, concentration camps and holy wars. I do claim, however, that the symbol of God as the creator, sustainer, and perfecter of our humanity through love and forgiveness provides a powerful and significant object of devotion for such causes. In comparison with the potential of this symbol, secular appeals to our deepest rational self-interest as the basis for overcoming our selfishness and self-centeredness seem somewhat feeble, and possibly inconsistent. We need a center of devotion outside the self, a center powerful enough to draw the self out of its own narcissism, if our self-centeredness and our ethnocenteredness and our anthropocenteredness are to be overcome. The symbol "God" can provide such a focus for human devotion.

But the symbol "God" will function in this way, truly promoting our further humanization, only if it is conceived properly. Many different conceptions of God have been proposed in the past, many different sorts of gods have been worshipped, and certainly not all of them have conduced to the further humanization of our species. A god conceived as an arbitrary tyrant who "has mercy upon whomever he wills, and [who] hardens the heart of whomever he wills" (Rom. 9:18), will hardly inspire in devotees respect and care for all their fellow creatures. A god portrayed as manifesting fearful and all-destructive wrath against all who violate the divine will, will hardly inspire patience with or forgiveness of those who offend us or with whom we thoroughly disagree. God has often been conceived as an all-powerful demon to whom we must devote ourselves in fear of everlasting torment: such a god tends to call forth "authoritarian personalities" (T. W. Adorno), spirits that cower obsequiously before authority but become braggarts and bullies when dealing with those who are weaker or of subordinate social status—hardly truly free spirits, humane and just and loving. From the point of view of our further humanization, some images of God—including some with roots in the Bible and in certain strands of Christian tradition—are exceedingly dangerous, and worship of such gods will only further human depravity. It is not enough, then, to advocate devotion to God, if humanization is our concern; devotion to some conceptions of God is dehumanizing, and it is little wonder that many great humanitarian reformers in past and present have found it necessary to dissociate themselves from traditional Christian beliefs, taking agnostic or atheistic positions. We must be prepared radically to criticize and reconstruct traditional ideas of God, if God is to continue to serve as an appropriate object of devotion for our time, one who truly mediates to us salvation (humanization).[2]

What should be the basis of our criticism and reconstruction? Are we cut adrift here in a sea of vagaries and opinions, each person constructing whatever image of God seems fit to her or him and bowing down in worship? If this were to be our conclusion, it is doubtful that theological reflection would be worth the effort. For the gods which we would construct could not move us significantly beyond our present insights and ideals, of which they would simply be personifications. Such a move is essentially idolatrous: bowing down before that which our own hands and minds have made. Relativistic and parochial idols of this sort could hardly help move us toward a more universal community inclusive of all women and men.

It is at this point that we can see the continuing importance of the other great symbol of Christian faith, "Jesus Christ." The Christian imperative has not been simply that we should worship God, God-in-general, just any God. On the contrary, it has been much more specific than that, contending that the true God, the one who brings genuine fulfillment to humanity, is not directly available and known in every image or action but has been revealed in and through Jesus: "He is the image of the invisible God," declares the author of the letter to the Colossians (1:15). "No one has ever seen God," says the writer of the Fourth Gospel; "the only Son, who is close to the Father's heart, . . . has made him known" (John 1:18). Christians themselves have not often taken with full seriousness these central declarations of their faith and have constructed their ideas of God from images and models other than that of the suffering Jesus. "Christ crucified," as an appropriate image for understanding who God really is, has been as much a "stumbling block" to the Christian churches as it was to the Jews of whom Paul wrote (1 Cor. 1:23), for Christians, like most others, have preferred to worship a God of power and glory rather than one humbled before the powerful, one suffering, weak and dying. So, although there has always been stress on God's love and mercy and forgiveness in Christian teaching, the *image* in terms of which God has been conceived—and thus the real center of devotion for Christian faith—has most often been the dazzling glory of almighty power. And to maintain that God in any way suffers or even is capable of suffering, to deny God's impassibility, was regarded as heresy. Not surprisingly, it was in the service of this God of might and glory that the worst horrors of Christian history were committed.

We should not go that way any longer. Modern historical studies, together with the growing secularization of much of our world, have enabled us to recognize that the Bible and the Christian tradition (like the other great religious traditions) are largely products of human creativity in the face of changing historical exigencies. We need no longer, therefore— indeed, we dare not—simply accept all biblical or traditional images or conceptions of God as authoritative or binding. To allow ourselves to be bound in that arbitrary way by our past is to be crippled and shackled as we try to deal with the immense problems humanity today faces. The only God we should worship today—the only God we can afford to worship— is the God who will further our humanization, the God who will help to make possible the creation of a universal and humane community.

The crisis of our situation, thus, frees us to consider radically reconstructing the Christian conception of God into a conception founded directly on the image of the suffering Jesus. Such a God would not be one who acts violently in the face of opposition but rather one who lovingly and patiently suffers the evil men and women inflict in the hope of thus winning a free and loving response from them, who suffers crucifixion at their hands in hope of the resurrection of a new community of love and forgiveness in their midst. It would be a God who seeks to build community among humans not by power of nuclear terror but by evoking a spirit of free vicarious suffering for others. It would be a God for whom human fulfillment could not properly be understood in terms of a "kingdom" in which all commands from on high were carried through in legalistic perfection and detail, but rather in terms of communities of free spirits, living and working together in productiveness and love. It would not be a God, therefore, who exercised heteronomous or compulsive authority over humans, but rather one who encouraged and created free and autonomous women and men, and who recognized that community among such persons is possible only if they manifest self-giving and love toward each other and a willingness to forgive and suffer for each other.[3]

I do not claim that devotion to such a God would bring utopia; I certainly do not maintain that it would solve all our problems, either easily or quickly. The problems that we face today are massive, and how they are to be solved—if they can be solved at all—remains quite obscure. If we are the free beings that this God is supposedly in the process of creating, it is we who will have to take upon ourselves the responsibility of finding a way to the resolution of these issues without destroying ourselves in the process. And that means moving forward step by step with a faith and a hope that some resolution is truly possible, and a new and universal community—with new and better men and women to make up that community—can be created.

Such an awareness of full responsibility in our freedom, and hope for our future, could be engendered by faith in a God constructed in the image of Jesus Christ, and by the service of such a God. Such a faith and such a God, therefore, could serve well our further humanization in today's troubled world. Indeed, if such a truly humane God does not displace the gods of parochial groups and interests, the gods of prejudice and of blind conviction of right in the pursuit of power—whether by revolutionaries or reactionaries—there seems little basis for great hopes for the human future.

III

I have been suggesting how a criterion of humanization might guide our reconstruction of Christian belief. Let us turn now to consider the relevance of this criterion to the great non-Christian traditions. Here too, that which will further humanization as we move into the future is to be regarded as justifiable and good; that which is dehumanizing, or which is seriously distracting in the struggle to build a humane society, must be judged negatively. It is clear that the acceptance of this criterion involves some important preferences and decisions. We have already noted the way in which it gives present problems and needs precedence over the claims of tradition, particularly those claims about a supernatural order or "other world" which might distract attention from the urgent concerns of this life. There is certainly warrant for this emphasis in the prophetic strands of the Hebraic-Christian tradition, with their contention that the requirements of justice and mercy in meeting present social problems weigh more heavily with God than religious ritual. But the sharp way in which I have formulated the matter goes considerably beyond this traditional leaning in the direction of this-worldly claims, for I have argued that the very idea of God itself is to be criticized and reconstructed (or rejected) in light of the requirements of this humanistic criterion. All claims to truth made simply on the grounds of religious authority are in question: theological truth-claims are to be assessed strictly in terms of today's vast needs and our best moral insight (educated as much as possible, of course, by past experience and by tradition). Although it can be claimed that a moral-humanistic criterion of this sort has been implicitly invoked in religious criticism and theological reconstruction from the time of the eighth-century prophets, it has seldom been stated this unequivocally, thus bringing its theological significance and consequences clearly into view. It should not surprise us, therefore, that despite its biblical heritage and background this criterion may have quite radical consequences when applied seriously to central traditional Christian claims.

Whatever be the historical roots of this criterion, I have invoked it here because it seems to me to express the deepest longings and hopes of many contemporary women and men the world over, a growing consensus in many places around the world—particularly among the oppressed and underprivileged—that the time has come to rebuild our human world into an order more genuinely humane. It is a criterion, therefore, which can properly be applied not only to western religious practice and thought but to other traditions and institutions as well. There is a tremendous push toward both modernization and humanization throughout the world today, and all the great religious traditions must come to terms with this fact. The criterion of humanization pinpoints what is at stake here for the religions. It will not be surprising, of course, if some traditions fare better at its hands than others.

All of the great non-Christian traditions manifest much variation and diversity, and the tensions and strains in them are immense in the present struggles for modernization and humanization throughout Africa, Asia, and Latin America. I am not competent to examine any of these traditions in detail or to make judgments about them. I must limit myself here, therefore, to some general comments about what seems to be occurring and the significance this has for a theological interpretation of religious pluralism.

Anyone from the West who has lived among some of the peoples of the so-called less developed nations cannot help but be impressed with the way in which dehumanizing social institutions, superstitious beliefs, and religious sanctions are often thoroughly intertwined, mutually reinforcing each other. In India, for example, the caste system—which assigns persons a role and destiny simply and completely on the basis of birth, and makes it difficult if not impossible for low-caste or out-caste persons to move out of a life that is very degrading—is sustained and supported by the belief in karma and reincarnation. These beliefs, defining one's present condition as the necessary and entirely just outcome of one's deeds in previous incarnations, and as therefore simply to be accepted, imply that to struggle against one's situation is rebellion against the very order of righteousness and justice that governs the universe. Within this general framework special afflictions of disease or other misery are often believed to be caused by demons or evil spirits in no way subject to human control. To persons living within this conceptual world, the whole order of life, and the major events of life, seem imposed from without and cannot be significantly reshaped by human efforts in the present. Religious beliefs of this sort, accepted by and acceptable to vast numbers of ordinary people, greatly hamper efforts toward humanizing life in India, and help to maintain inhuman living conditions for many millions. For this reason the leadership of modern India from Jawaharlal Nehru on has been intent on breaking their hold and has insisted on building a new secular India in which the inhuman living conditions of the masses could and would be overcome. So a great struggle has been going on in India against some of the deepest-lying and most fundamental religious practices and beliefs that have shaped that civilization for millennia. It is in terms of what I have called the criterion of humanization that criticism of and attempts to reconstruct the traditional order and its religious sanctions have been developed.

Similar sorts of things could be said about the modernization of China, where totalitarian power has been used to wipe out as far as possible the old order to build a "new humanity"; about Latin America, where many have come to a new awakening with regard to the way in which the churches themselves have helped to legitimize and support massive injustice, and many church leaders have moved into the forefront of revolutionary activity; and about Africa. Among these peoples—despite repeated backlashes—modernization and humanization remain the watchwords of many leaders, however crude or ineffective or brutal their efforts may sometimes be. In all of this, of course, there is tremendous ambivalence, for modernity—especially in its technological aspects, but also in many of its social practices and institutions and in its beliefs about human nature, about justice and equality, about human possibilities of making and remaking the world—has been imported largely from the West and demands tremendous modification of traditional religious and cultural beliefs and practices. Whether modernization is undertaken through political democracy or through Marxist institutions or in some other way, its inspiration and basic ideology have been heavily shaped by western ideas and practices. So feelings of dissatisfaction with, perhaps even contempt for, some aspects of one's own cultural and religious past, are often combined with deep feelings of uncertainty and guilt about being disloyal and unfaithful to all that had been held dear for so long. Deep desires to appropriate (some aspects of) western ideology and praxis are mixed with feelings of revulsion toward crass western pragmatism, materialism, and secularism, hatred of (former) western colonialism and continuing western power and dominance, and a deep affection for much in one's own cultural and religious tradition. The contradictions and tensions must be almost unbearable. Though the political imperialism of the West may be coming to an end, economic and cultural imperialism are far from over; and they are the more deeply resented just because so much seemingly must be adopted from them if a new order is to be built.

What is to be our attitude in the face of these tensions and struggles? Surely a Troeltschian or sociological relativism will not do, however humane and right-minded it might have seemed to a previous generation. Not so many years ago it was possible (and no doubt correct) to think in terms of a number of great world-civilizations, each with a distinctiveness and integrity of its own. That the values, institutions, styles of life in each should be cherished and respected, and that missionary and imperialistic activity on the part of Christendom was a highly questionable intrusion into societies that should be granted their own autonomy, seemed a humane and highly persuasive thesis. This thesis could even be extended—and was—to primal tribal cultures, whose values and autonomy, it was held, should not be interfered with by the so-called more advanced societies. "Nothing human is alien to me" was the motto, and that slogan still has great appeal. We should glory in the fullness of our pluralism.

An attitude of that sort was surely an advance over the stuffy imperialistic pride with which westerners had been colonizing and ruling the world for the previous two centuries, convinced that their culture and their religion represented all that was high and good and true, and that all others should either be converted to western views and practices or deserved to be dominated by the West, politically and economically. But such a relativistic position is really not appropriate to the realities of today's world. We are no longer a group of largely independent great cultures, each with its own integrity and dignity, each to be preserved in and through its own great traditional institutions, ideologies, and values. We are in the midst of tremendous transformations and tensions and turmoil, through which the multiplicity of separate human cultures is rapidly being transformed into a single intraconnected fabric of human civilization, the many constituent parts of which are culturally and socially and spiritually interdependent and interrelated in countless ways. We are still a pluralized world, and we will probably always remain so, but humanity no longer consists of several great independent societies or cultures. Our pluralism increasingly exists within and is formed by the powerful movement everywhere toward modernization. It is not a question any longer of whether this is good or bad, whether it should be encouraged or resisted. It is a tide that is transforming all human life on this globe—whatever we may think about the current western modernity/postmodernity debates—and will continue to do so for the foreseeable future. It is a basic fact of our lives, of our moment in human history, and we do well, therefore, to take this into account as we seek to order our existence today.

If we return now to our criterion of humanization, we will quickly see that for Christian faith a relativistic aloofness toward other cultures and religions is no more appropriate to this contemporary historical situation than is a patronizing paternalism. We must attempt, rather, to work in and through all the forces of modernization presently alive in the world (in both East and West) toward the establishment worldwide of civilizations that are genuinely humane. We must assist the modernizing processes, in whatever ways we can, to be humanizing processes. This imperative should not, of course, be used as a warrant for further western cultural and religious imperialism. But at the same time it suggests that we should not deplore, out of some romantic notion about the glory and the integrity of every human culture, the eroding away and ultimate destruction of old and outmoded values and institutions which now are found to be seriously dehumanizing. On the contrary, we should do all we can to help make the transition through which the cultures of the world are going—both our own culture and others—less painful and difficult. We should seek the overcoming of inhumane religious and cultural institutions and beliefs in other cultures as well as in our own, for we are rapidly all becoming one humanity. To be a Christian—indeed, to be a modern/postmodern human being—is no longer to participate simply or primarily in one cultural tradition; it is to be participant with and involved in the worldwide struggle for a fuller and more humane social order, a struggle in and through which older religious institutions and practices everywhere will have to pass away, and new and more humane ones are created.

Our criterion of humanization, thus, does not permit us any longer to take up a monolithic attitude toward other cultures and religious traditions, either attempting to conquer them completely or allowing them simply to stand in the integrity of what they have been in the past. We must be discriminating and selective, supporting that which furthers a more humane order, opposing that which is dehumanizing. Though it is true that the humanistic criterion which I have been sketching is largely descendant from western religious and cultural traditions, to invoke it is not simply to further western spiritual imperialism in the old style. For it is a criterion which, as we have seen, requires radical reconstruction of our western religious traditions quite as much as of others. Moreover, it has already been implicitly accepted as a proper basis of judgment in much of the modernizing (nonwestern) world, and it is too simple, therefore, to regard it as being imposed entirely from without. Above all, it is a criterion directed toward the fulfillment of all human beings and all societies, no matter what their cultural or religious traditions and commitments. It is centered on the men and women concerned and their needs, and is not the imperialism of an ideology.

It will be protested, of course, that this focusing of attention on human needs and welfare in this life is itself simply one more ideology competing with all the others; and from one point of view that is true. But the implied conclusion, that therefore no greater warrant for this position can be offered than for any other, that we are caught in a relativism of ideologies among which no justifiable discriminations can be made, is misleading. As we noted earlier in this chapter, all ideas, ideologies, claims to truth, faiths, are held by human beings for human purposes. Their ultimate *raison d'etre* is to serve certain human needs and intentions. It is impossible to break out of an ultimate relativism of viewpoints so long as we continue simply to weigh one truth-claim against another, since each proceeds from different premises and is coherent and reasonable in terms of the overall worldview that it presupposes and expresses. Here there is an unending warfare of religious, cultural, and philosophical positions that can never be rationally settled, since each position invokes its own criteria in assessing its own and others' claims, and there are no universal criteria for arbitrating the dis-agreements. Once we recognize, however, that each of these perspectives is in fact simply a *human* position—whatever may be claimed (by its advo-cates) about divine revelation as its foundation—serving certain human needs and promoting certain forms of human life while inhibiting others, it becomes possible to find a way through the relativistic impasse and to assess the alternatives. One can ask which human needs are met by each position—which forms of human life sustained and enhanced, which downgraded or suppressed. One can, in short, ask about the *human* mean-ing and significance of each religious claim or worldview, and one can ask if that human significance and consequence are indeed humanly desirable or justifiable.

Every religious tradition promises salvation in some form or other, that is, promises true human fulfillment, or at least rescue from the pit into which we humans have fallen. Every religious tradition thus implicitly invokes a human or humane criterion to justify (at least to its adherents) its existence and its claims. My proposal that we make humanization our explicit criterion for evaluating the several religious traditions and their claims is thus based on recognition of something implicit in them all. In this sense, a humanistic orientation of the sort described here should not be regarded as just one more ideology among others. For it can claim both to be implicit in the others and also to offer a perspective on the great diversi-ty of religious life and truth which makes possible truly significant—that is, *humanly* significant—comparison and evaluation. Once we recognize this, we have a criterion that can give us guidance in the present religiously plu-ralistic situation. (The criterion of humanization will be defined with more specificity, and developed more fully, below in Chapters 4–5.)

It must be admitted that there is little agreement among religious tradi-tions on conceptions of the human or on the understanding of what consti-tutes human fulfillment. But the formulation I am proposing makes that an issue that can be directly argued and debated, each party invoking in its own support whatever experiential and other evidence is available publicly in our present human existence. Each disputant needs to show why his or her interpretation of the human is most adequate to the actual realities of human life today, and therefore can most properly lay claim to our alle-giance in this life. Admittedly this discriminates against the appeals to supernatural or otherworldly sanctions that all the religions (except, per-haps, some forms of Buddhism) have traditionally made for their claims. But, as we have seen, it is just in their appeals to (mythic) sanctions or authorities outside our ordinary human reach and assessment that the unlimited diversity of religious interpretations gets much of its strength.

Because of this diversity in their ultimate courts of appeal, and with respect to it, the different religions become very difficult to compare, and impartial judgments among them become almost impossible. What is needed in this circumstance is to abstract from this diversity and relativity (as much as possible) to the common point of interest in the human that all the religions share. This can then provide a basis for comparison and evaluation.

In insisting that each tradition present its interpretation of human existence and fulfillment in terms of what is directly and publicly available to all, rather than in terms of its own ideology, we are only laying down ground rules without which the debate could not proceed. Nevertheless, they are rules which clearly disadvantage all contestants that wish to base their claims on esoteric revelations or on other sorts of special privileged authority.[4] But that, of course, is precisely what the present worldwide cry for humanization is all about: breaking out of our bondage to structures of authority and power that are not subject to open and impartial inspection, and which thus are in the nature of the case dehumanizing. The question is: Do we recognize the validity of this cry against the inhuman and this appeal to that which fulfills the human? If we do, then we have an arbiter before whom each of the religious traditions can quite properly be asked to justify its claims.

IV

I shall not attempt any assessment here of the claims of the several great religious traditions in terms of the criterion of humaneness and humanization. That is a task which is already being taken up around the world, as each culture faces the problems of modernization, and which, in any case, others are much better equipped to pursue. Rather, I want to turn now to a question that some must feel increasingly urgent as they read these pages: whatever pragmatic value the criterion of humanization may have in thinking about the place of religion in the modern world, can this criterion be justified as properly Christian, and not just humanistic? Can one legitimately claim that a position which gives such prominence to this criterion is theologically adequate?

From a traditional point of view the interpretation of Christian symbolism that I have sketched with the aid of the criterion of humanization might well be regarded as very spare. Nothing has been said here about human entrapment in sin or about the atoning work of the cross. There was no mention of the doctrine of the deity of Christ or the trinity, nor of the church and the sacraments. Even the question whether God can be regarded as a heavenly being or infinite person who intervenes in human affairs has gone undiscussed.

Some of these matters will, of course, be taken up in later chapters of this book. They were not discussed here because at this point I have been interested in formulating a conception that would enable us to bring Christian faith into a position to enter directly into conversation with other traditions on matters affecting us all, as we continue to undergo radical modernization and (one hopes) humanization. At the points where Christians make special claims about the divinity of Christ or about God's special concern for specifically *Christian* belief, entering into such free and open dialogue becomes difficult if not impossible; precisely these sorts of claims suggest the superiority of Christianity over other religions and have been employed to argue this in a most unbecoming way. Such a stance is neither appropriate nor useful when we are considering the present worldwide struggle to reorder societies in ways that grant each person and each community its own proper dignity. When concerns of this sort are under consideration, we may not begin by asserting, or even implying, our own superiority to all partners, or potential partners, in dialogue. Rather we must enter into conversation as equals, hoping to be able to contribute something of significance to our common objective of building a more humane world, expecting also to learn much of significance from the other parties to the conversation, hoping and expecting that we will all grow into deeper community with and respect for each other as we converse together.

Because of the urgency that genuine dialogue with other religious and nonreligious positions get underway, I have confined myself here to this somewhat spare or minimalist interpretation of Christian beliefs. I want to maintain, however, that this has not involved shortchanging or "selling out" Christianity in some fundamental way. Rather, in my opinion, it is strictly in accord with deep interests and concerns of Christian faith itself. Here we come to a great divide in the understandings of faith. Should the central concern of Christianity be understood to be the presentation of certain indispensable *truth(s)* to humanity so that "whoever believes . . . should not perish but have eternal life" (John 3:16); or should it be seen as primarily a *ministry of reconciliation* among all humankind inspired by the love of God manifested in Christ (2 Cor. 5:17-20)? Most Christians have maintained that it is both these things, though in actuality they may have emphasized one more than the other. It is my contention, however, that it is important to make a choice regarding which is to be given priority and which should be considered secondary.

If the business of Christianity is most fundamentally to present truth-claims about God and Christ and ourselves, then our stance toward those others with whom we are speaking will be basically argumentative and combative: we will be concerned to persuade them to accept what we understand to be the truth, the unchanging truth, let the chips fall where they may. However, if the fundamental business of Christianity is a ministry of reconciliation among humans, building community where there is dissension, promoting understanding and acceptance where there has been estrangement and rejection—because the God to whom we are devoted is one who loves and forgives and reconciles—then our stance will have to be different. Our concern first and foremost will be to enter into community with those others with whom we are speaking, and where estrangement or separation exist to seek reconciliation with them. It will be, in short, not to make claims for ourselves or our truth against our neighbors, but to love and accept our neighbors as ourselves.

Downgrading the importance of the more peculiar and controversial traditional Christian affirmations, as I am doing here, and highlighting the ministry of love and reconciliation that builds community among humans and thus seeks to contribute directly toward the establishment of a more humane world, does not involve compromising the essentials of Christian faith but is directly expressive of those essentials.[5] The Christian concern for the salvation of all women and men is primarily a concern for their full humanization. At this point the contemporary worldwide struggle for a truly humane social order coincides completely with the central thrust of Christian faith (though conceptions of how this goal is to be achieved may differ profoundly); and there is no reason for Christians to set themselves apart, or to stand aloof, from major forces presently at work toward this objective in other religious traditions and in secular society. Indeed, from a Christian point of view, precisely this striving toward humanization should be regarded as the preeminent activity of God—the source and fulfiller of our humanness—in today's historical struggles.

The theological stance I have been sketching here involves a modernization of Christianity appropriate to and correlative with the modernization (in the direction of fuller humanization) of the other great religious traditions, as well as with the powerful movements in contemporary secular society toward that end. It provides an interpretation of Christian faith, and the Christian God, that will facilitate and encourage the full yet critical participation of Christians in the struggles for a more humane social order that are so widespread in the world today. And it provides a basis for encounter on equal terms with the other great religious traditions, and for discriminating and intelligent dialogue with them about what is humanly significant in the several faiths of humankind. Moreover, it gives an intelligible interpretation to the central and enduring Christian claim: the claim about God, and about the significance for our time of faith in this God who is conceived and defined in terms paradigmatically represented by the person, ministry, and death of the man Jesus—the God of love and mercy and self-sacrifice. I am contending that devotion to this God, and action in accord with the "will" of this God, are not only wholly appropriate to the life and struggles of our time, but that they have a significant contribution to make to all of us involved in these struggles.

I am not claiming thereby that the other great religious and secular traditions do not also have important, perhaps indispensable, contributions to make toward the fuller humanization of us all. That matter is, of course, primarily for their own adherents to ascertain and to explain; and the rest of us should gladly listen to what they have to say, seeking to learn from them whatever we can. Doubtless Buddhism can teach us much about human suffering, and about the relativity of all our religious symbols and conceptions and the dangers of their hypostatization and literalization. And Hinduism (as well as Buddhism) will have claims to make about the importance of spiritual discipline and insight and the dangers of devotion to a too-anthropomorphically conceived God. Judaism and Islam have significant testimonies to make with regard to God's incomparable uniqueness and the unqualified demands upon us which faith in God requires—insights which, as both these traditions have long realized, suggest that much Christian talk about Jesus as "divine" or as "God and savior" has been idolatrous. Secular humanism has much to teach all the religious traditions about human freedom, and Marxist humanism can enable us to understand better the economic and social requirements that must be met if there is to be genuine justice and equality. Each of these forms of humanism can help alert us to some of the profound evils to which the various kinds of human religiousness have all too often become allied. In this many-sided conversation Christians may dare to hope, perhaps, that faith in and devotion to the God who is working to "make human life more human" (as Paul Lehmann often put it) may commend itself as right and proper and good to many who had oriented themselves and their activities principally in terms of secular humanism or some other religious tradition.

The coming new age of a thoroughly interconnected and interdependent worldwide humanity must build upon the best insights and disciplines of all our long and varied human experience, as conserved for us in the many religious and cultural traditions alive and meaningful today. We must be open to all, in conversation with all. But we dare not be uncritically receptive to every claim that is made, whether by perspectives strange to us or by the traditions we ourselves hold dear. Each must be examined and assessed in light of the criterion of humanization. It is the task of theology—and of the corresponding modes, in other traditions, of reflection on our humanity and what is ultimately significant for us humans—to define and clarify and interpret the criterion of humanization, to engage in reflection and discussion leading to deeper and fuller understanding of its significance and import, and to attempt to measure and assess in its terms the great claims and emphases about human life and destiny made by the various religious and cultural traditions of humankind. Thus, each of the great religious traditions should find its proper role in the coming world culture, and Christianity also will be able to show forth its distinctive significance.[6]

Chapter 2

Theology: Critical, Constructive, and Contextualized

The interpretation of Christian theology that I am presenting in this volume is based on an assumption so obvious that its importance has often gone unrecognized by theologians: namely, that theology is human work. Theology is done by women and men for human purposes. Theological work is assessed by human standards, and its judges are themselves always ordinary human beings. I mention these truisms because sometimes theologians have proceeded as though they were articulating superhuman divine truth, the very Word or words of God. They have held what they received from tradition in such reverence that they felt it inappropriate to criticize or reconstruct it in terms of their own best understandings or insights; instead they often reaffirmed in too uncritical a fashion what was handed on to them from the past as authoritative tradition or truth. But all religious practices, institutions, and beliefs have been humanly created and have changed and developed in traceable human histories, as they have come to serve new needs and have been adapted to new circumstances. This is just as true of Christian theology—of reflection on the language and ideas of faith—as of any other aspect of Christian life or praxis. Theology also serves human purposes and needs, and should be judged in terms of the adequacy with which it is fulfilling the objectives we humans have set for it. "The sabbath was made for humankind," Jesus said, "and not humankind for the sabbath" (Mark 2:27). That is, all religious institutions, practices, and ideas—including the idea of God—were made to serve human needs and to further our humanization (what has traditionally been called our "salvation"); humanity was not made for the sake of religious customs and ideas. It is right and proper, therefore, that theologians and

First published in *A Vision for Man: Essays in Honor of J. R. Chandran,* ed. Samuel Amirtham (Madras: Christian Literature Society, 1978); and later (with some alterations) as chap. 10 in *The Theological Imagination: Constructing a Concept of God* (Philadelphia: Westminster Press, 1981). Used with permission.

other thoughtful Christians be continually engaged in examining and reexamining received ideas of God, criticizing those ideas as sharply as they can in terms of the actual functions they perform in human life, and reconstructing them so they will serve more adequately as vehicles of our fuller humanization.

In this chapter I set forth an interpretation of theology as just such a critical and constructive task, performed by men and women for the sake of certain human needs and purposes. I do this in the form of an exposition of six theses, beginning with a statement of my understanding of theology; moving through an exposition of how theological work is to be done, and setting out the character of Christian as distinguished from other sorts of theology; then concluding with some comments on the contextualization of all Christian theologies. I hope these remarks will show in summary form the respects and extent to which Christian theology is bound to criteria and norms which should not be compromised, and the extent to which it is free to adapt itself to the forms and images and concepts of the context in which it is working and which it is attempting to serve. We begin with a general thesis on the nature of theology.

Thesis I. The proper business of theology (*theos-logos*) is the analysis, criticism, and reconstruction of the image/concept of God.*

Elucidation: This thesis, which may sound tautological, has a number of implications that should be made explicit, for it rules out certain traditional ways of understanding the theological enterprise. In the first place, this thesis means that theology is not to be understood as primarily exposition or interpretation of the several creeds of the church or the ideas of the Bible. Doubtless both Bible and creeds are relevant and important for understanding the image/concept of God and for judging what are proper, and what improper, uses or formulations of that symbol. But it is their utility for getting at the idea of God that gives the Bible and the creeds their importance for theology, not the other way around. That is, it is because we are trying to understand who God is that we are interested in the Bible and the creeds;

---

*When this essay was first written (two decades ago), I was defining theology in terms of the activity that specifically distinguished it from other disciplines, namely, construction of a conception of God. To the extent, however, that this may suggest that the question of God can be taken up independently of other related theological issues (e.g., concerning the nature of the world and of humanity), it needs to be qualified. In theological reflection and construction all issues are interdependent (as suggested, but not sufficiently emphasized, in the elucidations of this thesis and some that follow); and they should, thus, be developed in interconnection with each other, as we seek a "wide reflective equilibrium" (Francis Schüssler Fiorenza). A holistic approach of this latter sort is exemplified in Part Two below. For a discussion of theological method that brings out, more adequately than this chapter, what is at stake here, see chap. 2 of *In Face of Mystery*.

it is not because we are obliged to accept what is taught in creeds and Bible that we are interested in God. Bible and creeds are secondary to and derivative in their significance from that primary theological focus. Both creeds and Bible are thus subject to a standard other than themselves in terms of which they must continually be judged, namely, the understanding of God. This is the primary subject matter of theology and that to which everything else must be subordinated. It is not theologically adequate, then, to show that a particular conception is biblical, or that it conforms to a creedal statement. On the contrary, biblical and creedal conceptions can properly be introduced into theological work only if they themselves conform to requirements laid down by the image/concept of God.

It should be clear that our first thesis has similar implications for other sorts of claims sometimes made about theology. It is often held, for instance, that Christian theology is primarily the exposition of Christian doctrines or dogmas, as though these doctrines and dogmas were givens that the theologian must simply accept, and that he or she is then called upon to explain or interpret. But according to our thesis this is once again the wrong way around. The only given (and this is a very peculiar "given") with which the theologian works is God: the various doctrines and dogmas are attempts to express and interpret what we mean by the word "God," and they have their significance in the degree to which they are successful in doing that. Doctrines and dogmas, then, are not simply to be accepted. They are to be examined, criticized, and often rejected, in light of the image/concept of God that finally commends itself to us. It is God who is the ultimate authority and point of reference for the theologian. No doctrine or dogma can be given that high place without falling into idolatry.

It is sometimes said that theology is primarily anthropology, an interpretation of the nature of the human, and that therefore the first task in theology is to develop a conception of the human. But this once again is putting the cart before the horse. Though we certainly cannot develop an interpretation of God without simultaneously working out an understanding of our human condition; and though different conceptions of human existence, and of human nature, will have diverse implications for what or who we understand God to be, the primary business of theology is to work out an understanding of that supreme focus for human service and devotion, God. And our understanding of humanity will have to be developed, ultimately, in relation to what we conclude God to be.

God, then, is the unique and peculiar focus of attention and interest in Christian theology. No other intellectual discipline has God as its special and peculiar object. The disciplines of biblical scholarship, church history,

history of doctrine, philosophical anthropology and the like are all indispensable to the theologian, but the primary task here is getting clear what is to be meant by "God." Doubtless it is not possible to address this question without considering God's relation to the world and to humanity—and thus doctrines of creation, of sin and salvation, of providence, of the church, and so on will all have contributions to make to the theological task. But in theological work these are ancillary to the task that distinguishes theology from all other disciplines: analysis, interpretation and reconstruction of the image/concept of God.

If this is the central business of theology, it is important for us to get as clear as we can just what sort of symbol this is, how it is constructed and how properly defined. That is the subject of my second thesis.

Thesis II. The image/concept of God, a human construct like all other symbols, is, and always has been, built up through extrapolation or development of certain finite metaphors or models, in such a way that it can serve as the ultimate point of reference for understanding and interpreting all of experience, life, and the world.

Elucidation. There are two points being made in this second thesis. The first is that by *God* we mean to be indicating what can be called our "ultimate point of reference," that in terms of which everything else is to be understood, that beyond which we cannot move in imagination, thought, or devotion. Traditional characterizations of God often make just this point. To refer to God as the "creator of all things visible and invisible," for example, is to say that everything that exists has its source in God's activity and can be understood rightly only in relation to God's purposes for it. To think of God as "lord" of history and of nature is to understand that everything that happens has its ultimate explanation in God's intentions and actions, that God's sovereign will rules the entire movement of nature and history, and the real meaning of that movement, therefore, cannot be grasped without reference to what God is doing. To speak of God as "the Alpha and the Omega" is explicitly to state that God defines or circumscribes everything else, and there is no way to get beyond God to something more ultimate or significant. By "God," then, we mean the ultimate point of reference for all understanding of anything. By "God" we mean the ultimate object of devotion for all human life.

It is precisely this ultimacy that distinguishes God from all idols, and it is only because of this ultimacy that God can be considered an appropriate object of worship, that to which persons, and entire communities, can properly give themselves in unlimited devotion. To give ourselves in worship and devotion to anything less than what we take to be the ultimate point of reference—anything less than God—is to fall into bondage to some finite reality or realities, eventually destroying both ourselves and our societies, making true human fulfillment (salvation) impossible. All idolatry is enslaving and destructive: by "God" we mean that which rescues us from all these enslavements into which we continually fall, that which brings human life to its full realization. But only that which is the ultimate point of reference for all experience, thought, and action can be the savior from all idols, that is, *God*. We may conveniently refer to this distinctive feature of the concept of God as "the principle of God's absoluteness."

If God has this kind of ultimacy—if God is in this way beyond everything finite, not to be identified with any of the realities of our experience in the world—then God is absolutely unique and cannot be grasped or understood through any of our ordinary concepts or images. This is the second point being made in our second thesis. At best, all of the concepts and images—always drawn from our experience in the world—that we use in seeking to grasp and understand God will be only metaphors or models, symbols or analogies. They will never be applicable literally. The concept of God is built up in our minds by playing off one metaphor against another, by criticizing and qualifying this image through juxtaposing it with that concept, by carefully selecting finite models that will enable us to gain some sense of that which is behind and beyond everything finite, and which must not be identified directly with anything finite. Our concept of God, thus—if it is the ultimate point of reference we are attempting to conceive—will never be finished or fixed in some definitive form or definition. Rather, it will always be that which escapes our every definition but to which we aspire as we formulate our definitions. By "God" we mean that, as Anselm so well put it, "than which nothing greater can be conceived," that is, that which is beyond our every finite conception.

So that these two points implicit in Thesis II are completely clear and explicit, I shall summarize them in two subtheses.

Subthesis A. The ultimate point of reference—that to which every item of experience and every object within the world, as well as the world itself, is to be related—transcends all experience and the world, and may not be confused or identified with any item of experience or object within the world (principle of God's absoluteness).

Subthesis B. All concepts and images that are used to give content or concreteness to the image/concept of God are drawn from particular human experiences within the world; they must be regarded, therefore, as only models or metaphors or analogies on the basis of which the symbol of God is built up.

These two subtheses, taken together, give us Thesis II. They state that whatever else we mean by "God," we mean at least that which transcends the world and all that is in it,* that which shows everything finite to be an idol if treated as an object of worship or devotion. This implies that in our speech of and to what we call "God," we must always treat our concepts— all of which are drawn from our experience of realities within the world— as models or metaphors or analogies, never as literally defining or properly characterizing the divine.

Thesis II makes it clear that the way in which God is conceived will always be heavily dependent on the particular models and metaphors that we use. A God conceived in terms of the metaphor of creativity or constructive power, for example, will be very different from a God conceived in terms of violent destructiveness; a God conceived by means of images of loving-kindness and merciful forgiveness will be quite different from one conceived as impersonal process or abstract unity. There are many different notions of God abroad, and that which distinguishes the specifically *Christian* conception of God from others is the configuration of metaphors and images in terms of which it is constructed. The next question to which we must address ourselves, therefore, has to do with the models and metaphors that define and characterize the Christian conception of God. That is the subject of Thesis III.

Thesis III. The received Christian image/concept of God draws heavily on human metaphors and models—for example, father, lord, judge, son, word, love, mercy, forgiveness, suffering—thus suggesting that the ultimate point of reference may properly be understood in terms of human, or at least humane, metaphors and analogies, and that God relates Godself to humankind in ways that promote and enhance human development and fulfillment; to the extent that Jesus of Nazareth is regarded as the final or definitive revelation of God, God's humaneness becomes further specified as essentially suffering love.†

---

*When this essay was written, I depended heavily on the spatial metaphor of transcendence to facilitate distinguishing God from both the world as a whole and every particular being in the world. This widely used metaphor, however, to the extent that it suggests that God is to be thought of as somehow "outside" or "beyond" the world, must be used with caution. More recently I have been employing the notion of creativity to indicate what is meant by "God" (see chap. 6 below), thus qualifying in significant ways the metaphor of transcendence.

†This statement of Thesis III (concerned with God's "humaneness") and its elucidation are formulated largely in terms drawn from the highly personalistic language of the tradition. Though such language continues to be useful (in my present view), it requires more careful qualification than could be supplied in this text. A fuller and more adequate treatment of these matters will be found in chaps. 6, 7, and 9 below. For full discussion of the problems this sort of anthropomorphic language poses, see *In Face of Mystery*, Part IV.

Elucidation: The Christian conception of God was built upon foundations drawn from the Old Testament, where anthropomorphic metaphors
like lord, king, mighty warrior, creator, and judge were heavily used and in
fact provided the defining images. God was conceived as a mighty personal
being, creator of the world and lord of history. The characteristically Christian metaphors qualify this conception in the direction of de-emphasizing
God's arbitrary imperial power and highlighting God's personal and
humane character: God is depicted preeminently as loving, gracious, forgiving, faithful, a "father." In radical forms of Christianity, where Jesus is
taken as the definitive revelation of God—that is, as the defining image or
model in terms of which God is finally to be understood—the notion of God
is significantly transformed, from its Old Testament origins in the image of
a "mighty warrior" who "lords it over" all others, into a conception (also
originating in the Old Testament) of one who is essentially a "suffering servant" who in love and forgiveness sacrifices self completely that humans
might have fulfillment and life (cf. Mark 10:42-45). With Jesus as the key
model in terms of which God is understood, God is grasped as essentially
suffering and forgiving love. At the very heart of Christian faith, thus, are
images which depict God as essentially *humane*.

We can say, then, that alongside the principle of God's absoluteness
(which characterizes monotheistic notions of God generally), Christian
faith sets, as equally central, a principle of God's humaneness. In some
ways, these two principles correspond to what in traditional Christian theology were developed as the first and second persons of the trinity—God
the transcendent creator, and God the incarnate savior; to these two the
Holy Spirit was added as the third person of the trinity, "proceeding" from
the Father and the Son. The Spirit was the continuous presence of God—of
the Father and the Son, of Absoluteness and Humaneness—in all times and
places, and acknowledged especially in the community of the faithful. In
terms of our formulation here, the doctrine of the third person stresses that
God, properly characterized as both truly absolute and truly humane, must
also be understood as always and everywhere present; and thus, in particular, as present here and now.[1]

The central features of the Christian concept of God have now been
sketched. There are three principal criteria in terms of which every proposed idea of God is to be assessed, criticized, and reconstructed: absoluteness, humaneness, and presence, corresponding to the three principles that
define the essentials of the Christian view. We are now in a position, therefore, to state more directly the task of specifically Christian theology. That
is the burden of Thesis IV.

Thesis IV. The task of Christian theology is to assess and criticize received ideas of God in terms of their adequacy in expressing God's *absoluteness* and God's *humaneness,* and to reconstruct the image/concept of God so that it will present these motifs as clearly and meaningfully as possible in the contemporary situation, that is, so that God's *presence* in contemporary life becomes intelligible.

Elucidation: We can now see more clearly the significance of something noted under Thesis I, that theology is not properly understood either as primarily biblical exegesis or as the exposition of traditional dogma or doctrine. Christian theology is essentially *construction*—construction, as carefully as possible, of a Christian view of God (in connection, of course, with a view of the world and of humanity). Doubtless the Bible has a great deal to contribute to this constructive work; indeed, it would not have been possible to formulate our three criteria for construction of the image/concept of God—absoluteness, humaneness, and presence—without recourse to biblical materials. It is in these materials that we have the principal record of the origins and growth of the notion of God in Israel's history; and here also are to be found the principal extant reports of the life and ministry of Jesus of Nazareth, regarded by Christians as central to God's definitive revelation. The conception of God, thus, is in a number of important respects biblically rooted. No theologian, however, has been satisfied simply with reproducing biblical ideas: theologians have always been engaged in the work of translating these ideas into terms that would be effective and meaningful in their own time and place and culture. That is, they have concerned themselves with analyzing, criticizing, and reconstructing received ideas of God into terms that seemed more appropriate and adequate and true for the situation in which they found themselves. This critical and reconstructive work was already going on in the Bible itself—as can easily be seen in the development of the conception of God from Moses through the Yahwist, Amos, and others to Second Isaiah, and then finally to Jesus, Paul, and John—and it continued in the work of the second-century Apologists, in Origen, Athanasius, Augustine, Anselm, Aquinas, Luther, and Calvin, and all the way down to Karl Barth and Paul Tillich in the last generation.

Theology thus cannot be regarded as primarily biblical exegesis, however important biblical study is to the constructive work of the theologian. Nor can theology be regarded as essentially the reproduction and exposition of traditional doctrines and dogmas. The long history of Christian experience and reflection is doubtless a great help to the theologian's understanding of God, but it never directly provides the theologian with that construction: that is the theologian's own peculiar work. The central thing to be learned from this long history (as the recital of names just given ought to indicate) is that in each new era the image/concept of God has to be further (re)constructed, bringing in new elements not thought of before, eliminating motifs that now seem inadequate, misleading, even false, correcting what now appear to be the misconceptions or misinterpretations of previous generations. However important biblical and historical materials are to the reflection of the theologian, they never can function as final authorities. In every generation it is the theologian herself or himself who makes the final decision about what contours the notion of God will have on the pages being written.

Construction of the concept of God is today, as always in the past, central to theological work. That is both the glory and the frailty of theology: glory, in that it is the conception of God, certainly one of the highest and most complex ideas known to the human mind, which is being contemplated and constructed; frailty, in that every such conception is, after all, only one more human conception, subject to all the limitations of finitude, relativity, prejudice, and sin that infect every piece of human work, thus necessarily to be criticized and corrected by others.

Once we recognize that the most fundamental task of our theology is construction of a notion of God appropriate for our time, we will see that we cannot divest ourselves from taking full responsibility for every feature of that notion. We are the ones who must persuade ourselves what the principles of absoluteness and humaneness can properly mean for our time and our world and our experience. And we are the ones who must decide how these are to be conjoined in a symbol appropriate to focus the worship and devotion of women and men in today's world. We are the ones, in short, who must construct image/concepts of God that will be meaningful and significant for our day. To be called to the vocation of Christian theologian is to be called to just this task of construction.

How, now, is constructive work appropriate to contemporary life and culture to be done? That question brings us to Thesis V.

Thesis V. Criticism and reconstruction of the image/concept of God will involve continuous reference to contemporary forms of experience and life—personal, social, moral, political, aesthetic, scientific, and others—all of which must be related to, and thus relativized and humanized by, the concept of God, if God is indeed to function as the ultimate point of reference for our living and thinking today.

Elucidation: The task of theology is not only to speak of God's absoluteness and God's humaneness (the first and second persons of the trinity), but also to show that this absoluteness and humaneness are present and effective today (the third person of the trinity). That is, it is to show that God can be and in fact is the ultimate point of reference for *our* lives, our world, our experience, our devotion. This means that theologians must be prepared to portray, at least in principle, all contemporary life and experience—in Asia and Africa as well as Europe and the Americas—in relation to what God is believed to be, so that no nook or cranny of life or the world remains disconnected from or out of relation to God. To the extent that segments or portions of contemporary life and experience remain unrelated to God, God is not in fact the ultimate point of reference for the entirety of our world. And thus what we are calling God is not indeed *God*, and we are not God's worshippers: we are polytheists and idolaters. Just as important, therefore, as formulating an adequate notion of God—or rather, an essential part of the formulation of such a notion—is showing the way in which God is related to every segment and every dimension of today's experience and world. Theologians must begin to develop understandings of human culture and life that take into account not only what is known and believed about all these matters in western religious traditions but also what can be learned from nonwestern religions and cultures as well as from modern wisdom and science. No domain of culture or of learning may be overlooked if God is to be not only "the God of our fathers and mothers" but also the proper and true ultimate point of reference for our time and our world.

As we bring the various segments of contemporary life and experience into connection with our understanding of God, they are simultaneously brought under the criticism and judgment of God's absoluteness and humaneness. Our awareness of God's absoluteness will show every point of view, every custom, every institution, every style of life of which we know, to be finite and limited and relative; and we will begin to see how frequently we and others falsely absolutize one or another of these into idols before whom we bow in worship. As God, the great relativizer of all false absolutes, unmasks these idols of ours, we are enabled better to understand who (or what) God is in our time and place. And we begin to see more clearly the evils that corrupt and threaten to destroy our common life.

God is also conceived as truly humane. So as we bring the customs and institutions and practices of human life today into connection with the image/concept of God, we are enabled better to see the respects in which they are inhuman, depersonalizing, destructive of our own humanity as well as the humanity of others. To be aware of God's humaneness is to be aware of a demand upon us to humanize these inhuman structures in our

world, to work toward freeing those in bondage to degrading and depersonalizing institutions and practices.

The theological task of bringing all of life and the world into relation
with God facilitates and requires criticism of idolatries and inhumanities
wherever they continue to degrade and destroy contemporary human
beings. Theology, if it truly speaks of God, always simultaneously becomes
social criticism and ethics. This brings us to a point where we can ask
about the way in which, and the degree to which, Christian theological
thinking must be contextualized in each culture within which it is being
undertaken, the subject of my sixth and last thesis.

Thesis VI. It is appropriate and correct—in our construction of an
image/concept of God within a particular cultural context—to employ
freely whatever indigenous metaphors, models, and concepts commend
themselves (even if this leads to significant departures from biblical or traditional ways of understanding God); and at those points where indigenous social and cultural forces, ideas, and institutions reach for idolatrous
absolutization, or are responsible for continuing injustice and dehumaniza-
tion, they must be identified, relativized, and resisted as they are brought
into relation with that God who is both absolute and humane.

Elucidation: Once we recognize clearly that theology is (and always has
been) fresh construction of the concept of God in terms of the experience
and needs and demands of each new situation in which women and men
find themselves, we can see that the question of contextualization is neither
a new nor a particularly unusual one for Christian theology. Theological
thinking has always been involved in reconceiving and reinterpreting the
concept of God (and other related concepts) in terms indigenous to new
historical situations that posed issues significantly different from those that
had previously been addressed theologically. The history of theology has,
in fact, been essentially a story of the appropriation of such new terms and
concepts, thus transforming and developing the concept of God in important ways, showing God's relevance to ever wider reaches of experience.
Doubtless as theological reflection moves from cultures that have long spoken of the Christian God to cultures formed religiously and philosophical-
ly according to other patterns and vocabularies, the demands placed on
human imagination and creativity by constructive theological work
become greater. But in principle nothing is changed. It is only that in such
cases we can see, more sharply and clearly, just what theological thinking
must always involve: creative imaginative construction at every important
point. Proper contextualizing of all theological metaphors and concepts is
essential to all good theology.

It is equally important, of course, as the image/concept of God is constructed in terms supplied by a new historical or cultural context, that God's absoluteness and humaneness become significant norms, in terms of which the false idols and the inhuman and unjust ideologies and institutions of that cultural setting are effectively exposed, criticized, and (as liberation theologians have rightly insisted) reformed or overthrown. The conception of God as both truly absolute and truly humane is never completely "at home" in the relativities and imperfections and inhumanities of any culture. However, to the extent that it becomes and remains vital and significant in the life of a people, it provides an effective basis of criticism and of motivation for reform, even for revolution. Thus, successful contextualization of the symbol "God" can never mean its full adaptation to the norms and values of a culture. It must involve, rather, articulation in concepts and metaphors that make its critical bearing on that culture relevant and effective for those living there.

As God becomes the ultimate point of reference in terms of which all human life and experience (in a particular time and place) are understood, the institutions and practices and beliefs of that culture necessarily become exposed to theological judgments on their idolatries and their inhumanities. Thus, God no longer remains merely the God of an ancient tradition but becomes instead the *living* God for those living in that world.

Christian theology is completely free—indeed, theology is under the imperative—to become fully contextualized within each culture in which Christians live and work, but neither the principle of God's absoluteness nor the principle of God's humaneness may be compromised. The central task of theologians in every culture is to construct an image/concept of God appropriate to that objective.

Chapter 3

Religious Diversity, Historical Consciousness, and Christian Theology

Hour can persons and communities with radically differing conceptions of the world and of human life, and quite diverse views of the most urgent problems facing human beings and the most effective ways to address those problems, come to understanding and appreciation of each others' ways of being human? How, in all our diversity, can we humans learn to live together fruitfully, productively, and in peace in today's complexly interconnected world, instead of regularly moving into the sort of conflict and struggle that easily erupts into terribly destructive warfare? These questions raise special issues for Christians because of the absolutistic claims about divine revelation and ultimate truth they have often regarded as central to faith. Such claims require careful theological scrutiny in light of the situatedness of Christian faith in a thoroughly pluralized human world, scrutiny that will move us toward fundamental revisions in our understanding of the tasks and methods of Christian theology. I shall try to explain these contentions in this chapter.

Among ordinary Christian believers, as well as most theologians, it is usually taken for granted that the fundamental truths and values needed for the proper ordering of human life are available and known in and to the Christian tradition: they have been provided by divine revelation (however that may be understood). The task of theologians and other teachers in the church, thus, is taken to be interpreting and passing on these truths and values of the tradition, not fundamentally questioning, criticizing, or reconstructing them. Hence, when other religious (or secular) positions making divergent or even contradictory claims are encountered, these

First published in *The Myth of Christian Uniqueness: Toward a Pluralistic Theology of Religions*, ed. John Hick and Paul Knitter (Maryknoll, N.Y.: Orbis Books, 1987), 3–15. Used with permission.

should either be refuted as mistaken or interpreted in light of the basic principles that Christians already accept.[1]

To many Christians today, however, this sort of practice, which has stood the churches in good stead for two millennia, increasingly seems to be faulty and dangerous. In the first place, it is apparent that there are a number of other religious (and secular) communities and traditions—Buddhism, Judaism, certain forms of secular humanism, and so forth—that have quite impressive resources for interpreting and orienting human existence, and for giving significant formation to human individual and social life. It seems a narrow sort of self-impoverishment to refuse to learn from these differing ways of being human, however alien some of them may at first appear. Second, and much more important, it has become obvious today that if we humans do not learn to appreciate each others' commitments well enough to enable us to live together in our diversity, if we continue to attempt (as most communities and traditions have throughout the past) to live largely from and to ourselves—even moving willingly at times to destroy those whom we regard as enemies—we will not be able to address effectively the enormous problems now threatening humankind worldwide. We live today in a single intraconnected and intradependent world, whether we like it or not, and it is no longer possible either to ignore the many other ways of being human that surround us or to move toward eliminating them. We must learn instead to encounter these others on equal terms, seeking, as sympathetically as we can, to understand and appreciate both their insights into the human condition and the forms of belief and practice they recommend and inculcate.

With these considerations in mind, I wish to propose in this chapter certain theological moves for Christians that will, I think, help to open our self-understanding in such a way as to facilitate significant interchange with others on matters of fundamental conviction and faith. If we are to take other faiths, other life-orientations, with full seriousness, we must reexamine some of the theological claims that Christians often make. I shall suggest that modern historical consciousness helps bring into focus the sort of reassessment and theological reconstruction that is called for here.

I

It should be clear that if our objective is to proceed toward greater mutual understanding with those with whom we now disagree on fundamental issues, we cannot continue to follow our usual practice of simply taking it for granted that our received religious traditions provide us with every-

thing we need. It is just this sort of provincial approach to thinking and living that gives rise to the problems we are taking up in this chapter.

Some suggest we should attempt to overcome our traditional parochial-
ism by moving to what they claim is a "universally human" position, one
that penetrates beneath all the "accidental" and "historical" differences
among humans and their religions to some supposed "essential oneness"
we all share. Then, on the basis of this deep unity underlying everything
human, we can understand and negotiate the differences with which the
several great religious traditions confront us. But there really is no such
universally human position available to us; every religious (or secular)
understanding and way of life we might uncover is a *particular* one, that
has grown up in a particular history, makes particular claims, is accompanied by particular practices and injunctions, and hence is to be distinguished from all other particular religious and secular orientations. Doubtless there are similarities, parallels, and overlappings of many different
sorts within this enormous human diversity—and it is just as important to
grasp these connections as to apprehend the differences—but it seems
undeniable that every position to which we might turn is itself historically
specific. A universal frame of orientation for human understanding and life
is no more available to us than a universal language. (These issues will be
discussed more fully below, especially in Chapter 12.)

Instead of searching for a single "universal position" that sets forth,
supposedly, the "essence" of the human or of human religiousness, I want
to acknowledge immediately that in my view it is impossible to move out
of and leave behind the particular symbolic, linguistic, and conceptual
frames of reference within which we ordinarily do our thinking and living.
Nevertheless, if we are to approach sympathetically, and enter into dialogue with, others of quite different commitments and convictions, we
must find ways of relativizing and opening up our basic symbol-system.
The tendencies toward absoluteness and exclusivity in traditional Christian
faith and reflection easily lead to a kind of idolatry that makes it difficult to
take other faiths seriously in their own terms, searching out their insights
into human existence and the deepest human problems, attending carefully
to their proposals regarding how those problems should be approached.[2]

To address this problem inherent in traditional Christian faith and theology, I want to make a relatively simple proposal: that we follow out certain implications of our modern historical consciousness and the kind of
reflection it engenders as we work out our theological understanding of
Christian faith. Many Christians already accept modern historical methods
as appropriate for understanding the origins of Christianity as well as the
institutions, practices, and beliefs of other religious traditions. I want to

suggest now that the complex of attitudes and consciousness that underlies modern attempts to engage in historical and comparative studies of human religiousness can provide a way to break through the tendencies toward absoluteness and self-idolatry that often obstruct interaction between Christians and others.

Modern historical and comparative studies direct attention to precisely the particularity and concreteness of communities and traditions, in this way seeking to grasp their full human significance and import. As we begin to appreciate the richness and meaning of life in a specific community or tradition, it becomes possible for us to take more seriously its integrity and its unique claims. We gradually come to see how it has gained its distinctive structure, emphasis, and character in and through the history in which it was created. We grasp its unique historicity.

Let us take note of what it means to understand a religious position in this historical way. It means grasping the patterns of life before us, the ritual practices, the customs, the values, the ideas, the ways of thinking and meditating, the worldviews, all in connection with their specific historical context, in order to see how and why they came into being with just the special qualities and characteristics they have come to have. It is clear that widely diverse patterns of life, structures of roles and institutions, religious practices and experiences, have developed in the various societies around the globe and in different historical periods. Thus, the women and men who grew up in those societies and historical periods were formed in different ways, came to have different skills, different interests, different needs, different patterns of relationship to other humans. They became quite different persons than they would had they grown up in some other society or some other period. Each of us would be very different had we grown to maturity in, say, an Indian village (as a low-caste Hindu), in a commune in central China, or in a Roman emperor's family. (These sorts of observations are, of course, commonplace in modern historical understanding.)

With our human historicity in mind in this way, let us turn for a moment to consider the rise and development of human religiousness. Human life, as we today believe, gradually evolved from its animal origins to forms shaped by cultural activity, and only over the course of many generations did it become historical in the sense we have just been noting. The development of language and culture enabled women and men to become conscious of themselves and of the world around them in respects not possible for other forms of animal life, and they increasingly oriented themselves and their lives in terms of this growing linguistic and cultural consciousness. In time, unifying ideas or pictures of the world began to appear to the more imaginative and poetic, ideas that enabled persons to see and understand their world better, making it possible to adapt and live within it more effectively. And notions of what humans themselves are, what their deepest needs are and how these needs are to be met, also began to be formulated.

The earliest versions of these conceptions of the human and of the world were apparently in the form of stories, poems, and songs told and sung generation after generation. These presented imaginative pictures of human life, showing the problems that must be faced and the tasks to be performed. They enabled men and women to gain some idea of what the world in which they lived was like, what were the powers or beings that must be dealt with in human existence. Human life could be seen, for example, as a journey through hazardous territory where one might encounter wild beasts and evil monsters as one sought to get to the safety of home; or it might be depicted as participation in a great warfare between the forces of light and the forces of darkness. It might be set forth essentially as responsible citizenship in a quasi-political order, the kingdom of God; or as but one stage in a never-ending transmigration of the soul from one form of life to another. The human individual or self might be seen as a soul, fallen out of its proper home in heaven above, which had become trapped in a physical body from which it must find some way to escape. Or, in sharp contrast, the very sense of self or soul might be regard-ed as an illusion, the product of ignorance, the veil of *maya*, which right insight alone can dispel, thus dissolving the profound human problems that arise out of this false consciousness. Or human existence might be understood to be a product of the accidental collocation of material atoms, or of blind evolutionary processes that could just as well have gone in other directions and formed other patterns.

In the course of history, women and men have developed many diverse worldviews, many different conceptions of what life in the world is all about, of what the central human problems are and what solutions to them might be available. Every great civilization, indeed every isolated tribe, has worked out one or more such conceptual or imagistic frames for under-standing, interpreting, and orienting human life. And humans have shaped and reshaped their lives, institutions, values, and practices in accord with these various visions of reality and the human. It is out of primordial visions of this sort, and the practices that gave rise to or accompanied them, that the different religious traditions have grown. In their religious practices, institutions, and rituals humans have found orientation in life, have found an interpretation of what existence is all about and how it is to be lived. Or rather, we should say, it was in their search for orientation in life, in their attempt to come to terms with the problems of human exis-tence and how it is to be lived, that humans created and developed the various religious traditions, thus giving life the wide range of meanings it has come to have.

Of course the great religious poets, prophets, and storytellers have rarely understood themselves to be directly creating traditions of value and meaning to serve in this way as interpretations of the ultimate mystery of things, as bulwarks against the void. They have thought of themselves, rather, as simply depicting what human life is all about, what happens to men and women in life. Since humans have always come to consciousness and self-consciousness within communities and traditions already there, which had been handed down by the elders—the mothers and fathers—as the wisdom about life, no one ever experienced himself or herself building up a conception of the world and the human simply from scratch. Living and working within the framework of understanding handed down to it, each new generation made only such changes and additions—and subtractions—as its activities and experience demanded. Men and women seldom (if ever) understood themselves to be creating or constructing a picture of the world and of the human within the world. Rather, each was, at most, making small corrections in received pictures regarded as substantially true. From our modern historical vantage point, however, looking back at the many great and diverse cultural and religious traditions that have appeared in human history, all these conceptions and pictures seem best understood as the product of many generations of human imaginative creativity in face of the ultimate mystery that life is to us all. Out of and on the basis of such traditions of meaning, value, and truth, all women and men live. (Some of the larger anthropological and theological implications of these matters will be developed below in Chapters 4–6.)

II

Such a historical approach to the understanding of human religiousness, its origins and functions, has long been accepted in the scholarly study of religion (including the study of Christianity), but it has not often been made a point of departure for Christian theological construction. I want to suggest, now, that theological self-understanding informed by modern historical consciousness can provide an approach to Christian faith that will—without destroying or undercutting the fundamental significance of the central symbols of God and Christ for the orientation of life—enable Christians to give other religious traditions their full integrity and meaning, neither patronizing nor otherwise demeaning them.

If our self-understanding is informed by a historical conception of human existence of the sort I have outlined, we must think of ourselves as historical beings like everyone else; and we will see the traditions of value, meaning, and truth by which we are living and which orient our lives as themselves historical in character—that is, as creations of the human imagination in and through history, like those of any other people or community. This sort of historicist self-interpretation, of course, gives rise to some theological questions that must be faced squarely. Some may believe it undermines the very meaning of Christian faith. If we agree that everything religious—including our own commitments and convictions—is historical in character, is not the normative significance of faith undercut? If the Christian meanings and values, insights and understandings, by which we live are taken to be basically products of certain specific historical developments, instead of held to be grounded simply and directly in divine revelation, do they not lose their point?

I do not think these consequences need follow from the proposal I am making, though it must be granted that the sense of *absoluteness* connected with our religious convictions will be weakened. This does not mean, however, that they are thereby rendered inoperative or ineffective. In fact, an understanding of human existence as historical in the way I am proposing—precisely because it emphasizes the functions and importance of worldviews and conceptual frameworks for ongoing human life—shows clearly how humanly significant, indeed indispensable, are religious language and reflection. There is no reason to suppose that imaginative construction of holistic frames of orientation, of world-pictures, either can or should be discontinued today. It is as necessary for contemporary women and men to have a conceptual frame or worldview for ordering and understanding their lives as it has been for any other generation; but (in light of modern historical understanding) the role that human imaginative creativity has played in producing such frames of orientation should now be made explicit and taken much more seriously into account than heretofore. Our religious activities are still to be carried on, but now in a critical and self-conscious way that was not possible earlier.

What does this mean for Christian theology? If we understand human historicity in the sense I am urging, Christian faith (like every other faith) will be seen as one perspective, one worldview, which has developed in and through a long history alongside other traditions, many of which are vying for the attention and loyalty of us all. When one applies the concept of worldview to one's own tradition in this way, one simultaneously distinguishes it from and relates it to other worldviews. This involves a certain distancing of oneself from one's tradition, taking a step back from simple, unmediated commitment to it. We now see the great theologians of Christian history, for example, not simply as setting out the truth that is ultimately salvific for all humanity (as they have often been understood in the past), but rather as essentially engaged in discerning and articulating one particular perspective on life among many others.

This change in theologians' self-understanding transforms the critical questions for Christian theology. In the past theologians asked, What are the principal doctrines or ideas prescribed by tradition for Christians to believe, and how should these be interpreted today? It now becomes necessary, however, to direct attention to questions like, How does one articulate a worldview—specifically, the Christian worldview—and how does one assess its significance for human life today? Refocusing religious reflection in this way leads one to attend to a rather different agenda from that followed by most theologians in the past. Instead of concentrating on familiar doctrines and dogmas, one is led to inquire into the fundamental categories—the basic conceptual and symbolic framework—that have given Christian perspectives their unique structure, order, and experiential flavor. If these can be ascertained, one can begin to explore the ways and respects in which these categories can order and provide orientation for contemporary human life.

A human frame of orientation, of course, is given its full character and meaning by complex patterns of institutions and customs, words and symbols, liturgical practices and moral claims, stories and myths handed down from generation to generation, shaping and interpreting the experience of those living within it. Not all these expressions, patterns, and practices are of equal weight, however: the basic structure and character of a worldview is defined largely by a few fundamental categories that give it a distinctive shape and order. These are connected and interrelated in various ways by the wider vocabulary of terms and symbols used in ritual and meditation, ideology and story, thus providing concreteness and filling in details of an overall picture, or developing complex of pictures, that can accommodate and interpret the infinite variations and nuances of the experience of many generations. This configuration of defining terms and symbols—often elaborated in quite diverse ways with different nuances of meaning and of behavioral and institutional implications—I call the *categorial structure* of the worldview. The task of Christian theologians today (according to the view I am presenting here) is to penetrate through the multiplicity of Christian philosophies, theologies, and myths, to the basic historically developing categorial pattern that informs them all. With this pattern in mind, theologians are in a position, on the one hand, to engage in analysis and criticism of Christian worldviews that takes into account insights and understandings provided by other religious and secular positions, both ancient and modern; as well as, on the other hand, to move forward with the construction of contemporary Christian understandings of human life, the world, and God.

I cannot here provide a detailed analysis, criticism, and reconstruction of the Christian categorial scheme.[3] Instead I will briefly sketch what I take to be the four principal symbols or categories that give Christian worldviews their basic structure and character: God, world, humanity, Christ. (The first three of these categories, it may be noted, are not uniquely Christian; they have also figured importantly in Jewish and Muslim perspectives.) These four categories provide principal benchmarks or reference points in terms of which Christian maps of reality are drawn. Or, to change the metaphor, they are principal hooks or fasteners to which Christian webs of experience, life, and interpretation are attached, shaping their patterns and character. Here I can say only a few words about each of these categories.

"God" is, of course, the ultimate point of reference in Christian perspectives. Christian traditions have expressed this by speaking of God as the source of all that is, the ultimate ground of all reality, the creator of the world and the lord of history. In the biblical documents God is portrayed as a quasi-personal or agential reality—that is, the model in terms of which the notion of God is constructed is the human self or agent. In classic Christian theology, however, this was greatly complicated by the development of trinitarian conceptions.[4] Just how this ultimate point of reference for all human life and thought can properly be conceived today is a major issue for contemporary constructive theology. (In Chapter 6 below I present a sketch of my present construction of the concept of God, in relation to a contemporary understanding of the world.)

The second term of the categorial scheme, "world," refers to the overall context within which human life takes place. In the earlier mythopoetic versions of the Christian perspective, this context was characterized simply as "the heavens and the earth." But today we are obliged to think of it as an unimaginably immense universe hundreds of millions of light years across and billions of years old. Within this universe are millions of galaxies, and within one of these galaxies is the solar system that provides the immediate context for planet Earth. Earth in turn is a complex ecosystem apart from which human life would not be possible. All of this, in Christian worldviews, is understood to be God's "creation."

The third principal category, "humanity," refers to those creatures living here on earth who are sufficiently self-conscious and capable of taking responsibility for their own actions and lives (for they were "created in God's image") as to require that they have symbolical frameworks for orienting and ordering all their activities (for elaboration, see Chapter 4 below). Orientation has been gained, as we have noted, as humans imaginatively created world-pictures and interpretations of human existence that set out various possibilities, problems, and parameters of life in ways relevant to their historical experience and their accumulated knowledge. It is a principal part of the task of contemporary Christian theology to show how and why an adequate modern world-picture and understanding of the human requires—or at least can usefully employ—the symbols "God" and "Christ" to help orient life today.

The fourth category is "Christ," that figure from human history who is believed by Christians to reveal or define, on the one hand, who or what God really is, and, on the other hand, what true humanity consists in. The historical figure of Jesus Christ thus gives concreteness and specificity to the understanding of both God and humanity, in this way significantly shaping these central symbols that define what is normative for orienting human existence in Christian terms. (A somewhat "wider view" of Christ than that suggested here is sketched below in Chapter 7.)

This fourfold categorial scheme—God/world/humanity/Christ—has largely defined and given shape to Christian understandings of life and the world. Other terms in the Christian vocabulary—for example, sin, salvation, church, sacrament, trinity, faith, hope, love, creation, revelation, holy spirit, and the like—all help to elaborate and fill out this categorial structure so that it can give a full interpretation or picture of what human life is all about, how it is carried on in the world, and toward what human devotion, worship, love, and service should be directed.

Careful and thoughtful reflection on the four terms of this categorial pattern is essential in developing a Christian theology informed (as I am proposing here) by modern historical consciousness. It is necessary for theologians to learn as much as possible about the different ways of thinking about God and the world, humanity and Christ, that have appeared in Christian history; and they must seek to understand the principal arguments for these various views. They will then be in a position to raise some important questions that others in the past have often failed to ask: Which of these Christian views (and in what circumstances) have been destructive, damaging, or oppressive to humans, and thus evil? Which ones (and under what conditions) have promoted the love, creativity, peace, and justice—human fulfillment—for which Christian faith hopes? Which ones (and in what respects) must now be regarded as archaic and misleading, the "mythology" of another age? Which may be expected (and in what ways) to provide adequate, full, and insightful understanding of our contemporary existence, its problems and possibilities? Theologians working with the sort of historical self-consciousness I am advocating are in a position to

examine and to assess traditional theological positions both sympathetically and critically.

This attempt at comprehensive and critical historical assessment should
prepare the way for developing a constructive interpretation of the Christian perspective on life and the world, an interpretation intended to effectively orient the existence of women and men today. In some instances,
however, it may bring a theologian to the conclusion that the traditional
categorial scheme orders and interprets human life in a way no longer
viable or helpful. Perhaps one or more of the principal categories requires
drastic revision, drawing on ideas suggested by other religious or secular
traditions. The theologian may even feel forced to conclude (as some have
in recent years) that such central Christian symbols as "God" or "Christ"
must be given up entirely, other images or concepts being given categorial
status in their stead. There is, of course, an almost unlimited range of theological possibilities and permutations. For a theology that wishes to remain
"Christian," however, the fundamental task is quite straightforward: to
work carefully and critically through the proposals for understanding
human life and the world presented by the Christian tradition (and by theological reflection on that tradition); to try to grasp our contemporary
experience and life in terms of these categories, images, and concepts; and
to reconstruct them in whatever respects are required to enable them to
serve as the framework for a world-picture that can provide adequate orientation for life today.

A contemporary theology, informed in this way by a thoroughgoing historical consciousness, would not be in a position to claim—as Christian
theology has so often in the past—that its assertions were directly and
uniquely authorized or warranted by divine revelation. (This does not
mean, of course, that they are not in some significant sense grounded in
God, as ultimate point of reference; nor does it mean that there are no
ways at all in which the concept of revelation might be used to articulate
that grounding.)[5] Christian theology would understand itself in essentially
the same terms that it understands other religious activity and reflection—
namely, as human imaginative response to the necessity to find orientation
for life in a particular historical situation. It would, thus, keep itself open
to insights, criticism, and correction from other points of view, including
other religious and secular perspectives and worldviews.

Surely this is an enormous gain over more traditional approaches. As
our modern historical knowledge vividly shows, every theological position
has always been taken, and every claim been made, by some particular,
limited, finite, human being, whether named Paul of Tarsus or Thomas
Aquinas or John Calvin or Karl Barth. Beliefs about divine inspiration and

revelation have all too often enabled theologians in the past to obscure this fact by claiming that this or that affirmation or position is grounded direct-ly in the very truth of God. And heretics were burned at the stake for not properly acknowledging what God had so distinctly revealed, and what this or that theologian or church official knew with such certainty. To acknowledge forthrightly and regularly that our theological statements and claims are simply *ours*—that they are the product of our own human study and reflection, and of the spontaneity and creativity of our human powers imaginatively to envision a world and our human place within that world—is to set us free from these all too easy but false moves toward authoritarianism, which have characterized so much Christian theology in the past. And simultaneously we are opened to the broad ranges of experi-ence, life, and insight lying outside our own tradition, and provided with a powerful incentive to engage in dialogue and other interchange—on equal terms—with representatives of other religious and secular points of view.

III

I would like now to draw together the points I have been making. None of us—Christian or non-Christian—possesses absolute or final truth, truth adequate to orient humankind in face of the enormous problems we con-front in today's world.[6] (This point is developed in more formally theolog-ical terms in Chapter 6, with reference to the concept of *mystery*.) At best we Christians, like all others, have available to ourselves the insights and understanding of our forebears. But these were, in all cases, their own imaginative constructions, formed under the influence of their own experi-ence and of the problems they faced in their time, and thus finite, limited, relative. They have been corrected, amplified, and transformed in the past by other imaginative and creative women and men. And they can surely benefit today from exposure to images and concepts, perspectives and worldviews, developed in other quite different traditions. The problems with which modernity confronts us—extending even to the possibility that we may obliterate humankind completely in a nuclear holocaust or total ecological collapse—demand that we bring together all the wisdom, devo-tion, and insight that humanity has accumulated in its long history, as we attempt to find orientation in today's world. We simply cannot afford not to enter into conversation with representatives of other traditions, making available to each other whatever resources we each have to offer, and learning from each other whatever we can.

Such dialogue today should not have as its objective just talking togeth-er to get information about points of view different from our own. We

must enter into serious exchange with each other in order to help humanity—including, of course, ourselves—find adequate orientation in today's
world; in order, that is, to enable us to construct religious (and secular)
frameworks that can provide guidance with respect to the unprecedented
problems we today confront. We must learn how to discern the basic patterns and frameworks of the several great religious and secular traditions
of orientation that have been created by humankind in its long history—
to discern what I have called their fundamental categorial structures—and
this should facilitate our comparing them with each other more intelli-
gently, evaluating the strong and the weak points of each as frames of orientation for life today. Thus we will come into a better position to construct frames of orientation that can provide guidance for contemporary
human existence.

Religious claims have always had to make their way, finally, in the open
marketplace of human experience and ideas. Though dogmatic appeal to
revelatory authority, or to special insight, enlightenment, or truth, might
for a time have given a position special attention and credence, in the long
run of history only the power to explain, interpret, and orient actual
human life has enabled some positions and claims to survive and to grow
in intellectual and cultural power, whereas others, gradually or quickly,
have died out. Acknowledgment that our religious reflection is *our own*
imaginative and intellectual (individual and communal) activity—not a
direct expression of divine revelation—will be salutary in forcing us to do
our work as well as we can, even while we are open to insights and understandings from other quite different religious and secular perspectives.

In the twentieth century particularly, humankind—which for most of its
history developed in quite diverse ways in various geographical settings
around the globe—has been growing together into one humanity. Now the
threats of nuclear war, population explosion, and ecological collapse have
irrevocably bound us all together in one common fate, whether we like it
or not. It is no longer possible, therefore, or desirable, for us to continue
living simply and uncritically out of the parochial religious and cultural
traditions we have inherited. Entering into dialogue with others and trying
to understand each other, exposing the weaknesses and problems of our
own perspectives to each other as well as their respective values and
strengths, learning to appreciate the insights and conceptions of positions
quite different from our own—these sorts of moves are increasingly
demanded of us all.

I have tried to sketch here a way to understand the task of Christian theology today that will help Christians move more easily and wholeheartedly
into genuine interreligious understanding and fruitful dialogue. This per-

spective, as we have seen, grows out of modern western historical thinking, and it is in that respect, of course—like all other perspectives—particular, relative, and limited. We do not know what sorts of theological self-understanding may succeed it at some later time. But it is an approach that enables us to break the grip of the absolutistic commitments that have characterized much traditional Christian faith and theology, thus enabling us to encounter other significant religious and secular traditions *in their own terms* instead of as defined by our categories. Moves of this sort can help provide us with the understanding and sympathy for others that is so much needed to help bring peace in our time. Only as we find ways of stepping back from, and thus not remaining confined within, those features of our own traditions (both religious and secular) that wall us off from others, can we hope to come into genuine understanding of and community with them. Building such community is today's most profound religious necessity. Promoting it, therefore, is the most important task to which Christian theology can now attend.

Part Two

Rethinking Some Central Christian Themes

What bearing does the understanding of theology that I am proposing in this volume—the ongoing imaginative construction and reconstruction of the basic Christian symbols—have on our conceptions today of God and Christ, of humanity and the world? In particular, what sort of reconception of these symbols does our present consciousness of the radical diversity of forms of human life, and our increasing awareness of the profundity of other great world religions, require of us? It is to these questions that Part Two, the theological core of this book, is devoted. The three principal chapters of this section (Chapters 4, 6, and 7) have not been previously published; they present in compact form, and with an eye to theological problems posed by religious and cultural pluralism, ideas worked out more fully in my book, *In Face of Mystery: A Constructive Theology.*

Chapter 4, "A Biohistorical Understanding of the Human," deals with two large issues: (1) I present here a conception of the human which, on the one hand, takes with full seriousness the biological grounding of every feature of our existence, and, on the other hand, seeks to make intelligible—through its emphasis on the radical *historicity* of human being—the enormous variety of ways of being human that have developed in the course of history. (2) I seek to show that despite this great diversity, and the historical relativity of everything human that accompanies it, the conception of human existence as *biohistorical* provides us with criteria for making significant cross-cultural judgments respecting diverse forms of human life (and the configurations of value, meaning, and truth that accompany these). The criterion of humanization (initially sketched in Chapter 1) here begins to obtain a fuller anthropological grounding and thus clearer meaning and content.

In Chapter 5 the implications of this conception of the human for the (religious) notions of evil and salvation are briefly explored in relation to their distinctively biological and historical roots. This helps to focus some of the specifically theological features of the criterion of humanization, and makes it possible to define it with more precision. Chapters 4 and 5 taken together, thus, not only sketch a theological anthropology with the means to understand and interpret human historical and cultural life in all its diversity as well as its interconnectedness with its biological base: they also propose a way in which cross-cultural *normative* issues, with which our emerging global civilization increasingly confronts us, can be addressed.

This brings us into a position, then, to turn to the two principal normative symbols in terms of which Christian forms of life have sought to orient themselves, *God* and *Christ*. In Chapter 6, with the ultimate mystery of human life and the world as backdrop, a conception of God that can stand in significant relation to contemporary scientific understandings of the world, as well as in openness to the diversity of religious and sociocultural orientations that have emerged in human history, is outlined. In place of the somewhat reifying traditional ideas of God as the creator of the world and the lord of history, the metaphor of "serendipitous creativity," expressing itself in and through a variety of evolutionary and historical directional movements or trajectories, is employed in working out an understanding of God appropriate for today. When this notion is then combined, in Chapter 7, with a reconsideration of the normative christic images that have so powerfully shaped Christian faith and life, the basic outlines of an overall world-picture that can order and orient Christian existence in today's multicultural and religiously pluralistic world have been drawn.

With the faith-stance sketched in these chapters in mind, we are in a position to move forward into the wider extra-Christian world within which we today are so conscious of living. Part Three takes up some of the issues posed for Christians when they enter into direct dialogue with Buddhists. And in Part Four a pluralistic/dialogical notion of religious truth is presented, a notion that can help us think in a significantly different way about our radically pluralized human world, thus facilitating more sympathetic, and more effective, engagement with those many others who have commitments sharply different from ours.

Chapter 4

A Biohistorical Understanding of the Human

In Chapter 3 I argued that Christians have an obligation to take seriously, and attempt to understand sympathetically, the religious faiths of others around the globe who do not call themselves Christian. There have been in the past—and this will probably continue far into the future—many different ways of being human, and many different understandings of what humans are and how they ought to live. How should we respond to this pluralism in human living, and in human thinking about life—about what life is most fundamentally and how it ought to be conducted? Is human existence pluralistic at every level and in every respect, or are there some basic universal threads that run through life everywhere? These questions are of importance today not only because they are so prominent in the pluralistic/relativistic consciousness of modern/postmodern culture, but also because of the implications they have for our understanding of Christian faith and its claims. We Christians are also a part and an expression of this panorama of diversity. How should we today understand the significance of this fact? Do traditional Christian ideas of human being and the human story enable us to grasp everything that is important here? If not, what kind of conceptions should we develop to help us better understand and respond to these matters?

I

In my recent book, *In Face of Mystery: A Constructive Theology,* I have worked out a pluralistic/historicistic understanding of human being as a way of accounting for and interpreting the significance of the great diversity and widespread disagreement about values, meanings, ways of living,

This chapter draws on a range of materials published in *In Face of Mystery* (Cambridge, Mass.: Harvard University Press, 1993), esp. in Part II. Used with permission.

conceptions of what is true about life and the world, and so on, with which we are continually confronted today. I propose what I call a biohistorical understanding of the human, one that takes account of, and holds together, both the biological grounding of human existence in the web of life on planet Earth and the many different sorts of historical development of humankind in and through the growth, over thousands of generations, of the varied sociocultural patterns of life around the planet. This efflorescence of human cultures—which increasingly came to include flexible and complex languages, a great variety of forms of differentiated social organization, the development of skills of many different sorts, the creation of innumerable kinds of artifacts, including especially tools that extended human powers in new directions, and so on—appears to have shaped the actual biological development of the predecessors of *homo sapiens*. So the biological organism that finally emerged as human was, as the anthropologist Clifford Geertz has said, "both a cultural and a biological product." Our present biological organisms, if left simply to themselves, would be so seriously deficient that they could not function. Geertz sums up the matter in this way:

> We are . . . incomplete or unfinished animals who complete or finish ourselves through culture—and not through culture in general but through highly particular forms of it: Dobuan and Javanese, Hopi and Italian, upper-class and lower-class, academic and commercial.[1]

Thus our culture—the roles we learn, the language we speak, the skills we acquire, the ideologies we accept, the values we cherish—is an indispensable feature of our human nature. Without the particular culture which has formed each of us in a quite specific way, we would not exist as human at all—though it is also true, of course, that we might just as well have been formed in some quite different way, by a different cultural context. There actually are, then, we might say, many different sorts of human nature, as diverse and variegated as the plurality of human cultures and subcultures. The only thing that is common to us all is our basic biological structure—a structure of great plasticity, open to a wide range of patterns of development, requiring external programming by a culture in order to function. Our capacity for language, for symbol-using and symbol-making, is innate; but our capacity for English, for speaking and thinking and experiencing in this particular way, is acquired. And along with it we also acquire particular ways of being human—particular ways of seeing and understanding ourselves, particular likes and dislikes, particular possibilities of thinking and experiencing, particular conceptions of the meaning of human life and of the nature of the world in which we live.

This cultural inbuilding of our human nature means that our humanity has been created as much by history as by biological evolution. To be sure, the possibility of there being humans at all resulted from a process of evolution through some billions of years. But the actual emergence of distinctively *human* beings came about through the growth of historico-cultural processes that helped to push the development of *homo sapiens* in surprising but decisively important directions. We are, then, all the way down to our deepest roots as humans not simply biological beings, animals. We are biohistorical beings, and it is our historicity that gives our existence its distinctively human character. Though all humans probably come from one original genetic stock, our foreparents migrated over the face of the earth, settling down in extremely various living conditions, from the tropics to arctic cold, from deserts to rain forests, from rugged mountains to rolling prairies to seacoasts. Not surprisingly, these different human groups developed a great variety of patterns of life, distinctive languages and social institutions, and sharply contrasting religious beliefs and practices, as they sought to adapt themselves to the climatic, topographical, and other conditions of their diverse locations. Hence, many different cultures emerged in history, each with a certain appropriateness to the setting in which it appeared.

In these general remarks all I have done is rehearse briefly a widely accepted picture of human origins well known to educated persons (at least in the West). I want to emphasize now that this characterization of the emergence and growth of humankind on planet Earth applies also, of course, to religious and cultural developments in the Ancient Near East. Scholarly studies of the Old and New Testaments today, buttressed by much archeological and other historical work, reveal that the actual beginnings and growth of Israelite religion, and later on Christianity, were quite different from what might be gathered by a straightforward reading of the Bible. As we seek to construct an adequate theological understanding of human being, it is important that we give full recognition to this wider human story within which the appearance and development of our own religious traditions occurred. If we do this, we will be in a better position to see the proper place and the real significance—amidst all the pluralities and relativities and particularities of human life—of Christian faith.

Christian faith makes certain universalistic claims: about humankind, about the world, and about God. One of the major questions with which we must come to terms in this book is how such claims are to be understood in light of our knowledge that they, like everything else religious and cultural, have emerged within highly particular historical developments, and thus are in a significant sense relative to those developments.

In what respects and with what limitations may we today regard it as justifiable for any religiously and culturally formed standpoint to make such claims? If we conclude that it is still possible and appropriate to attempt to formulate human values and truth that can be regarded as (in some sense) universal, we must make certain that we do this in a way that does not imply neglect or repudiation of our understanding of humans as bio-historical. Given this understanding, deeply rooted (as I have suggested) in today's biological, anthropological, and historical knowledges, it would be highly inappropriate to work out a theological position that, for example, presupposes or implies a more or less static-structural conception of an unchanging human nature, together with notions of permanent truth and value or of eternal "natural law" (ideas that often accompany such static-structural views). What is required of us instead is that we take a further step in our understanding of the significance of our historicity and see what theological interpretations of human nature, truth, value, and meaning are appropriate to it.

II

It is the unfolding of history itself that has brought us to the position in which we today find ourselves, needing some sort of new universal vision of the human, one that takes into account more adequately the enormous diversity of human life—and the significance of that diversity—than have the traditional views we have inherited. Happily, recent historical developments suggest that just such a new vision may now be in the making. The process of human cultural creativity that had for hundreds of generations flowed through many relatively separate and distinct channels has in this century, with the growing interdependence of all human life in the limited space available on planet Earth, brought the various separated segments of humanity into increasingly complex interconnections. And it has become necessary, as never before, to find a way for all of us to live together without destroying one another. In previous ages even the most disastrous events of human destructivity affected only particular limited segments of humankind; and life elsewhere went on. Today, however, whether we think of nuclear war or the population explosion or continued ecological breakdown, it is humankind worldwide (and much else on our planet) that is affected by our continuing destructiveness. Humans everywhere, therefore, must begin to take collective responsibility for our common situation in a manner unlike anything hitherto known to us.

This issue is thrust upon us by the history in and through which we are today living; and it is because we are in such a decisive way historical beings that we find the demands it makes upon us so powerful. For beings with *historicity*—beings shaped by their past and with powers to, in significant ways, take responsibility for their future—the crucial questions always are: What is the actual historical situation in which we are living? What demands does this place upon us? What alternative ways of addressing these demands are available? To respond effectively to these questions we need values and ideas, institutions and practices, that are relevant to this situation in which we find ourselves—and thus *relative* to it. If we are unable to respond responsibly and effectively today, humankind may not long survive; for, as we have come to realize in this century, we may be about to obliterate ourselves. Thus, if we now find ourselves searching in a *new* way for values and truths with a certain claim to universality—that is, a claim to significance for all human beings—this does not mean that our historical relativity has been either forgotten or surpassed. This search cannot succeed, however, unless we find ways to move beyond, or at least make significant allowances for, the cultural and religious *parochialisms* that have heretofore been so destructive in human affairs. The nihilistic consequences of much earlier thinking about relativism must be overcome as we open ourselves to the new worldwide humanity of which we all are part and to which we must contribute.

Let us go back now and collect our thoughts. In this chapter we are engaged in trying to think through more adequately our conception of the human, our understanding, that is to say, of what sort of beings we men and women are. This turns out to be a complicated matter. It has become clear that we cannot come to an understanding of our humanness simply by looking at individual persons, or even particular groups or societies, hoping thereby to discover the needs and capacities, the basic structures and activities, of human beings, thus putting together a conception of the human. Individual men and women and the various human groups and societies are all members of a particular species of life and are complexly related to all other living beings, on the one hand. And they have emerged and gained their individuality and uniqueness in specific social and cultural settings that have formed and shaped them into these particular personalities and groups, on the other hand. So it is not really possible adequately to grasp what human beings are simply by directly observing them: we will understand them aright only when we see them as inseparably bound up with the vast human biohistorical process of which they are part. All human existence—that is, the existence of every individual woman and man, every community and society—is constituted fundamentally by this interlocked biology and history, and it is in terms of this biohistorical process that humans must today be conceived. That is, humanness does not belong simply and directly to each of us as an individual or even to our society as a whole. It exists, rather, only as the later phases of a very complex process of development (going back some millions of years) in which strictly biological evolution and change has, in the last 10,000 years or so, gradually become overshadowed by the historical cumulation of cultural change. With the advent of civilization and the invention of writing the process of historical development accelerated in a number of centers around the globe, each creating quite distinct traditions. And in the past two or three centuries these diverse and relatively independent civilizations have become increasingly open to each other. Now, especially since World War II, we have been moving rapidly toward a single intraconnected human world. That there are now enormous momentums in this direction—despite many profoundly destructive and utterly inhuman local conflicts—seems hardly disputable.

According to this reading of history, human nature today—that is, the historico-cultural dimensions of our nature—is being asked to give up the parochial patterns that have characterized it ever since the Stone Age and to take on a new universal—though definitely pluralistic—form. This is a demand that today's historical situation apparently places upon contemporary humanity as a whole. It is not the case, of course, that all women and men are prepared to acknowledge this demand or are even aware of it. The exigencies of many local situations make it virtually impossible for such a consciousness to develop. But those of us who have become aware of this movement of our history toward a new unity and a new universality can hardly help but feel drawn (or driven) to orient ourselves, not simply by the particular values and customs, institutions and forms of life, characteristic of our own provincial traditions, but instead by a *global consciousness*. We feel a demand on us to move beyond our limited loyalties to American, western, or traditional Christian consciousness and institutions and traditions into a universalistic—but pluralistic—human consciousness and into social and cultural forms appropriate to that.

How should such a universalistic pluralistic consciousness be conceived? What institutions would best express it? What attitudes, motivations, practices, ideals promote it? None of this is clear, yet obviously these are among the most important questions now facing men and women. We shall be concerned with them throughout the rest of this book. In my view precisely these sorts of issues are the proper business of theology. The creation of worldviews, of conceptions of the human, of symbols to focus human work and worship, has always been central to the religious strand of human life; and Christian theology emerged as the need for careful criticism and systematic reconstruction of these matters gradually became apparent. As we have seen, in the course of human history innumerable religious visions have been produced, each having some appropriateness to its own situation, to the needs of women and men for meaning and orientation in that place and time; each, thus, having a significant justification and integrity. To the extent that a particular world-picture provided adequate orientation—so that life could go on, and women and men found meaning in their activities, and some sense of who they were and what they should do—the religious tradition survived and developed. If, however, it failed to provide sufficient orientation and motivation for survival and growth, the perspective either died and was replaced by some other (as happened in many great and small religious changes in history) or poets and prophets, reformers and revolutionaries appeared, persons able to criticize and transform the tradition so it could adapt itself better to the circumstances it had to address. This latter, of course, is what happened with those great religious traditions, such as the Hebraic, Hindu, Zoroastrian, which developed relatively continuously over many generations from ancient times to the present. Sometimes, in a moment of crisis and creativity, what had begun as a movement of reformation and transformation of older patterns turned into the birth of a significantly new and distinct vision of human existence, as with Christianity, Buddhism, and Islam. After becoming established as distinctive practices and symbolic frames of orientation within their own communities, these religious orientations also have gone through long histories of development and transformation as new conditions arose to which they had to adapt.

Humankind today is confronting a similar historical moment of crisis and possibility: we live increasingly in a single "global village," and we are faced now with the possibility of population, ecological, and nuclear calamities that could destroy us all. All of the great religious—and secular—traditions are thus called upon today to reconsider the practices and the symbolic structures within and through which they have grasped, interpreted, and formed human life and the world. They are called to see whether it is possible to uncover or create symbols and practices and institutions suitable to the new age into which we are rapidly moving, that is, structures that will enable us to truly *live* in this new age, creatively and fruitfully and in ecological balance with our environment, and not to destroy ourselves utterly. This is a daunting assignment, perhaps an impossible one. But to provide orientation for life in this way, through creating appropriate and meaningful sociocultural dimensions of human existence, has always been the part of the religions. And the criticism and reconstruction of religious symbols and practices in order to facilitate this, however ambitious and difficult, has always (in the West) been a central feature of theological work (though this has not often been clearly acknowledged). It is, therefore, quite appropriate that Christian theological reflection address itself to this task today, in face of the new historical situation into which humanity—that is, all of us—has moved.

These reflections on the historical situation in which humankind now finds itself—human existence understood to be radically diverse to very deep levels, but humankind as a whole confronted with global problems crying for attention—force us to face directly what is perhaps the deepest religious, cultural, and intellectual problem of our time (a problem at the heart of many of the debates in the West about modernity/postmodernity): Can criteria for making the kind of quasi-universal judgments now required of humankind with respect to our quite various social institutions and practices be formulated? Can criteria be developed which will assist us in assessing in pertinent ways the religious and cultural complexes of meaning and value which have hitherto ordered human life?

III

The biohistorical understanding of human being that I am sketching here (and which I believe sums up many assumptions about the human widely taken for granted among educated people in the West today) does not present us with a merely *descriptive* account of what we humans are; *normative* implications, bearing on our existence and the biological, social, cultural, psychological, and interpersonal conditions that make it possible, are also implied by it. Humans (like any other living beings) can be crippled or ill or deficient in various ways. An important function of our conceptions of the human (whatever they may be) is that they provide us with criteria by means of which we distinguish what we call "healthy" human life (for example) from sickness or disease; "normal" behavior (or attitudes, or social relationships) from abnormal; "wholeness" in contrast with various kinds of deficiencies. We need to ask ourselves now, What norms are implicit in the conception of humans as biohistorical beings? Can these provide us with criteria that will assist us in identifying and addressing major environmental, sociocultural, political, economic, and other moral/ethical issues with which women and men today must come to terms? Can they provide us with criteria appropriate for assessing the great diversity of human institutions and practices, patterns of belief and value and meaning, that confront us in today's world, thus assisting us in our search for a better, more sustainable order in our intraconnected global society? If so, they will begin to put some flesh on the bare bones of the criterion of humanization called for in Chapter 1, above.

I cannot here work out in any detail the ethic implicit in this biohistorical conception of human existence. However, I would like to point out features of this conception on which one can draw in developing an ethic for today. I wish to make five points in this connection. The first is a general remark about our *historicity* and the normative implications that lie within it. The next three present more detailed specification and elaboration of what it means to take historicity as having normative significance. The last returns this whole discussion to our full *bio*historical being, setting the normative significance of our historicity in its larger context.[2]

(1) What most sharply distinguishes human beings from other forms of life, I have suggested in this book, is their historicity, their having been shaped by processes of *historical* change and development and their having gradually acquired some control over the further unfolding of these processes. The centrality of our historicity to our very being as human implies that an optimal realization of our biohistorical existence depends in important respects upon an optimal realization of our historicity. (What that optimality can be and how it is to be determined will be specified somewhat in the following points.)

(2) It is clear that historical existence—that is, history and historicity— would not be possible without the maintenance of delicate balances between order and freedom, continuity and creativity. The maintenance of such balances in communal institutions and practices, and in individual agents and their actions, is what can be called "responsible" ordering and acting. An optimal realization of human historicity in any particular concrete situation, therefore, can occur only to the extent that communities and selves are able and willing to take significant responsibility for their institutions, practices and actions. What actually constitutes such responsibility will, of course, be understood quite differently in different sociocultural and historical contexts.

(3) The exercise of our historicity in responsible ordering and action— shaping not only our own communities and selves but future history and thus future humanity as well—can continue to grow only through the increasing development of well-ordered freedom in individuals and societies. The enormous increase of human technological power in recent centuries, culminating now in the power to destroy all of humankind along with many other species of life, means that only as we humans succeed in taking much greater responsibility for the effects of our actions (on both the environment and the ongoing movement and direction of history and culture) is it likely that we will survive at all, let alone flourish.

(4) Our historicity, especially with respect to our capacity to take responsibility for ourselves and for the direction history is going, would

not be possible apart from at least some historical consciousness. (Again, the form that this takes and how it expresses itself in different situations and for different persons and communities will vary widely.) The functioning of our historicity depends significantly, that is to say, on our awareness of our situation in the world and of what our real possibilities in life are, as well as on the existence, in the society in which we live, of practices and institutions that facilitate this functioning. There are, thus, inducements in human historical situatedness itself, inducements toward more adequate awareness of our historicity and its significance, as well as toward historically viable patterns of societal organization and practices.

(5) Our historicity cannot function optimally, of course, unless it is working harmoniously with its biological base (which, in turn, it significantly qualifies); and only if that biological base is itself functioning well. Taking responsibility for ourselves as historical beings must ultimately include, therefore, taking significant responsibility for the wider organic and physical networks of which we are part.

These normative tendencies or propensities in our humanness, as thus far sketched, are quite formal. In that respect they violate the very concern for historicity that I am trying to express here. To point to a kind of over-arching imperative, for example, toward the "optimal realization of our historicity" is to leave this central contention in much too abstract a form. This norm, as it actually gets invoked, is concerned with the realization of human historicity in the many diverse particular contexts in which we humans today live: what is "optimal" for one sociohistorical situation and natural setting may well be quite different from what is "optimal" in other significantly different contexts. "Historicity" means that our understanding of what is required of us is always significantly shaped by the concrete historico-natural contexts within which our communal institutions and practices have emerged, and within which we have grown into selfhood and now live. For example, one particular feature of our (contemporary) historical context with which we are especially concerned in this book— namely our becoming a single intraconnected worldwide humanity—may shape the way in which the notion of optimal realization of our historicity is understood by (at least some of) those reading these lines. With many others, however, living in quite different sociohistorical contexts (for example, in remote villages in "less developed" nations) this idea would carry virtually no weight, other matters being felt as much more urgent. The conception of ourselves as fundamentally historical beings has itself developed in a particular context (largely among intellectuals in the West). And like all other such conceptions it is principally within that context that it is seen as having meaning, significance, truth. The extent to which it will be taken seriously in other situations will depend very much on those situations themselves.

Thus, given our modern/postmodern understanding of humans as biohistorical beings—beings who have emerged within, but whose very existence as historical drastically qualifies, the biological process of evolution—several distinct normative factors useful in assessing different forms of human life, and their orientations toward the future directions they might move, can be discerned. These taken together suggest the normativity of our historicity itself; and this, then, can be further articulated as involving responsibility, historical consciousness, well-ordered freedom, and concern for the organic and physical world to which we belong. As historical, culture-creating, and in some respects self-determining beings, humans must decide what they are to be, how they should shape and order and orient their lives, toward what sort of future they will work in this world in which they find themselves. These normative notions can help us address those matters.

I am not claiming, of course, that all women and men today think of themselves as free and creative, as able to shape and determine their own future and their children's future. In some cultures ideas of this sort have not appeared or have been downplayed; and in most cultures they have been de-emphasized for women. Thus, the historical forms in which experience comes to many individuals and groups often inhibit these notes from coming to consciousness. From our modern western standpoint, however, which sees the great variety of cultures, religions, and societies that the human spirit has produced, it is hard to avoid thinking of that spirit as possessing great creative power and freedom. It is difficult, therefore (for those of us who are aware of these matters), to evade a sense of the necessity for societies and individuals to take significant responsibility for themselves and their world. For we are well aware that what humans decide today—this is especially, and most frighteningly, evident in the realms of international politics and economics, population growth, and ecological concern—will shape future generations, will even determine whether there are any future generations.

I hope that I have said enough to show that on the basis of our historicity (the mark that most sharply distinguishes our humanness from other forms of life) criteria can be developed in terms of which judgments can be made, policies formulated, and practices encouraged respecting moral, religious, and other sociocultural matters of all sorts—judgments and policies and practices that respect the integrity and distinctiveness of the wide range of cultural and religious traditions with which we today find ourselves interacting, while at the same time providing a basis for their critical assessment. Our international political arrangements have put the gradually cumulating growth of human power over our long history into the hands of nations—and now, more recently, corporations—competing with one another. And our moral and religious commitments and values and suspicions—especially in some of the fundamentalistic versions appearing in many places around the globe—focus our energies and interests on these diverse and warring political, economic, and cultural fragments of humanity, rather than on the well-being of humanity as a whole. So our moralities and our religions and our value-loyalties, instead of facilitating some sort of salvation from the evils that confront us, tend to increase the possibilities of disastrous wars. It will not be possible to avoid these, it seems clear, unless we humans worldwide find ways to take up our full responsibilities and act in behalf of humanity-as-a-whole—and the environment on earth which makes all life possible—rather than according to the demands of our present social, political, economic, religious, and cultural arrangements and commitments. We must, that is to say, move toward taking greater responsibility for life on earth, not less; we must move toward a more universal human consciousness, not backward toward more limited and provincial cultural, religious, ethnic, and political commitments. In all of this we can be encouraged, I think, by the fact that people worldwide appear increasingly to be attempting (both socioculturally and as individuals) to take charge of their lives in new ways, seeking to transform them in accordance with deliberately posited goals, which, they hope, will enable greater human fulfillment in life—for their children if not for themselves—than would a continuation of the older practices and ideas.

IV

What I have been sketching here, one could say, is a contemporary (pluralistic and historicistic) version of a central Pauline assumption about human existence, namely, that it is profoundly *moral* in character, laying the demand upon us that we take full responsibility for our (social and individual) moral failures. As Paul puts the matter: we are always "without excuse" in whatever we think or do (Rom. 1:20). I am seeking, however, to articulate this notion in a way that avoids the highly judgmental stance toward alien styles of life that is so sharply expressed by Paul (in Romans and elsewhere), a way that opens us to sympathetic understanding of and appreciation for patterns of human belief, practice, and institutions that are very different from those to which we are accustomed (and which for that reason seem right and good to us). This sort of understanding in turn opens for us the possibility of living and acting in a truly *reconciling* manner toward others very different from ourselves, as we attempt to carry out the "ministry of reconciliation" to which (according to Paul) Christians have been especially called (2 Cor. 5:18).

Relativizing our own Christian standpoint in the way this biohistorical understanding requires—thus encouraging us to enter into serious dialogue with persons from other quite different perspectives than our own—does not mean that we no longer are able to make judgments about right and wrong; about good and evil; about which ways of thinking of human existence and the world we should accept and which oppose; about which proposals for addressing major social and cultural problems we should today support and which reject. On the contrary, as I have suggested, a normative ethic that can deal sympathetically with problems posed by religious and cultural pluralism is directly implied in the biohistorical conception of the human itself. Far from leaving us stranded in a relativistic morass, this way of thinking about our humanness enables us to move forward to address the major problems we today confront.

According to Christian faith, however, we need more than a conception of human being simply by itself—even an ecologically and pluralistically informed holistic conception of the sort I have sketched here. If we are to be adequately oriented in life and the world, we also must have some sense of the ultimate reality or power(s) with which we humans have to do, some notion of that which gives us our very being and sustains us in life, that to which we can devote ourselves without reservation—some idea of what many (including Christians) have called God. In Chapter 6 I shall present a way to think about God appropriate to the conception of the human we have before us, an understanding capable not only of giving our worship and devotion sharp focus, but also of providing us with significant orientation for the tasks we must address in today's world. But before we turn to that, it will be useful, in Chapter 5, to develop further our biohistorical conception of the human by looking briefly at its implications for our understanding of evil and salvation. This will facilitate further specification of what I have been calling the criterion of humanization.

Chapter 5

A Note on Evil, Salvation, and the Criterion of Humanization

Every theological position must deal with the questions of evil and salvation. It could be maintained, in fact, that these are the central themes in human life that generate the religious consciousness and that every religion seeks to address. In any critical and carefully constructed theology it is important, therefore, to consider how the notions of evil and salvation are built up and what justification is offered for holding them. In the following remarks I offer some suggestions about the way in which a biohistorical approach to the concepts of evil and salvation might be developed, and in connection with this elaborate further the criterion of humanization proposed in Chapter 1 and filled out more fully in the discussion of historicity in Chapter 4.

I

In taking up issues of this sort, it is necessary to distinguish carefully the conceptual and interpretive images and frameworks that we employ in our reflection from the raw existential and experiential data to which they give form and meaning. It is, of course, never possible to disentangle these dimensions of experience completely, but once we become aware of the extent to which our linguistic and religious traditions shape our apprehensions of these matters, we can see the importance of at least attempting to examine this question as sensitively and critically as we can. This is especially the case with the issues of evil and salvation, because here we seek to articulate, on the one hand, some of the roots of our sense that humans are caught up in deep predicaments, and, on the other, the belief found in most religions that there is a "way out" of or solution to this situation. Since we

First published as chap. 6 in *The Theological Imagination* (Philadelphia: Westminster Press, 1981). Used with permission.

will be trying here to get back (behind commonly accepted formulations) to certain characteristics of human existence generally, it is especially important that we not too quickly or naively buy into the linguistic and conceptual apparatus supplied by our own (doubtless provincial) religious and philosophical traditions. Though there is no way to jump out of our skins here, it is well that we try, so far as possible, to discern just what sorts of skins we have.

I begin with the conceptual and interpretive aspect of this problem since there is no way for us to consider or discuss these matters without doing so in and with some concepts and terms. The terms we are examining here, "evil" and "salvation," fall within, and gain their specific meaning in relationship to, configurations of other similar terms, such as "pain," "suffering," "sin," "destruction," "despair," "guilt," "disease," "catastrophe," "horror," and the like, on the one hand; and "fulfillment," "meaningfulness," "redemption," "joy," "peace," "happiness," "hope," "health," "ecstasy," "beauty," "goodness," and "God," on the other. An adequate analysis of what is meant by "evil" and "salvation" would require careful mapping of the interrelations and interdependence of these various terms with each other and with other similar concepts, enabling us to come to a clearer understanding of the structure of this region of the English language. It would be useful to compare this mapping with mappings of similar terms and concepts drawn from other religious and linguistic traditions, for only in this way can we become aware of the hidden limitations and biases of the tradition within which we are working and become open to other possibilities of experience and consciousness that might decisively illuminate and transform our sense of the problems with which we are attempting to deal. None of this, however, can be done within the compass of these brief remarks, even had I the competence to do so.

I shall limit myself, then, to some general observations. First, it is to be noted that one of the configurations mentioned above is positive (with respect to human concerns), the other negative. Human disaster or failure and human well-being and fulfillment seem to be the major issues in terms of which the configurations surrounding *evil* and *salvation* are generated: the framework of valuation here is anthropocentric—at least initially. (One wonders how it could be otherwise: since all these terms are *our* terms, generated in response to concerns and problems that emerge as we humans seek to deal with our world and our experience, is it really surprising to discover that our most primitive or foundational valuations point toward that which fulfills, and that which frustrates, *our* human existence and its projects?)[1] The acts of generalization that occur as these complexes of terms are developed, however, move toward transcendence of their anthropocentric origins. Concepts like health and beauty as well as pain and disease and catastrophe may be applied quite as well to other than human beings. And with the conception of God—though the name "God" initially designated, perhaps, that reality believed to be ultimately salvific of the human—there is clearly an attempt to indicate a point of reference in terms of which all else (including, of course, the human itself) can be assessed and judged. Thus, in a theistic scheme evil is defined ultimately with reference to *God's* will and judgment, not ours, and our originally anthropocentric apprehensions of evil are reconstructed in light of what God is believed to require. Similarly with salvation: though this doubtless was originally a largely anthropocentric conception, defined by what (some) *humans* recognized as fulfilling or salvific, in monotheistic world-pictures (such as those that have decisively shaped western notions of evil and salvation) it is God alone who knows and determines what is truly saving of the human—and this may go counter to deep human instincts, perceptions, and desires. It is important that we be critically aware of the way in which these matters color our (western) perceptions and interpretations.

I am suggesting that, although the primitive experiences out of which language about evil and salvation developed must have been largely anthropocentric, at least in western languages and the Abrahamic religions certain *conceptual* developments occurred that significantly qualified this anthropocentrism. Are movements toward the transcendence of anthropocentrism in human consciousness and reflection always largely of a conceptual sort? Why and how have such conceptual developments occurred in (some) monotheistic traditions? It would be illuminating to explore whether analogous developments have occurred in other religious traditions.

These remarks (though very sketchy) pose, with increasing urgency, questions about the experiential elements underlying these conceptual developments. Since there is no way to abstract completely from all concepts (and their interpretive features), it is impossible to address this issue directly. What seems called for is a reflective movement in the opposite direction from the one of increasing generality and objectivity that we have just noted. I cannot pursue that suggestion here, but I can propose a hypothesis that might be worth exploring: that the experiential root of what becomes characterized as evil is to be found in the capacity of living organisms to feel pain. Pain is a feeling that (unlike the other modes of negative consciousness mentioned above) occurs in many forms of life less complex than the human; it apparently does not, thus, always involve conceptual elements, though for instances of higher-level consciousness (for example, humans after infancy) some conceptual dimensions must (nearly) always be present. Feelings of pain are the mode in and through which threats of danger or destruction most primordially impress themselves on living organisms; I suggest, now, that it is this sensing of potential destruction, and (in some organisms) the consequent awareness of power(s) capable of and bent on such destruction, that is the germ of the concept of evil. According to this hypothesis, at least three increasingly complex levels of awareness, each elaborating on the preceding one(s), underlie the consciousness of evil: awareness of pain, a sensing of the danger of destruction, some sense of powers working such destruction. Consciousness of salvation would, from this perspective, seem to be a reactive or second-order consciousness: of being *rescued* from those powers which are bringing about such destruction—and thus of being rescued from the danger of destruction and from pain.

In religious consciousness of evil and of salvation these primitive roots may, of course, be generalized, objectified, and elaborated to the point where—as in radical monotheisms—the original awareness of evil as bound up with one's own pain and destruction is completely concealed or even reversed (as in, for instance, the Calvinist triumphant willingness to be "damned for the glory of God"). Such is the power of an effective symbolical and conceptual frame. When this happens, contradictory moments and paradoxical tensions become incorporated into the notions of evil and of salvation, and they develop an internal dynamic pushing toward greater complexity and depths of meaning. These notions, thus, become vehicles of profound religious and human insight (for example, in concepts of self-sacrifice, of vicarious suffering, of ordinary everyday suffering as morally and religiously significant, and the like). Obviously the Christian consciousness has drunk deeply from this well.

It seems, then, that—though they could not exist at all apart from the complex and changing experiential matters that call them forth—the conceptual dimensions of the consciousness of evil and salvation which emerge are in certain respects of greater theological significance. It is they that determine how the experiential elements will be understood and interpreted, even how they are experienced. If that is the case, it is important to inquire how and why certain conceptual frameworks or configurations of symbols come to be preferred to others. In seeking answers to this question, it will not do to say simply that they more accurately reflect or interpret experience: for it is precisely the question of the grounds for making such a claim that are at issue here. To address this question we must move "below" the level of experience and inquire into the human nature that is doing the experiencing. That is, we have to develop a theological anthropology. The biohistorical anthropology that I sketched in the previous chapter will be helpful as we consider further now the problem posed by the diversity of interpretations.

II

Doctrines of evil and salvation present beliefs or assertions about rescue from "bondage" or healing of "disease," and about human fulfillment or realization. None of these can be stated clearly apart from some conception of the human. The negative notions of bondage and sickness gain their meaning by dialectical contrast with positive conceptions of what constitutes human freedom and health. And positive notions of human realization and fulfillment presuppose some awareness of the range of human possibilities, those that distort or skew human being as well as those that complete or satisfy its inner tendencies, needs, and capacities. The understanding of the human that comes to dominate a culture defines broadly (for that culture) the needs that must be met and how they are to be met. Thus distinctive value preferences develop and eventually are given institutional and ideological expression. If theological interpretations of evil and salvation are to be adequate for today, they must be developed in terms of conceptions of the human which grasp and articulate human possibilities and problems as we experience and understand them today. Here I can offer only a bare outline of an approach to these large and difficult issues.[2]

Our modern awareness that Christian patterns of understanding and of action, like all others, are culturally and historically relative in many respects, together with our recognition that other traditions and viewpoints have achieved insights into and have explored potentialities of the human that are overlooked or denigrated in western Christian reflection, requires us to develop our theological anthropologies today in broader and more comprehensive terms than the Christian tradition envisioned through most of its history. It was never supposed, of course, that such notions as "reason" or "freedom," "*imago Dei*" or "sin," applied only to Christians. These were regarded as appropriate characterizations for all human beings. Nevertheless, they were inevitably understood in terms of western Christian experience and were so defined and interpreted in western theologies. We can now see that these notions are themselves historically relative and are probably not adequate for understanding the variegated experience—and thus the capacities and possibilities—of all human beings. This latter question must be left open, as we attempt to take seriously the ways in which other traditions and perspectives have defined and understood human reality. As yet too little comparative work on these matters has become available to enable western theologians to know in what respects or to what degree traditional Christian notions must be modified to take account of insights drawn from other points of view. For this reason contemporary Christian conceptions of the human should include a definite openness to unfamiliar experiences and conceptions and a willingness to be self-critical at every point. Anthropologies that do this obviously cannot be developed in simple extension or extrapolation of traditional concepts. They require a "stepping back" from such concepts to allow full examination and careful assessment of traditional Christian metaphors, images, and notions, alongside others that seem to merit close scrutiny and possible adoption.

The biohistorical anthropology sketched briefly in Chapter 4 can help us address precisely these matters. This understanding of the human, as biologically founded and yet open to far-reaching cultural and historical development, is able to interpret the variety, differentiation, and complexity that human existence has come to have around the globe; and through its emphasis on the way in which cultures develop historically, it can give an account of how the several great cultural and religious traditions emerged and grew to their present character and proportions. It must be acknowledged, of course, that this conception itself grew up in the West and owes much to Jewish and Christian traditions. However, it is not simply an extrapolation of traditional views: (1) It takes into account the fact that there are other significant traditions and viewpoints that must be considered, as well as social scientific and biological studies of the human. (2) It provides a standpoint from which traditional western religious and philosophical claims about the human can themselves be criticized and assessed.

No doubt representatives of other faiths and traditions and points of view will not regard this conception as neutral or unbiased. They may well, therefore, wish to call it into question in various ways, proposing alternative views of their own. That is, of course, their right and their responsibility. Such moves will advance the gradually emerging effort today to develop conceptions of the human that will help us deal with the increasing convergence, of the several great cultures and civilizations, toward one intraconnected worldwide humanity. Pending the development of some consensus on these matters, however, it is important to press forward with such provisional concepts and hypotheses as can now be formulated, always remaining open to criticism and correction by advocates of other positions. In my view the conception of humans as biohistorical beings provides the most promising base at present on which to develop a more comprehensive understanding of human existence.

III

What light does this conception throw on the way in which the question of salvation arises for humans? As living organisms (animals) humans, in pursuit of certain necessities without which they would die, are in continuous interaction with their environment; and the threat of destruction always hangs over them. The most elemental of their needs are no doubt biological, and physical pain signals biological need. But, as we have seen, humans are historical beings through and through as well as biological, and our consciousness is structured and stocked by language that has been created and acquired in social interaction. Accordingly, most of our felt needs are culturally defined and culturally relative. Even needs directly rooted in our biological makeup, such as for food, always come to consciousness in a culturally defined form: we hunger for steak and ice cream but are repelled by items that in another culture may be regarded as delicacies. For biohistorical beings, then (as we have seen), conceptions of evil and of salvation—that is, conceptions of that which most fundamentally threatens human existence and that which overcomes the threat—always have double roots, biological and cultural.

By the time these concepts become ingredients in religious consciousness, however, they have developed a distinctive meaning and integrity of their own, and biological survival may no longer be emphasized as the most fundamental value. Rather "devotion to God," "loyalty to the community," "love of country," "pursuit of truth," "keeping the faith," come to be of central significance for many women and men, and they are often prepared to sacrifice their lives, if need be, for such "spiritual" values. It is obvious that the double-sided makeup of human nature allows for a wide range of possible conceptions of both evil and salvation. It is not surprising, therefore, that a great variety of religious and moral orientations have appeared in the course of human history. Doubtless these many value orientations each contribute significantly to the enhancement of human life and the preservation of human communities—indeed, they help to constitute (as I argued in Chapter 4) what distinguishes characteristicly human existence from that which is merely animal. But they may also be (in some respects) disruptive of human community and destructive of the biological basis of human existence.

These observations enable us to move our anthropological reflections from descriptive to normative concerns. The biohistorical understanding that I am sketching in this book identifies the human power to transcend and transform its animal base—through creating those complexes of symbols and practices, values and ideologies and institutions, that we call cultures—as the most distinctive characteristic of humans. Thus, the well-being of humanity depends absolutely on the enhancement of the sociohistorical activities and processes and institutions that promote creativity of this sort in us all. These facts provide (as suggested in the discussion of historicity in Chapter 4) the basis for a normative principle that can be used in assessing the diverse views of evil and salvation that have appeared in history: whatever tends to enhance and strengthen the culture-creating processes through which our original animality is transformed into humanity is good; whatever tends to corrupt, block, or destroy these processes of humanization—in any human beings, regardless of race, class, nationality, or gender—is evil; whatever rescues us from or otherwise overcomes such evil processes, powers, or events is salvific.

This principle—which I call the criterion of humanization (as proposed in Chapters 1 and 4, above)—provides a means for assessing the most diverse aspects of human life and culture: family patterns and child-rearing practices; social institutions and class structures; methods of socialization and processes of social interaction; patterns and conceptions of community and of individuality; political and economic and educational institutions and practices; scientific and technological developments and institutions; moral, religious, and aesthetic values, institutions, and ideologies; and so on. Every dimension of social, cultural, and personal life has its direct or indirect effects, positive or negative, on the processes of humanization. Doubtless we know much less about these matters than we should, but relevant wisdom is to be found in all the great religious traditions as well as in modern secular humanisms (as represented by such figures as Karl Marx, Friedrich Nietzsche, Sigmund Freud, John Dewey, Jean Piaget, Michel Foucault, and others).

Though the criterion of humanization, and thus of authentic human existence, solves no problems in itself, it provides a critical reference point for assessing the claims of the several religious and secular traditions and enables clearer perceptions of the major human problems to which we must address ourselves. It is a criterion already accepted (implicitly) and used in many circles. In contemporary Christian thought, for example, the criticism of traditional Christian institutions, beliefs, and practices by liberation theologians (whether African American, female, or "third world") is based largely on something like this criterion. But interest in this criterion is not limited to Christians: the worldwide demand for more humane social institutions, for greater economic justice and equality, for liberation from every sort of oppression, is evidence of an emerging consciousness of the criterion of humanization in many different settings.[3]

This criterion can be understood as a secularization and universalization of certain fundamental Judeo-Christian themes. The goodness of creation as a whole and specifically of human existence, the significance of history and of what transpires within history, the importance of human communal existence and of just social institutions, a high valuation of morally responsible selfhood and such virtues as mercy, forgiveness, love, faithfulness, and the like—these all have been central emphases of Jewish and Christian faiths. And they have led to forms of community and selfhood, and to institutions and ideologies, that have taken human historical existence to be of central importance; as something, therefore, for which humans must take full responsibility. God—the ultimate point of reference for these traditions and the ultimate ground of all legitimation—has been understood as the creator of the world and of these human physical selves that inhabit it. And God has also been thought of as continuously involved with worldly history, moving it toward a consummation of perfect peace, justice, and freedom. Such Jewish and Christian talk about God expresses a belief that both the striving of all persons toward genuine humanization, and those worldly processes that promote and enhance that humanization, have an ultimate metaphysical foundation, a foundation in that Reality which grounds all that is (see the Introduction and Chapters 1–2, above, and 6, below). The serious concern with human social institutions, with possibilities of realization for every individual, and with the quality of interpersonal relations—to which the criterion of humanization directs us—can thus be seen as representing a configuration of valuations in many ways similar to, and in some respects derived from, Judeo-Christian understandings of human life in the world. The specifically Christian affirmation of Christ as at once "true humanity" and "true divinity" carries this emphasis further, in its claim that the paradigmatically human has appeared in history. The symbol of Christ represents both what is genuinely human and that which ultimately grounds our humanization, God (see Chapter 7). The major task of specifically Christian theology is to show that and how these central symbols of Christian faith ("God" and "Christ") are still important today for specifying and clarifying what humanization is and, thus, where salvation for women and men is to be found.

IV

These brief remarks do not present a full Christian theological view of evil and salvation, but they do sketch what I believe to be a promising approach. To work out this approach in detail, one would need to explore the relevance and richness of important Christian notions not explicated here, for example, vicarious suffering and original sin, Christ and the Holy Spirit, certain eschatological themes and images, the "Christian virtues" of faith, hope, and love, and so on. This approach makes possible theological reflection on human existence and salvation that is open to conversation with and insights from other religious and secular traditions and viewpoints, and that stands in close connection with the understandings of the human that are developing in the modern social sciences, history, and biology—major extra-Christian dimensions of our modern consciousness and experience of the human that must be given serious consideration in theological anthropologies seeking to address today's needs.

Chapter 6

Mystery, God, and Human Diversity

We are all aware at some level, I think, that life confronts us humans as mystery. Karl Rahner puts it this way:

> What is made intelligible is grounded ultimately in the one thing that is self-evident, in mystery. Mystery is something with which we are always familiar, something that we love, even when we are terrified by it or perhaps even annoyed and angered, and want to be done with it. . . . what is more self-evident than the silent question that goes beyond everything which has already been mastered and controlled. . . ? In the ultimate depths of [our] being [we know] nothing more surely than that [our] knowledge, that is, what is called knowledge in everyday parlance, is only a small island in a vast sea that has not been traveled. It is a floating island, and it might be more familiar to us than the sea, but ultimately it is borne by the sea. . . . Hence the [deepest] question for [us humans] is this. Which [do we] love more, the small island of [our] so-called knowledge or the sea of infinite mystery?[1]

This profound mystery—or better: the many mysteries—of life provides the ultimate context of our existence as self-conscious beings. Paradoxically, then, it is in terms of that which is beyond our ken that we must, in the last analysis, understand ourselves.

I

"Mystery" (as I am using the word here) does not refer to a direct perceptual experience of something, as do words like "darkness" or "dense fog" (when we cannot see anything), or words like "unclear" or "obscure"

Materials for this chapter, here revised and expanded, were drawn largely from two articles, "Mystery, Theology and Conversation" (*Harvard Divinity Bulletin* 21, no. 2 [1991]: 12–14) and "Nature, History, and God: Toward an Integrated Conceptualization" (*Zygon: Journal of Religion and Science* 27 [1992]: 379–401). Used with permission. A much more comprehensive discussion of the issues taken up in this chapter will be found in chap. 5 and Parts III and IV of *In Face of Mystery*.

(when used of some distant object that we cannot discern well enough to identify with confidence). "Mystery" is fundamentally an intellectual term, not an experiential one. It refers to bafflement of mind more than obscurity of perception. A mystery is something which we cannot think clearly, cannot get our minds around, cannot manage to grasp. If we say that "life confronts us as mystery," or "whether life has any meaning is a mystery," or "why anything at all exists, instead of nothing, is a mystery," we are speaking about intellectual bafflements. We are indicating that what we are dealing with here seems to be beyond what our minds can handle. Thus when, in theological discourse, we call attention to the mystery of human existence, the mysteries in which we live, we are reminding ourselves that in theology we are dealing with matters at the very limits of our intellectual capacities; we are involved with profound puzzles, conundrums that we cannot solve and that we should not expect to solve. We must be cautious at every point, therefore, about what we take ourselves to be achieving in our reflection. In theology a question mark must be placed behind everything that is said.

Sometimes (as in the ancient Greek mystery religions, from whence our modern word comes) "mystery" is thought of as descriptive of some object of arcane theological awareness or knowledge—perhaps God—rather than as prescriptively applying to us, to the limitedness of our knowledge and the questionableness of our attitudes. This way of thinking opens the door to obscure—but often exciting—claims, claims for which no grounds can be offered but which may seem theologically important. Speakers or writers may announce, for example, that they are in a position to "unveil" some particular mystery for us, allowing us to see what we could not otherwise see—like a landscape after the fog has lifted, or a dark room after a light has been turned on. The use of perceptual metaphors in talk of this kind only helps to encourage confusions; for this way of speaking leads us to suppose that we are being given information about realities hidden from others, possibly "secrets known only to God." However, I want to point out that when we say of something that "it is a mystery," this does not in fact tell us anything specific about that of which we are speaking, or which we are seeking to understand. Rather, it calls attention to something about ourselves: that we seem to have reached a limit to our powers at this point, and we may, if we are not careful, easily become confused or misled. The word "mystery" in its theological employment, thus, should be taken as a kind of warning that our ordinary ways of speaking and thinking are beginning to fail us and that special rules in our use of language should now be followed: take unusual care; beware of what is being said; the speaker may be misleading you; you may be misleading yourself; attend to what is being said with critical sensitivity to its problematic character. When we introduce the concept of mystery into our theological work, this does not mean that we may now cease employing our faculties in a thoroughly critical way. On the contrary, it alerts us to the necessity at this point to employ our critical capacities to their utmost.

As we have noted in previous chapters, a major function of religions (and of theologies) is to present human beings with visions of the whole of reality. That is, religions (and theologies) provide construals of the ultimate mystery within which human life transpires—construals that are sufficiently meaningful and intelligible to enable us humans to come to some understanding of ourselves in relation to the enigmatic context within which our lives proceed, and which are sufficiently attractive to motivate women and men to live fruitfully and meaningfully within this context. Although many such visions of the ultimate reality with which we humans have to do, and of the significance of human life, have appeared in the course of history, none has succeeded in comprehending the ultimate mystery of things.

Unfortunately our religious traditions have seldom been completely candid about this, especially when they claimed they were offering what had been revealed by God on high to be the true salvation of humanity from the deepest ills of life. Although claims of this sort have enabled religious groups to attract faithful—and often fanatical!—adherents, it is important to note that by downplaying in this way the ultimate mystery within which we all live, they in fact falsified our actual human condition, and frequently became, thereby, dangerous threats to human life and flourishing rather than trustworthy guides. Examples of this can be seen today in the emergence of fundamentalisms of various sorts—religious and secular—around the globe. The only possible check against the monumental deceits that our religiosity works on our gullibility—and on our desire for certainty in a terrifying world—is the constant reminding of ourselves that it is indeed *mystery* with which we humans ultimately have to do. Therefore, we dare not claim certitude with respect to our ideas of the right and the true, the good and the real, but must acknowledge that in these matters we men and women always, in fact, proceed in faith, as we move forward through life into the uncertain future before us. Precisely because of the mystery, we must give a prominent place in our vision of reality to forthright acknowledgment of our ultimate *unknowing* with respect to the deepest questions of life and death. Precisely because of the mystery, we must engage in relentless theological criticism of our human faiths, their symbols, and the practices they inspire. Precisely because of the mystery, we must undertake disciplined but imaginative construction of the visions of the world to which we give ourselves in faith.

One of the most important features of the understanding of theology as our own imaginative construction is that it requires us not to confuse *our* ideas and reflection—especially when we speak of God—with that ultimate mystery with which we are attempting to come to terms. This helps keep us honest in our theological work, on the one hand, and it acknowledges, on the other, the full independence of God from what *we* may think or say. In reminding ourselves that God is mystery to us, we allow God in God's concrete actuality to be whatever God is, quite apart from our conceptualizations. In this respect, the concept of mystery, just because of its emptiness and openness, can help us face in a very direct way what it means to take God's reality seriously, to confess the God that is truly *God*, the ultimate reality not to be confused with any of our human imaginative constructions.

II

Although in our culture God has often been identified with the ultimate mystery of things, a moment's reflection makes clear that the symbol "God" has significantly more definiteness and specificity than the concept of mystery. "God" is the name ordinarily used to designate that reality (whatever it might be) that grounds and undergirds all that exists, including us humans; that reality which provides us humans with such fulfillment or salvation as we may find; that reality toward which we must turn, therefore, if we would flourish. The symbol "God," thus, leads us to attend to and reflect on the ultimate mystery of things in a very particular way, namely, in connection with the respects in which it creates, sustains, and enhances human (as well as other modes of) existence. How should we today think of this reality so important to human being and well-being? According to contemporary scientific and historical understandings, what actually creates and sustains human life are the physical, biological, and historical processes that provide its context. It is with these matters, therefore, that a theological perspective for today should connect what it calls "God." The name "God" can take up and hold together these vast and complex processes in a distinct and powerful symbol, a symbol that places them in a wider setting that accents both their meaning for human existence and their contextualization in the ultimate mystery of things. The symbol "God" can help focus our consciousness, devotion, and work, and provide orientation and direction for our everyday concrete decisions and actions, as we men and women seek to order our lives and our activities in terms of a vision of human existence as situated among many other realities in a vast mysterious ecosystem.

This symbol has, in fact, always functioned in this way, as the focus for a worldview. For example, in the biblical world-picture in which this symbol was given its most influential form, however much God's radical independence and self-subsistence were emphasized, God was seldom (if ever) portrayed as a being whom humans encountered directly in its solitary splendor: on the contrary, a central biblical theme was that no one ever has direct or immediate contact with or experience of God. Even Moses, through whom God is said to have made Godself known decisively, was not allowed to see God's "face," we are told, but only God's "back" (Exod. 33:23), for no one can see "[God's] face . . . and live" (33:20). This inaccessibility of God is a theme that is frequently repeated; for example Job, in the midst of his tribulations, seeks God for an explanation, but God is nowhere to be found:

> Look, he passes by me, and I do not see him; he moves on, but I do not perceive him. . . . if I go forward, he is not there; or backward, I cannot perceive him; on the left he hides, and I cannot behold him; I turn to the right, but I cannot see him. (9:11; 23:8-9)

In the Fourth Gospel (1:18) and again in 1 John (4:12), we are told that "No one has ever seen God." For the biblical traditions in the main, then, God is not the sort of reality that is available to direct observation or experience.[2] For the most part subsequent theological reflection has taken this same line: it has held that all knowledge of God is analogical or symbolical. That is, it is never direct or unmediated but is based on likenesses drawn from ordinary objects of experience.

If we take this theme in the biblical picture seriously, we are led to conclude that human awareness of God or knowledge of God did not actually arise out of direct perceptions or experiences of the divine being itself, as has often been assumed. Rather, it emerged in connection with the creation of a particular *world-picture* in the Ancient Near East, especially in Israel. In this picture, constructed by the human imagination over many generations, the dominant active power in the universe came to be thought of as a creator/lord/father ruling from on high. That is, the idea of God was constituted—was given its content and defining meaning—largely by a configuration of such image/concepts as king, creator, father, lord, all of them drawn from everyday human language and experiences but now put together in a conception believed to represent the all-dominant power in the universe. Although it was found necessary, over the centuries of Jewish and Christian history, to introduce many other metaphors and images into religious reflection and devotion (in order to elaborate and further develop the image/concept of God, thus enhancing its intelligibility and deepening its meaning)—for example, "the Alpha and the Omega, the first and the last" (Rev. 22:13; cf. Isa. 44:6), the first cause, being-itself, ultimate reality, and so on—in most Christian and Jewish piety and faith the originating political and familial biblical images and metaphors have continued to be largely definitive of the God-symbol. The image/concept of the creator/lord/father enabled believers' imaginations to bind together every-thing in their world into a meaningful whole within which all life's vicissi-tudes would have a proper place and significance. It provided an ample focus for human devotion, meditation, and service, a focus to which women and men believed it proper to give themselves without reservation.

The meaning of the idea of God has, thus, derived principally not from direct encounters with a super-human being which some women and men had from time to time, but from its employment as the symbolic center and focus for a particular overall world-picture. A principal question that must be faced in theological reflection today is whether a notion of God consti-tuted largely by anthropomorphic political and familial metaphors such as father, lord, and king can continue to function effectively as a focus for the sort of world-pictures—conceptions of the universe and our human place within it—which most of us now take for granted.

III

Let us keep these remarks—about the symbol "God" gaining its principal content and meaning as part of an overall world-picture—in mind as we consider the modern world-picture that increasingly informs the way in which educated women and men worldwide think about the universe in which we live. We conceive our universe in terms very different from those which constituted the ancient worldview found in the Bible (or, for that matter, in any other religious tradition)—"big bang," cosmic evolution, emergence and evolutionary development of life on planet Earth, life as an ecosystem, humans as biohistorical beings, and so on. I would like at this point, with the help of two concepts of my own, to bring out certain fea-tures of this relatively new "common creation story" (as some have called it),[3] features which are often overlooked but which will facilitate our con-structing an image/concept of God that can (in my view) significantly help orient the lives of women and men in today's world.

First, I will present a conception of what I call "serendipitous creativi-ty," manifest throughout the universe—the continuous coming into being of the new and the novel, whether this leads to what appear (from human and humane perspectives) to be horrifying evils or great goods. Second, since the traditional Christian picture of the world, as dominated by a powerful teleological movement underlying and ordering all cosmic and historical processes—a movement closely connected with the idea of God as a kind of person or agent—has become quite problematical in the twentieth century, I propose to replace it. Today's way of thinking about these matters can be better expressed by a more modest conception emphasizing "directional movements" or "trajectories" that emerge in the course of evolutionary and historical developments. This more open (even random) notion—the serendipitous creativity manifest in evolutionary and historical trajectories of various sorts—can be combined quite comfortably, I think, with the way we have come to think about cosmic processes today. It is a notion that can interpret the enormous expansion and complexification of the physical universe (from the "big bang" onward) as well as the evolution of life here on earth and the gradual emergence of human historical existence. The whole vast cosmic process manifests (in varying degrees) serendipitous creativity: an everflowing coming into being of new modes of reality. It is a process that has often produced much more than would have been expected, given previously prevailing circumstances, indeed, more than might have seemed possible—even moving eventually, along one of its lines, into the creation of human beings with their distinctive history and historicity.

There are, of course, other plausible ways to view today's universe. Taking up such a position as this involves, therefore, a step of faith.[4] Since this is a notion that can (as I shall attempt to show) be quite useful in helping to orient human existence today, I propose that—as a tentative preliminary step of and toward faith in God for our time—we agree (for now) to think of the overarching context of human life, the universe, as a serendipitously creative process or movement. We can fill out more fully what this idea involves if we take note of some important implications of cosmic and (especially) biological evolution, as these are widely understood today.

First, consider certain features of the concept of time implied by evolutionary theory. Movement in and through time, as traced today through the long history of the universe and particularly through the evolution of life on earth, seems to be irreversible and in this respect unidirectional. That is, although many whirls and eddies and dead ends appear in the evolutionary development, and although many cycles of night and day, of seasonal changes, and of birth, growth, and decay are to be found here on earth, there seems to be an essentially continuous movement onward toward new forms, toward unprecedented developments—not simply patterns which forever repeat themselves. Moreover, these novel developments, to the extent they involve the appearance of new evolutionary lines —for example, new species—each have specific potentialities for developing further in some directions but not in others. Such tendencies, as biologist Ernst Mayr says, "are the necessary consequence of the unity of the genotype which greatly constrains evolutionary potential."[5] To the extent that a new evolutionary tendency enables a species to adapt to its environment more successfully than its predecessors, a certain momentum of development in a particular direction is set up. Increasingly effective adaptation over successive generations may occur, leading to the emergence of further new species. From our human vantage point, with our awareness that in this way ever more complex species have emerged along some evolutionary lines, we can discern *trajectories* of a sort eventuating in these new forms. These are visible, however, only to our retrospective or backward-looking view, and there is no reason (from a biological standpoint) to suppose that the process of evolution has actually been directed, somehow, toward this or that specific goal or toward any goal whatsoever. The processes of natural selection, it appears, are themselves able to bring about the directional momentums that emerge along the various lines down which life has evolved. And time, in this evolutionary process, takes on an increasingly linear character. Further evidence of this appears from another side: when living forms that have emerged become extinct, as many if not all eventually do, they do not reappear again at some later point, but are forever left behind. In view of all this, Jacob Bronowski goes so far as to state flatly that "It is evolution, physical and biological, that gives time its direction."[6] Cosmic time, then, to the extent that it is understood in light of evolutionary processes continually branching out and developing in many different directions, is irreversible, creative of the new, and in that respect linear and unidirectional.

Second, evolutionary development here on earth has not stayed on a level plane. Some of these momentums set up by natural selection eventuate in what (from our human standpoint) we cannot but regard as "higher" forms;[7] along one line (our own) such developments have given rise to what is actually a new order of reality: history. This is a very important point, and we must be careful how we express it. It is not that the evolution of life has been a sort of straight-line movement, up from the primeval slime to humanity with its historicity and complex history. Obviously, that is a misleading image: evolutionary developments have gone in many directions. Most of these lines have died out, although some have achieved a basic equilibrium with their environment and thus become stabilized. Others continue to evolve. Moreover, it is not evident that the human form is as biologically viable as are, for example, some insects. So from a strictly *biological* point of view (with its emphasis on survival, perpetuation of the species), there is little reason to think that human life is the most successful product of the evolutionary process. However, in our reflections here we are not confining ourselves to strictly biological considerations: our principal concern is with our profoundly human need to find a way to orient ourselves in this evolutionary world. We humans live within the order of history, which, with its high development of cultures and modes of social organization, is the only context (so far as we know) within which beings with freedom, creativity, self-consciousness, and responsible agency have appeared, characteristics not fully explicable in strictly biological terms such as nutrition, metabolism, reproduction, and the like. Although beings with historicity are in important respects but one among many forms of life, in some significant ways they have moved beyond the strictly biological into a distinctly new order of reality.

As we noted in Chapter 4, fully human beings (beings with *historicity*) did not appear as the last stage of what was simply a long biological process: it was only after many millennia of distinctly *historical* developments (in combination with continuing biological evolution) that human existence as we presently think of it came on the scene. The beings that we humans now are, thus, are quite as much a product of long and complex historical and cultural developments (going in significantly different directions in different parts of the world) as of evolutionary biological processes. Moreover (it is important to note), only with the emergence of the particular *historical standpoint* of late modernity has this long biological-historical movement eventuating in contemporary humankind come into view. But as we humans today look back over the gradually cumulating evolutionary and historical movement that produced us, the outlines of a cosmic trajectory, eventuating in the creation of beings with historicity, begin to become discernible. (There are, no doubt, many other cosmic trajectories as well, moving in quite different directions.) From where we stand—with our human interests and contemporary values—it would be strange indeed were we not to affirm that the emergence of this trajectory is to be valued highly (at least by us humans); as the source of our very existence, we cannot but consider it a wonderful manifestation of the serendipitous creativity characteristic of the cosmos that is our home.

Thinking about our distinctively human existence—our humanness, our historicity—as grounded in the creativity in the ultimate nature of things, the ultimate mystery, clearly requires an act of faith of much greater specificity and human significance than the general affirmation of pervasive creativity in the universe (our initial step of faith). It is an act of faith, moreover, that is not as uncommon among intellectuals these days as might at first be supposed. All speculation about, and search for, intelligent life in other parts of the universe rests on precisely this assumption of some underlying tendency in the cosmos pressing toward what we have here been calling historicity—humanlike reality—and on the hope that we may, if we search long enough and carefully enough, eventually uncover signs of highly complex forms of life in regions far removed from planet Earth. Where the particular trajectory that brought human existence into being on our planet will move in the future, we do not, of course, know—perhaps toward the opening of ever new possibilities for human beings, as we increasingly take responsibility for our lives and our future; perhaps going beyond humanity and historicity altogether, however difficult it may be to image what that might be; perhaps coming to an end in the total destruction of human life.

I am suggesting, thus, that with the introduction of two basic ideas—both consonant with modern evolutionary thinking, though not necessary to it—we can develop a world-picture that will assist us in finding our distinctive place within the evolutionary cosmos that is our home. The two basic ideas are: (1) the notion of cosmic serendipitous creativity, which (2) manifests itself through trajectories of various sorts working themselves out in longer and shorter stretches of time. With the emergence of distinctly historical modes of being—human being—purposive or teleological patterns have appeared in the world, as human intentions, consciousness, and actions began to become effective. We can say, then, that cosmic trajectories, which had their origins in what seem to have been mere physical movement or vibration, have (in some instances) gradually developed increasing directionality, ultimately creating a context within which deliberate purposive action could emerge.[8] These two basic ideas help to provide a framework for seeing the place of our human existence—its purposiveness, its social, moral, cultural, and religious values and meanings, its glorious creativity and its horrible failures and gross evils—within the vast (seemingly) impersonal cosmic order in which we find ourselves. We are beginning to gain some *orientation* in the universe as we think of it—imagine it—today.

Let us take note of five points in this connection. First, this approach provides a frame within which we can characterize quite accurately, and can unify into an overall vision, what seems actually to have happened, so far as we know, in the course of cosmic evolution and history. Second, this approach gives a significant, but not dominant, place and meaning to the *distinctive* character of human life and history within this cosmic process. Therefore, third, it can provide a basis for developing general principles of interpretation in terms of which communities (and individuals) can begin to understand the import of both the biological context of our lives and the historical developments through which we are living, in this way providing a basis for us to take responsible roles with respect to these contexts and developments. Fourth, this is an approach which can, because of the place that it uncovers within the cosmic order as a whole for the human and for the humane values so important to us, provide a ground for hope (though not certainty) about our future—a hope about the *overall* direction that human history may be moving, a hope for the possibility of movement toward a new humanity living in a new age of much greater ecological and moral responsibility. Finally, fifth, a hope with a cosmic grounding of this sort—even though carrying much less *assurance* than traditional religious expectations of, for example, the coming of God's kingdom—can help to motivate us men and women to devote our lives to bringing about this more humane world to which we all aspire.

This frame of orientation or vision of reality is not, of course, in any way forced upon us: it can be appropriated only by means of our own personal decisions, our own acts of faith. It will provide orientation for us only as we decide to commit ourselves to it, ordering our lives and building our futures in the terms it prescribes.

IV

Let us return, now, to the central question with which this chapter is concerned: how is this interpretation of the cosmos to be connected with the symbol "God"? We need to recall here my earlier remarks about the role(s) the symbol "God" plays in the traditional monotheistic picture of the world. What does this symbol add to, and how does it otherwise qualify, the ideas of the world and of humanity in this picture, thus giving theocentric frameworks of orientation a distinctive character? Putting this in somewhat different words: for those living within a monotheistic world-picture, how does the image/concept of God provide significant meaning and orientation for life? My summary answer to these questions is this: *the symbol "God" focuses human devotion and activity so as to orient human existence on that which is believed to bring human fulfillment (salvation).* Devotion to God (for those with faith) thus provides a kind of ultimate security in life, profound consolation in moments of deep sadness, healing in situations of despair. For God is that reality—and the symbol "God" is therefore taken to express that complex meaning—to which each person must give herself or himself, and on which communities must orient themselves, if human life is to gain wholeness, meaning, salvation.[9] I want to suggest now that the symbol "God" can, if properly interpreted, also focus and concentrate the evolutionary-historical conception of the world sketched above, while simultaneously relativizing it. In this way this symbol can continue significantly to orient human existence in the cosmic scheme of things (as we today understand these matters) and will help sustain positive human motivation for living in this world.

The world, I have suggested, is a serendipitous process that has produced a variety of trajectories, one of which has brought into being the historical order and may be continuing on in further creativity. This trajectory (on which we humans find ourselves) appears to represent at least one significant direction in which the cosmic process is moving, and we humans are being drawn beyond our present condition and order by this ongoing creative movement. But if we fail to respond appropriately to the historical and ecological forces now impinging upon us, we may not even survive. *God*, I am proposing, should be understood as the underlying reality (whatever it may be)—the ultimate creativity, ultimate mystery—that manifests itself throughout the universe and thus also in this evolutionary-historical trajectory culminating (to date) in our human historicity.

The symbol "God" holds together two motifs. On the one hand, as the irreducible mystery of things, God is understood to transcend everything human. On the other hand, God is regarded as having a significant connection with our humanness and our struggles for humaneness. (This point is expressed here by the notion of a cosmic-historical trajectory that has brought us humans into being and is moving, as we hope, toward a more idealized humanity and historicity.) These two motifs are held together (in the symbol "God") in a way that enables us to understand and to respond to this cosmic ground, source, and directionality, to respond to it as that which creates and sustains our humanity and undergirds our further humanization. As we have noted, when we introduce the name "God" into our discourse we suggest that the ultimate reality with which we have to do is not to be regarded simply as unqualified mystery: for this mystery is now taken to be that which creates and sustains the vast panorama of life, including the enormously differentiated and complex process which has given rise to, and continues to nourish, our human modes of being. To confess "faith in God" is to affirm that this mystery is the adequate and proper ground for confidence in and hope for human life and its prospects—that it is our "creator and redeemer" (to use the more familiar words of tradition)—and we declare our loyalty and devotion to it, and our intention to orient ourselves on it as we proceed through life. Devotion to God (as understood here) is significantly humanizing because it helps break our parochial and destructive idolatries, enabling us to become centered on the cosmic-historical creative movement that gives us our being. It helps focus our commitment on that which can draw us beyond what we presently are toward an existence more truly humane and better attuned to our environment.

The evolutionary/ecological conception of the world that I am sketching in this chapter—and which has supplied the basic metaphors and concepts employed in my reconstruction of the image/concept of God—has not been drawn directly from traditional Christian materials or from the resources of any other religious tradition. It was developed largely in modern astrophysical, biological, and anthropological theorizing. It is a conception that has gained increasing acceptance from educated women and men of quite diverse cultures and religions, as the most plausible account available today of the origins of life and the evolution of the cosmos. The notion of God that I have proposed involves a kind of extrapolation from and interpretive deepening of this transculturally accepted knowledge, even as it relativizes and limits this knowledge by reminding us that its ultimate context is *mystery*. Our inherited symbol "God," I am suggesting, has resources that can hold together in one our modern understandings of these matters and this ancient wisdom.

When the image/concept of God is reconstructed in this way, it becomes a focus that can provide vital and significant orientation for any women and men in our highly pluralized world who are learning to think of the cosmos and the evolution of life on planet Earth largely in terms of today's "common creation story"—orientation pertinent, thus, not only for Christians and Jews but also for other modern/postmodern women and men of quite diverse religious and secular persuasions. In this reconstruction the symbol "God" continues to present all of human life and its tasks (since they are grounded in the divine creative activity) as of profound meaning. In addition, through portraying the trajectory culminating in humanization and historicity as "God's activity," it provides those who accept it (as the focus for their lives) with means to identify and interpret what is of genuine importance to human existence, in both the natural world and the historical developments roundabout us. Finally, it helps to relativize, and thus provide critical leverage upon, every aspect of these (and other) pictures of humanity, the world, and God, through emphasizing that they are all grounded beyond that which is visible to and imaginable by us—that is, are grounded in what is (to us) ultimately mystery, in the God whom "no one has ever seen" (John 1:18).

When the symbol "God" is interpreted as identifying and holding together in one the ultimate mystery of things and the serendipitous creativity at work in the ecological order of which we are part, it can provide a valuable focus for human devotion, meditation, work in today's pluralized world. The triumphalistic, imperialistic, and authoritarian sting of traditional monotheisms is drawn—through interpreting the symbol in this open fashion, as construal of the ultimate mystery with which *all* women and men must come to terms—and God can thus continue to be an ultimate reference-point appropriate for our time. God is not thought of here as a particular being but rather as a particular form of ordering activity going on in the world, namely that serendipitous ordering which has given rise (among other things) to the evolution of life on planet Earth and the emergence of human beings, and which continues to sustain us and move us toward a more profound humanization. The symbol "God" holds before us in one the (otherwise seemingly disparate) cosmic and historical forces and movements which have produced human existence and its struggle for the humane. When we employ the name "God," we affirm the special significance (to us humans) of this growing unity of movement toward the human and the humane, which can be discerned and affirmed amid all the enormous diversity of cosmic and historical trajectories and powers.

If we do not take the name "God" to refer literally to an existent being, why continue to use it? Why not just speak of "cosmic and historical forces" moving toward humanization and ecological order? The symbol "God" has served as a focus for worship and for orientation in life for many centuries. In centering our attention and devotion with the aid of this symbol, thus, we are associating ourselves with those many generations of women and men—and those many communities from ancient times to the present—for whom it similarly evoked and focused commitments to humane and responsible ways of ordering life. We remind ourselves (and others) that we are not a generation basically disconnected from our forebears. We are, rather, participants in an ongoing history and community—a historical trajectory—the values and priorities and commitments of which have shaped our own, and from which, in fact, have come most of the beliefs (at least of those of us who are western and Christian) about the importance of the personal and the humane and the responsible. When we commit ourselves to God today, we acknowledge all this by accepting the central symbol of this community as our own and by confessing our desire to associate ourselves with this trajectory, insofar as it is moving toward true humanization for all women and men everywhere—despite the continuing movement of humankind on into a future in which anti-human and anti-ecological values and styles of life will likely be very powerful.

For those of us who understand the symbol "God" in this way, there is really no question about whether God "exists": for we are employing the name "God" to designate that creativity, that mystery, which undergirds our human existence in all its complexity and all its diversity. For us, it should be clear, faith in God, commitment to God, continues to provide a center for life that can nourish every dimension of our human being.

Chapter 7

The Meaning of Christ
in Our Pluralistic Age

In Chapter 6 on God and mystery, I treated the name "God" as a symbol that acquires its all-comprehensive meaning and significance not through direct human encounters with and experiences of God but rather through the role that it plays in a world-picture, first clearly formulated in ancient Israel. Regarding the world as created and governed by *God*—and thinking of God, thus, as lord of the universe whom alone we must worship and serve—is one way of construing the ultimate mystery of life and its meaning, a way that has provided orientation for and has helped to humanize a great many men and women over the centuries. How faith in God, devotion to God, is to be understood in our pluralistic age is not—I suggested—best addressed by claims and arguments about the existence of a divine being of this sort. We should pose the question somewhat differently, by asking whether and in what respects the *symbol* "God" can bring order and meaning—and thus significant orientation for life—into the evolutionary/ecological world-picture within which many of us today take ourselves to be living, thinking, acting. I argued that this ancient symbol, if properly reconstructed, can indeed provide significant orientation for contemporary women and men; and that faith in God, devotion to God, service of God, do indeed remain proper stances, therefore, for (at least some) humans in our modern/postmodern world.

The conception of God as thus far outlined, however, is at best a minimalist one: I suggested that when we speak of God we should understand ourselves to be construing the ultimate mystery of things as the serendipitous creativity manifest throughout the universe in the many evolutionary and (at least on planet Earth) historical trajectories through which new forms and configurations of reality and life have come into being—a pic-

Materials for this chapter, many of which are drawn from chaps. 25 and 26 of *In Face of Mystery*, were revised and expanded to show their bearing on issues connected with religious and cultural pluralism. Used with permission.

ture quite different from that of the creator/lord/father of Christian and Jewish traditions. This view, if properly filled out (I argued), can provide women and men today with significant faith and hope that can ground and sustain responsible living and acting in our desperately needy world. I want now to elaborate these claims further in connection with the other great Christian orienting symbol: *Christ*. But before I turn directly to that task, I think it important to make a few remarks about my use of the word "symbol" in this book.

I

When I speak of "Christ" as an important Christian *symbol*, I do not mean to dismiss or ignore the fact that Christians have ordinarily regarded this name (or title) as referring to a particular historical figure, Jesus of Nazareth. Nor do I mean to downplay the claim that Christ mediates to us the ultimate reality with which we have to do, God. Pointing out that "Christ" is a symbol for us simply means that Christ is present to us—and significant for us in the present—in a *symbolic* mode, rather than, for example, as some sort of immediate physical presence. That is, Christ is a reality within the Christian *symbolical world*, a central and (in my opinion) indispensable reality in that world. It is a reality carried in the ethos and liturgy of the Christian churches—but not a directly observable reality, accessible or available to all persons regardless of whether they know the Christian language and practices or not. Christ is present to Christians *symbolically*, that is, in and through Christian stories (particularly those in the New Testament), Christian preaching and teaching, Christian devotion and praxis, Christian reflection. The name "Christ" is a central symbol that orders and gives meaning to all of these. In a similar way the Buddha and Nirvana are symbols in terms of which Buddhists order their lives and experience. The Revolutionary War and Abraham Lincoln are symbolic realities in terms of which American patriots organize and orient their patriotic consciousness. Martin Luther King, Jr., and Mohandas Gandhi are symbols in terms of which transformative movements among today's poor and dispossessed order their hopes and activities. In saying, then, that Christ and God are important symbols for Christians, I do not mean to prejudice in any way the question of how those symbols will be understood or to what further reality (or realities) they may each refer. I am simply indicating the mode in which those realities become available to human consciousness, reflection, and action generation after generation: Christ and God become present to us in a symbolic mode.

All symbols have histories. They come into being in the course of time, and they may function as powerful resources of meaning and points of reference for women and men in particular communities for a time. But in due course most symbols die away and are replaced by others. What is it that brings religious symbols to life in history in the first place, and why do they lose their power and meaning after a time? A brief, but I think illuminating, answer can be given to these questions. Religious symbols become powerful in human affairs to the extent that they contribute to the efforts of women and men to orient themselves in the world, to gain some sense of who they are and what their tasks in life are, some sense of that to which they should devote themselves in order to find meaning, fulfillment, salvation. So it has been with the Buddha, and so with Yahweh. So it is with God and Christ. When symbols like these become important constituents of attractive, meaningful, and effective frames of orientation for human life, persuading men and women that they make sense of human existence and provide significant salvation from major ills of life, they survive and (may) grow in influence. As each generation passes on this sense of meaning and power to the next, the religious traditions focused by these symbols live and develop. Entire epochs may order their lives in terms of the symbolic resources they make available. However, if and when the effectiveness of a particular symbol in providing meaning and order for life begins to wane, and other symbolic foci for consciousness and devotion become more significant, the symbol may lose its power and eventually die—first, perhaps, among certain individuals or groups, then in an entire community, finally among all living humans.

Thus the central question for christology today, it seems to me, is about the ways and the respects in which the symbol "Christ" can continue to be significant for orienting the lives of women and men. What issues faced by contemporary human beings does "Christ" help us understand better and thus address more adequately? To which dimensions of our modern/postmodern lives does this symbol seem irrelevant? Does our contemporary consciousness of the significance of religious and cultural pluralism pose distinctly new questions for this symbol? Are there some features of the Christ-symbol which are especially pertinent to problems of contemporary human existence, and others that no longer seem to have significant meaning or weight? If so, which of these features should today be accented, which downplayed or even eliminated? Or, is it the case that the Christ-symbol has really become irrelevant to most modern human existence, as many claim? The Christian tradition has, over the years, found a wide range of images and concepts useful for articulating and explicating what it means by "Christ": logos, second person of the trinity, the man Jesus, son of God, lord, crucifixion, resurrection, a new community of which Christ is said to be head and spirit, a doctrine of "two natures," atonement, "second coming," and so on and on; and these have acquired and retained special significance through their use in a variety of devotional, liturgical, and moral contexts. Undoubtedly some of these traditional images and concepts tend to be connected with, and to foster, forms and practices of Christian life and devotion distinctly different from others. Which of these, if any, are pertinent to major features of human life today? Or are the problems of our time unique in respects that demand entirely new ways of thinking about Christ?

A fully worked out christology for today would need to take up all these issues and more. In this book, however, we are concerned primarily with the way Christian faith should understand and comport itself in today's pluralized world, the stance that Christians should take toward other religions. And that narrows considerably the matters on which we need to focus as we consider the symbol of Christ in this chapter.[1] Some have argued that this symbol, which so sharply and clearly marks Christian particularity and distinctiveness among the religious and secular traditions of the world, should be downplayed today, given our strong consciousness of the necessity to overcome the many barriers that divide humankind into fragments suspicious of and, indeed, warring with each other. The symbol "God" instead (it is suggested), with an ambiance reaching well beyond the parochial boundaries of the Christian churches, is more likely to facilitate the movement of Christians into positive relationships with others.

In my view to oppose these two premier Christian symbols to each other in this way, as we attempt to address issues raised by today's religious pluralism, is a serious error on at least two counts. First, the image/concept of God is itself but one more parochial symbol, certainly deeply cherished in some religious traditions, but not really relevant to, indeed rejected by, other quite prominent ones, such as Buddhism. In some feminist, Marxist, and secular humanist circles this symbol has become an object of deep suspicion, even bitter hatred. It is, thus, far from universally acceptable and meaningful. Second, the symbol "God" taken *simply by itself*—that is, abstracting from the particularistic (and thus provincial) concrete meaning given to it by one tradition or another—is (as we saw in the last chapter) rather vague and general. It is susceptible to enormous ranges of interpretation, from quite broad and abstract views that attempt to move beyond traditional religious boundaries—such as my proposal that takes up into itself the so-called common creation story widely accepted in educated circles today—to very narrow chauvinistic views that see God as a cosmic warrior authorizing and defending a tiny militant segment of humankind against all enemies. The symbol of Christ—especially in its emphasis on reconciliation, on willingness to give ourselves to others and for others, and on the building of communities of love and freedom, justice and equality—has, of course, done much to give *Christian* employment of the symbol "God" powerful humanizing and humane qualities (though in some Christian traditions these latter qualities almost disappear in an emphasis on Christ as himself a fierce and cruel divine warrior). I shall argue that the symbol "Christ" has important resources—going in significant ways beyond those made available by the bare symbol of God—for addressing certain dimensions of the problems posed by religious and cultural pluralism. In this connection it is important to remember, for example, that in traditional Christian faith Christ was apprehended both as normative for human being and action and as the definitive revelation of God. What does it mean for our consideration of issues posed by pluralism to give this symbol paradigmatic significance of this sort?

II

From its beginnings Christian faith has been characterized by a deep ambivalence symbolized by the cross of Jesus, on the one hand, and by Jesus' resurrection, on the other. The cross, standing as it does for Jesus' suffering, self-sacrifice, death, meant that for Christianity suffering would be seen as of central importance to human life, indeed as a vehicle of human salvation. As Isaiah 53, which was appropriated early by Christians to interpret the meaning of Jesus' crucifixion, put it: "He was wounded for our transgressions, crushed for our iniquities; upon him was the punishment that made us whole, and by his bruises we are healed." Enormous human suffering, then, even if brought on by crimes for which humans are clearly responsible, like torture and murder, is not simply evil: it may become, vicariously, an instrument of the redemption and transformation of others. The powerful Christian incentives toward self-giving, toward service of the weak, the poor, the unfortunate, toward self-sacrifice for others' well-being, which have always been central to the Christian ethic, are all expressions of this motif—symbolized by the cross—of the value and meaning of suffering for others. And the characteristic heroic figures of Christian history have not been those who exercised the magnificence of worldly power, but those, like Francis of Assisi or John Woolman or Mother Teresa, whose lives showed forth the virtues of patience, humility, kindness, and willingness to suffer.

But Christian faith has not been focused simply on self-giving. It has always had a strong motif of triumphalism also, and this was symbolized above all by the resurrection of Jesus. As the traditional story portrays it, Jesus' sacrifice was not for nothing: in the end he was exalted to the right hand of God the Father. And the sacrifices and self-giving of the faithful in this world will not be for nothing either: in the end they will receive their heavenly reward, the gift of eternal life in God's everlasting kingdom. Thus, what at first seemed to be a motif (in Christian symbolism) of absolute self-sacrifice for others turns out on closer inspection to be, all too often, essentially an expression of prudential self-interest—given the sort of cosmic order in which it was believed we live, an order ruled by a divine king and judge who will mete out eternal rewards and punishments at the end of life or the end of time. Paul expresses these ambiguities quite straightforwardly when he quotes an early Christian hymn in a familiar passage in Philippians 2. After reminding us that Jesus, though "in the form of God," took upon himself the "form of a slave" and then humbled himself even further to suffer death on a cross (2:6-8), Paul proudly declares that just because of this self-giving and self-humbling "God also highly exalted him," giving him a "name which is above every name, so that at the name of Jesus every knee should bend, in heaven and on earth and under the earth, and every tongue should confess that Jesus Christ is Lord, to the glory of God the Father" (2:9-11).

Such use of the symbolism of cross and resurrection not only drew the sting from the Christian motif of absolute self-sacrifice by transforming it into ultimate prudence and self-aggrandizement; it also laid the foundations for later Christian imperialism and arrogance. For it seemed to mean that Jesus is the only one through whom God's grace and salvation are mediated to women and men: "There is salvation in no one else," as Peter put it according to the account of his speech in Acts, "for there is no other name under heaven given among mortals by which we must be saved" (4:12). The true way of salvation for all humanity, thus, was known only to followers of Jesus. Symbols and doctrines were soon developed to express Jesus' special significance, interpreting him as God's unique son, the Logos of God, the second person of the divine trinity. And before long these increasingly exalted christological conceptions became reified and absolutized, and were taken to imply that the keys to all human fulfillment and salvation had been placed exclusively in the hands of the churches (cf. Matt. 16:18-19). It is hardly surprising that, given such exalted self-interpretations, churches in due course became corrupted into conducting crusades against the infidels and inquisitorial tortures and executions of heretics. And later they gave their blessing to western imperialism, and to the exploitation, enslavement, and even genocide of non-Christian peoples and cultures around the globe. The churches' central christological symbols are still being used today to authorize evils of this sort. It is important that we see that our traditional Christian symbolism must itself bear some responsibility for these matters.

Traditional christology is a deeply ambiguous amalgam in which the tragic story of Jesus' ministry and death is interpreted in terms of, and thus combined with, the conception of God known to the earliest believers: God the all-powerful, all-dominating creator/lord/father of humankind and the world. A contemporary christology will also be an amalgam, but of a different sort. It will similarly require interpretation of the stories of Jesus and the earliest Christians, but this time combined with a *contemporary* understanding of God—in our case, an understanding of God constructed in terms suggested by the serendipitous creativity manifest in evolutionary and historical processes.

III

Historians are agreed that we possess little reliable information about the man Jesus of Nazareth. He was apparently an itinerant preacher and healer in first-century Palestine who believed that the kingdom of God was beginning to break into human history, bringing it to an end. His own healings of suffering and sickness, and his forgiveness of sins, were dramatic signs of the kingdom's coming. In his teaching Jesus emphasized the imperative to love both God and our neighbors, and he gave this twofold love a radical meaning: it requires, for instance, repeatedly forgiving the offenses of others against us (we should forgive another "seventy times seven," he told Peter, according to Matt. 18:22), going out of our way to help suffering fellow humans (as the story of "the good Samaritan" suggests, Luke 10:29-37), always turning "the other cheek" and going "the second mile" (Matt. 5:39, 41), and all of this not only with friends but with enemies as well (Matt. 5:43-47). Jesus did not expect the wealthy and powerful to respond to his call: "It is easier for a camel to go through the eye of a needle," he said, "than for someone who is rich to enter the kingdom of God" (Mark 10:25). And he did not hesitate to bless the poor, "for yours is the kingdom of God" (Luke 6:20), and to call down woes on the rich and powerful and self-satisfied (Luke 6:24-26; Matt. 23:13-38). The life to which Jesus called his followers involved a reversal of ordinary political and social standards, where power over others signifies one's importance and serving others is regarded as demeaning: "Whoever wishes to become great among you must be your servant," he said, and "whoever wishes to be first among you must be slave of all" (Mark 10:43-44). All this was brought into sharp and unforgettable focus by the final events of Jesus' life: he refused to defend or protect himself against his enemies, accepting meekly their whips and curses and finally suffering a violent death at their hands.

Does this story still bear in some important way on our understanding of God and of the human—in particular, our understanding of how we should deal with non-Christian communities? How we should address the issues posed today by religious and cultural diversity?

This is not the place to examine the many New Testament texts which speak of Christ and of salvation, but if we could do that we would discover, I think, that although the name "Christ" often refers exclusively to the man Jesus of Nazareth, sometimes it seems to signify the whole web of saving and revelatory events within which early Christians found themselves.[2] This wider view, in which the name "Christ" is understood to refer to major features of the new communal ethos that grew up around and followed upon the ministry and death of Jesus, is particularly illuminating for the problems with which we are here concerned. Instead of narrowing the normatively human down to the image of a single metaphysically unique individual—with the limitations (some of which we will note later) that this brings to our conception of what is truly and properly humanizing and humane—this view presents the image of an inclusive egalitarian community welcoming all sorts and conditions of women and men, as the normative standard in terms of which humanity is to be understood. Though centering on the man Jesus, the Christ-symbol is regarded as referring not only to this solitary figure but also to the larger community of reconciliation that grew up in response to his work[3]—and in principle, thus, it can be extended to all similar communities of genuine healing, love, and justice. Any community that becomes a vehicle in history of more profoundly humane patterns of life—as paradigmatically epitomized in the christic (communal and individual) images of this seminal period—can be understood theologically as helping to constitute (in its own distinctive way) the fullness of Christ in human history. A view such as this allows us to develop a christology that fits well with, and proves quite illuminating of, both the conception of God I proposed in the last chapter and the relationship of Christianity to other religions.

I suggested in Chapter 6 that we interpret the traditional notion of God's working through all cosmic history—and in particular in human history—in terms of the modern conception of the evolutionary-historical process within which humanity has emerged and developed: the serendipitous creativity manifest throughout the universe has brought into being (over many aeons of time) a trajectory including the emergence of human existence—with its historicity, its freedom and ability to take significant responsibility for itself, and its dreams and hopes for forms of life that are truly humane, life lived within communities of love and care in a justly ordered and ecologically balanced world. A distinctive feature of *Christian* faith in God has been the conviction that it was in and through the appearance of Christ in history—that is, with the emergence of the particular new order of relationships among humans that occurred in the context of and following upon the ministry of Jesus of Nazareth—that dreams and hopes of this sort began to come more sharply into focus and, indeed, to achieve significant historical instantiation. To Christian faith, thus, the Christ-event has signified not only humankind in its most profound possibilities but also, in a unique way, *God's active presence* to humankind, creatively bringing into being a new age and a new humanity. (Given these convictions, it is not difficult to understand why and how a doctrine of God's incarnation in Christ appeared, as a major interpretive device of Christian faith. I shall not develop that line of interpretation here, however, since it would complicate this chapter unduly.)[4]

Thus far in this book both the biohistorical conception of the human and the image/concept of God have been developed in connection with somewhat vague talk about humanness and humaneness, conceived largely in terms of ideals of justice, peace, freedom, equality and the like. We have pictured a world in which persons would be granted their full dignity and integrity, as they sought to take responsibility for themselves and their futures. The historical emergence and development of ideals and values of this sort was, of course (at least in the West), significantly influenced by Christian experience and reflection. Nevertheless, there are striking differences between the basically humanistic theism, with which I have been thus far connecting these, and the explicitly Christian position that I am sketching now. For Christian faiths (as we have been noting) Jesus and the new communal order of peace and love that grew up around him have together provided the *defining paradigm* in terms of which both humanity and God have been understood. Even ideals of justice, love, peace, and the like could not, therefore, be appropriated simply in their conventional meanings: they were reconceived, rather, in light of the vision of the human and the humane that had become visible in Christ. In the humanistic theism with which we have heretofore been working normative humanness is not defined in this way, that is, with reference to a particular historical person and a specific communal order. Rather, its character is specified in terms of configurations of abstract ideals and values which are, in the nature of the case, never perfectly realized in any individual or society. Christian perspectives nail their normative ideas and values down in a much more definite and inescapable way than is possible for most humanisms, through binding them to this particular historical figure and community.

This makes the image of the truly human sharper and more specific while simultaneously radicalizing the Christian ethic. Christians are expected to live lives of love and self-giving, to work toward reconciliation with all others (including even those enemies seeking to destroy us), to be willing to sacrifice our own interests to the well-being of others—all of this being focused and made concrete in the dramatic image of the life, suffering, and death of the man on the cross and in the stories of his persecuted followers. In contrast with the looser and vaguer commitments that abstract idealizations ordinarily command, the New Testament stories of Jesus and the reconciling community make a powerfully evocative appeal in support of very heavy moral demands.

These very strengths, of course, carry with them the potential for serious perversions. In the past Christians have often been inclined to regard those who did not confess Jesus' lordship and deity as somehow excluded from God's love and care, even condemned to eternal torment. As Cyprian put it in a classical phrase, "There is no salvation outside the Church."[5] It is important that Christians never forget that the crusades against those regarded as infidel Muslims were conducted in the name of the crucified one, and the tortures of the Inquisition were intended to compel submission to precisely a church that claimed to be the exclusive mediator of Christ's salvation. These sorts of actions and claims, of which Christians have often been guilty, far from promoting the humane order for which Jesus died, have further undermined it by dividing humans from each other instead of reconciling them, by setting them at war with each other instead of bringing peace and love. Such perversions were made possible—indeed fostered—by the reification and absolutization of the churches' basic christic symbols. From early on Jews and Muslims realized that Christians were falling into idolatrous attitudes toward Christ (and the church), and they criticized these in the name of the One High God. But to this day most Christians have failed to acknowledge this quite proper theological critique of the ways in which they employed their central religious symbols.

The absolutized picture of Jesus as uniquely and exclusively God's son has helped to generate other theological problems: it has, for example, fostered a highly individualistic understanding of both humanity and God, an understanding in many ways incompatible with today's ecological and systemic ways of thinking. Since the normatively human was taken to be definitively represented in an *individual* man, traditional Christian faith (at least in western versions) has always had strong tendencies to understand human existence in essentially individualistic, atomistic terms—thus downplaying the defining significance of the communal or social, as emphasized by the wider conception of Christ that I

am proposing. Moreover, since this same individual man was regarded as
the definitive revelation of the divine, God also was often taken to be a
kind of atomic individual, a person—instead of, for example, an ecologi-
cal-processive reality, as I am suggesting. From these two points it clearly
followed in much traditional Christian faith and piety that the relationships between God and humanity would be conceived in essentially individualistic terms, as one-to-one relationships between each individual soul
and God.[6] In contrast, I have argued that humans are fundamentally
social realities—biohistorical beings—constituted by the relationships
(interpersonal and sociocultural, biological and physical) in which they
stand. Their relationship with God, therefore, should not be understood
as a kind of direct personal encounter but rather as mediated in and
through this social and ecological network.

I am not suggesting here that we must reject the traditional formulations
completely. If we are careful not to literalize and reify the christic symbolism, and if we interpret it in the wider sense that I have proposed, it can
remain significant and effective. It expresses in powerfully evocative images
the central Christian claim that the direction (and thus the ultimate meaning) of the evolutionary-historical trajectory that has produced humanness
is to be seen in its creative tension toward greater humaneness. For Christians the truly human and humane have become visible in the new sorts of
relationships within the community that emerged around, and in consequence of, the ministry and death of Jesus. Here also is disclosed, therefore, something of the character and quality of that creativity manifest in
and through the overall evolutionary-historical trajectory that has brought
humankind into being—that is, the character and quality of the ultimate
mystery we call *God*.

The central christic images and ideas present a dramatic and compelling
figure courageously facing death at the hands of those threatened by his
radical ministry and teachings, and of a communal life among his earliest
followers which seeks to overcome barriers to meaningful and fulfilling
forms of human existence that have been created by distinctions of status
and class, of religion, race, and gender. However difficult it may be to
instantiate in our lives today what these images portray, they present a picture of the human project that has strongly attracted many women and
men from the New Testament period onward. For centuries (in those societies deeply affected by the Christian story) these images have shaped
moral, religious, and more general cultural values and meanings, promoting the cultivation of loving, forgiving, and self-sacrificing attitudes and
practices. The Christian sense of the evolutionary-historical trajectory that
has brought us into being and continues to sustain us and to urge us on

toward a more profound humaneness is thus given a distinctive concreteness by these christic ideas and images.

IV

To many today—one thinks, for example, of Friedrich Nietzsche and Sigmund Freud as well as many feminist writers—the christic imagery of the New Testament, with its overriding emphasis on self-sacrificial love for others and on communal reconciliation and upbuilding, is regarded as a trap that is destructive of important human possibilities and thus of human reality. Others find the christic imagery and stories beautiful and romantic but virtually useless for orientation in the cold "real world" where quite different values and standards are in play. These images and meanings remain compelling, however, for they reveal something of great importance to human life. Notions of reconciliation, love, and peace, of self-giving, voluntary poverty, concern for our enemies, vicarious suffering, point to our deep interconnectedness with each other. Thus they show the direction in which communities and individuals must move if our human world is ever to become more truly humane. Societies whose members respect one another and work together steadily for the common good, societies characterized by equality of opportunity and by freedom and justice and concern for all, will not be created as long as our activities are directed largely toward our own self-aggrandizement, whatever the cost to others. Nor will our continuing celebration and exercise of violent power, whether political, economic, military, or religious—a particular problem in the United States, I am sorry to say—contribute much to their establishment. It is images (like those found in the New Testament) of communities of reconciliation—in which all recognize that they are "members one of another" (Rom. 12:5) with no discrimination among groups, classes, races, or genders—that can focus our attention and our lives on the commitments we today must make and the loyalties we must maintain if we are to align ourselves with those cosmic and historical forces pressing us toward a more humane world.

In this context of hopes and dreams the image of the self-sacrificial Jesus, who gives himself completely—and nonviolently—so that all might have "abundant life" (John 10:10), stands out in its full significance. Here is a vivid emblem of the radical transvaluation of values that is required if our world of violence and aggressive self-assertion is to become more truly humane and thus more human. It is an emblem that is simultaneously a powerful call for our commitment to this expected and hoped for coming "kingdom of God." The earliest Christians believed they had been called by God to just this sort of ministry of healing and reconciliation, and that it was the power of the divine spirit working among and within them—the power (in our language here) of those evolutionary and historical momentums that are moving in the direction of a more truly humane world—which led them to respond affirmatively to that call. This reconciling and healing power, imaged in and symbolized by the events surrounding and including Jesus, continues to call women and men today to respond to the need for, and to the forces working toward, such reconciling activity in the world.

Paul sometimes speaks of this new Christian orientation in life as being a "new creation" by God, a creation in and through which God is reconciling us to Godself, and calling us to become "ambassadors for Christ" (2 Cor. 5:17-20a). Elsewhere he speaks of a new "Spirit" that enlivens the Christian community, a Spirit the "fruit" of which is "love, joy, peace, patience, kindness, goodness, faithfulness, gentleness, self-control" (Gal. 5:16, 20-23). The Johannine writings go even further than Paul in their interpretation of the significance of the new life aspired to and experienced within the Christian communities, identifying it as the very presence of God: "Beloved, let us love one another; . . . love is from God; everyone who loves is born of God and knows God. . . . for *God is love*" (1 John 4:7-8; emphasis mine). The salvation—the relation to God—promised in these (and other) well-known texts is nothing else than the special quality human life is expected to take on within this new community, with its straining toward truly humane patterns of existence within itself, and its larger task of fostering further humanization in the world roundabout through its ministries of healing and reconciliation.

I have noted in earlier chapters that the various cultural streams of humanity seem today to be converging into a single intraconnected human history. And yet our world is fiercely divided into warring factions on every hand. At this portentous moment, perhaps more than ever before, we need conceptions of the human and visions of history that will facilitate our movement toward an ordering of our lives which is at once humane and universal, an ordering in which the integrity and significance of each tradition and each community are acknowledged and the rights of every individual are respected. New cultural patterns of association and cooperation must be developed, new institutions must be invented, new ideologies that are at once universalistic and truly pluralistic must be created. For these sorts of things to happen a spirit of self-sacrifice for the well-being of the whole of humanity will be widely needed, a spirit that can subdue the instincts for self-preservation and self-defense—perhaps among the strongest that we possess—which so dominate our communal and ethnic, our national and religious practices and institutions, as well as our personal lives. Just such a spirit of self-giving, love, reconciliation, the building of community, is what the symbol of Christ powerfully presents. And it is to a firm commitment to express this spirit—especially in our relations to those many others with whom we disagree and who appear to us as threats—that that symbol today calls us men and women, particularly those of us in the Christian churches.

It is pertinent, as we consider the difficult issues with which today's religious and cultural diversity faces us, to call to mind Jesus' parable of the last judgment (Matt. 25:31-46). Here we are told that it is not those who make a particular point of identifying themselves as Christian that will be acknowledged at the end of time as Jesus' true followers, but rather all those, whatever might be their explicit religious and other commitments, who perform simple acts of kindness or mercy to needy fellow-humans—giving a cup of cold water to the thirsty, clothing the naked, ministering to the sick and the imprisoned. In another connection Jesus is reported to have stated emphatically, "Not every one who says to me, 'Lord, Lord,' will enter the kingdom of heaven, but only the one who does the will of my Father in heaven" (Matt. 7.21). That is, it is through participation in actual ministries of healing and caring for the suffering and the estranged wherever they are found, in loving our neighbors and our enemies, in overcoming the barriers of alienation and hatred among humans and building communities of reconciliation with institutions to support them, that the ongoing work of humanization—the historical trajectory to which Jesus' followers are called to commit themselves—is carried out, not through pronouncing certain verbal confessions or being particularly concerned to associate ourselves with ecclesiastical institutions and practices. Precisely these sorts of reconciling and healing activities are urgently needed in today's world, as a historically, culturally, economically, and religiously divided humanity is being forced to grow together again, and human life on planet Earth becomes a single intraconnected network.

Obviously many (Christians as well as others) will not agree with this claim about the significance of the christic images: there are many other (religious and secular) ways of understanding the human situation, our deepest problems, the direction in which history should be (or is) going. Some of these alternatives present quite convincing cases, and there is no excuse for not taking them seriously. One thinks of Freudian, Marxist, existentialist, deconstructionist, feminist, and other secular humanist perspectives. One thinks of contemporary forms of Buddhism, Hinduism, Confucianism, Judaism, Islam, and others of the great religious traditions. One thinks also of other quite different interpretations of Christian faith.

Each of these alternatives presents and advocates its own (more or less fully defined) picture of the human condition today and its hopes for the future. My claim is not that the view of human existence and destiny that I have presented here is the only one to be taken seriously. It is, rather, the more modest one that this interpretation of the meaning of Christ for our pluralized world is (at the very least) an intelligible one, one that makes a certain kind of sense of the unfolding trajectory of human evolution and history, one that is directly pertinent to some of the most urgent problems with which we humans must today come to terms. It is a view, therefore, that men and women today can and should seriously consider when attempting to decide to what they should commit themselves, how they should orient themselves in life, to what complex of images, values, and meanings they should give their deepest loyalty, trust, devotion—that is, which God they should worship and serve.

Part Three

Reflections in Dialogue with Buddhists

In the preceding sections of this book I have attempted (1) to sketch my understanding of Christian theology and its tasks, (2) to make clear why Christians today must come to terms with the religious pluralism of our societies and our world in a new way, and (3) to suggest that fundamental reconstruction of some central Christian concepts and doctrines is required if these are to orient us appropriately in our religiously and culturally pluralistic world. These latter two claims, of course, remain largely abstract demands, the real significance of which continues to be somewhat vague, unless and until we begin to interact more directly with, and thus come to understand more fully, the various non-Christian religious and cultural traditions that today situate Christian faith and life. It is important, thus, that Christians generally, and western Christian theologians in particular, engage in study of and enter into dialogue with the extra-Christian and extrawestern world in which we live, much more seriously than we have in the past. Ongoing interchange with other ways of living, of being human, of orienting human life, is rapidly becoming indispensable for doing theology adequately.

For the last twenty years I have been attempting to inform myself on these sorts of issues, and to deepen my own theological understanding, by visiting—sometimes for extended periods—such places as India, Japan, Hong Kong, China, Korea, South Africa, and by participating in Buddhist-Christian and Jewish-Christian-Muslim dialogue groups. Since my deepest and most extended encounters of this sort have been with Japanese and American Buddhists, I have chosen to include here—as a kind of living example of the sorts of reflection to which a theologian may be led by such interchanges—four chapters based largely on papers or public lectures prepared in the course of my dialogues with Buddhists. I hope these will make clear some of the questions about, and problems with, the claims of other religious traditions that a theologian may be led to raise (see especially

Chapters 8, 10, and 11) and that they will also suggest the kind of unexpected new thinking about central contentions of Christian faith into
which one may be plunged (Chapters 9 and 11).

It is important in interreligious dialogues that the participants representing different traditions not only set out their own convictions and commitments as straightforwardly and clearly as they can, but also that they
examine carefully and thoroughly the claims, arguments, and overall positions of their dialogue partners. And they must speak candidly to each
other about what they see, how they understand, what problems trouble
them—if the dialogue is to be fruitful.

Chapter 8, "Shin Buddhism and Religious Truth: Some Questions," is a
considerably shortened, and otherwise edited, version of a lecture (originally entitled "Religious Diversity and Religious Truth") which was given at
Ryukoku University in Kyoto, Japan, in connection with its 350th anniversary celebration in 1989. This chapter takes up again my contention that
problems arising from the great diversity of human religious life can be
fruitfully illuminated by historical modes of understanding and interpretation of the various religious traditions. The history of the emergence of
Pure Land Buddhism is then briefly sketched, in order (1) to suggest what
such a historical approach might mean for the understanding of that tradition, and (2) to provide background for posing some questions—about
some of the principal *symbols* in terms of which Pure Land Buddhists
express their distinctive religious orientation—to which Christians need
answers if they are to understand and respond sensitively to Pure Land
Buddhists. In this chapter we are brought face to face, so to speak, with
issues that arise when Christians attempt to engage seriously in interreligious dialogue with representatives of this important strand of Buddhism.

Chapter 9, "God and Emptiness: An Experimental Essay," presents
some tentative rethinking of Christian ideas about God and Christ in light
of the Buddhist conception of "emptiness" (*Sunyata*). I was led to these
thoughts as I reflected on some of the comments on emptiness presented by
Buddhists at some meetings of the so-called Cobb-Abe Theological
Encounter Group, and as I dug deeper into some Buddhist materials on my
own. The paper was presented to the Group in October 1986.

Chapter 10, on "Some Buddhist Metaphysical Presuppositions" (originally presented to a meeting of the Theological Encounter Group in January 1984 as a response to a paper by Takeda Ryusei) is an attempt to state
clearly and candidly some problems I have with the Buddhist conviction
about the universality of *duhkha* (suffering). I attempt to lift into clear
view some of the massive assumptions (as they seem to me) that Buddhists
make about the world and human life in connection with this conviction,

assumptions that appear in many ways questionable from a western Protestant point of view. In the course of this chapter a number of central Buddhist themes are examined.

Finally, Chapter 11, "Christianity and Buddhism: Searching for Fruitful Dialogue," is based largely on a paper presented to the Third International Conference on Buddhism and Christianity, in Berkeley, California (August 1987). In this paper I identified two significantly different "root metaphors"—"holism" and "foundationalism"—which appear to have shaped, over many generations, certain distinctive sorts of thinking and practice that developed in these two traditions. It is suggested that such metaphor analysis of religious symbol-systems may enable us to get behind certain issues that arise among different traditions, thus helping us to learn significantly from each other rather than simply making debating points against each other. This prepares the way, then, for the movement to Part Four where this sort of analysis of Buddhism and Christianity is further expanded, and a pluralistic or dialogical conception of religious truth is proposed as appropriate for dealing constructively today with problems posed by religious pluralism.

Chapter 8

Shin Buddhism and Religious Truth: Some Questions

I feel very honored to have been invited to address this colloquium celebrating the 350th anniversary of the founding of Ryukoku University. My wife and I have visited your country and city on two previous occasions—the second time for several months—and we have found them beautiful and exciting places to be, where East and West meet and mix in creative and stimulating ways. We are pleased to have been invited to make another visit here, this time on such an auspicious occasion.

I would like, today, to set before you some thoughts on religious truth, about which I have been musing for a good many years, and in connection with that to raise some questions about some central Shin Buddhist assertions. As you know, I am a Christian theologian, and it has been my lifelong task to reflect on such questions as: What special meaning or significance does Christian faith have for our modern world, with its unprecedented problems? In what sense can Christian claims be regarded as true? How are such religious truth-claims to be related to scientific or historical or philosophical truths? And so on. In the course of this reflection I have become increasingly interested in the enormous diversity in religious claims about truth, as one moves from one tradition to another. Should—or can—we regard these various quite distinct claims as somehow all true? Or are they all false? Or is each such claim a partial and inadequate version of some ultimate truth toward which it reaches but which no religious tradition has succeeded in articulating adequately? None of these all too common answers to our questions about religious truth are satisfactory. In the first part of my remarks here I will suggest that a historical approach to these complicated issues can move us forward in coming to terms with them.[1]

Originally published in a Ryukoku University commemorative volume, *Shinran and the Contemporary World* (Kyoto, Japan: Ryukoku University, 1989). Some portions of this lecture as originally given have been omitted from this chapter; they now appear in Chapter 12 in revised form. Page numbers in the text refer to Ueda Yoshifumi and Hirota Dennis, *Shinran: An Introduction to His Thought* (Kyoto, Japan: Hongwanji International Center, 1989).

I

There has emerged in modernity an attempt to understand *historically* the many religious and cultural differences with which men and women must today come to terms; that is, to understand these differences in terms of the processes—the successions of historical events—through which they have developed, to understand them in terms of the historical experience and the historical activity and the historical creativity of human beings in their quite diverse historical settings around the globe. This mode of understanding and interpretation has proved convincing and illuminating to many. Modern "historical consciousness" (as it is often called)—both partially created by, and itself further contributing to, the development of modern methods of historical study—has gradually emerged in the past two centuries. With it has come a profoundly deepened sense of and respect for human diversity and pluralism. Historical and cultural-anthropological studies have supplied us with what Clifford Geertz has called "thick descriptions"[2] of the variant forms of human life that have developed in different times and places, and we have begun, in consequence, to appreciate much more fully the richness of meaning and value which these diverse forms of life have opened up for human beings.

My former Harvard colleague in the history of religions, Wilfred Cantwell Smith, argues that our growing awareness of the worldwide history of human religiousness has made available to us an overall framework within which each of the known religious traditions can be given a significant place and be meaningfully interpreted, without compromising its integrity. He points out

> that every religious tradition on earth has . . . developed in interaction with others; not in isolation, in some watertight compartment. . . . The practice of burial of the dead, . . . for instance, . . . extends back to palaeolithic times. The world history of the idea of the Devil, to take another instance, is quite specific, and cannot be understood within any one religious framework. . . . The idea of Hell, also [has had a] career in the global sweep of humankind's religious life. . . . Let us take a still more crucial example . . . the matter of scripture. . . . a world historian of religion can discern the growth, development, spread, and varied crystallizations of this massively important conception over the course of global history. . . . Finally . . . the Christian idea of God . . . has been . . . a part of the world history of the idea of God on earth, Christians receiving from, contributing to and participating in that total history. . . . We have all along been participants in the world history of religion; although we did not know it.[3]

Religious thinkers have known for a long time that no religious idea or text can be properly or fully grasped simply by itself: texts and ideas can be understood only if we know the language in which they are expressed; and then only if we see them in the context of other ideas and texts to which they are related and with which they are interconnected. Smith contends, however, that our knowledge and understanding have now grown sufficiently to make it clear that historical contextualization should no longer be confined to the particular community or tradition in which we happen to be interested: the wide religious history of humankind is a single intraconnected whole, and only this whole can today rightly be regarded as the proper context for understanding and interpreting the myriad particular expressions of human religiousness:

> The new emergence is the recognition of the unitary religious history of humankind. . . . [The] static notion of an "Islamic religion" [for example] gives way, once one looks more closely, to a dynamic notion of Islamic religious history, . . . [and] the notion . . . of Islamic religious history gives way to the truer concept of an *Islamic strand in the religious history of the world.* The same is even more obviously true for the Buddhist case, and is becoming increasingly visible for the Hindu, the Jewish, the Christian. . . . What is beginning to happen around the earth today is the incredibly exciting development that will eventually mean that each person, certainly each group, participates in the religious history of humankind; Muslims will participate in it as Muslims, Jews as Jews, Hindus as Hindus, Buddhists as Buddhists. . . . For ultimately, the only community there is . . . is the community, world-wide and history-long, of humankind.[4]

Our modern world no longer consists of nations or civilizations or peoples that can regard themselves as existing more or less autonomously, in independence of each other: we have become interconnected with each other in countless ways. What happens in one part of the world economically or politically has its effects on us all. We breathe a common atmosphere, and we all suffer from its growing pollution. We live together under the threat of nuclear and ecological disaster. Although culturally we are increasingly aware both of our diversity and of our interdependence, the meaning of this for our religious institutions and traditions, and for our religious self-understanding, has barely begun to dawn upon us. We need new and more adequate ways to think both the diversity and the interconnectedness of our human religiousness, if our various religious heritages are to contribute positively to the building of a world in which we, in all our differences, can live together productively and in peace. Historical understanding and interpretation of human religiousness can make that possible.

Today we are able to understand historically both how and why so many different types of religiousness have emerged. And we can understand why—as certain modes of thinking and acting, of meditation and practice, proved insightful in defining and diagnosing some of the more difficult problems and ills of human life, and made available treatments and remedies that were healing and in other ways effective—these modes of understanding and practice became increasingly honored and respected and preferred to others, became regarded as good and right and true, the patterns to be followed if humans were to find some measure of salvation from the terrors and evils of life. What is taken to be true in each religious tradition is closely connected with the way in which that tradition has learned to picture or conceive human life in its environment; and this symbolic conception or picture has itself been defined and shaped in many respects by the metaphors and images, and even the grammar and syntax, of the language in and through which it is articulated. Since the various religious traditions have become structured by significantly different symbolic patterns—and thus picture human life in the world in strikingly different ways—they have developed profoundly different understandings of reality and truth. (Additional elaboration of the importance of historical understanding of human religiousness can be found in Chapter 3, above.)

II

Any religious tradition could provide examples of this historically shaped growth of religious insight and the consequent emergence of widely differing religious truth-claims. I want to sketch briefly now the way in which the emergence and development of Shin Buddhism illustrates what I have been saying. In a recent book[5] Ueda Yoshifumi and Hirota Dennis provide—in illuminating chapters on "The Mahayana Mode of Thought" and the "Emergence of the Pure Land Path"—excellent historical background for the understanding of the insights and thinking of Shinran, the defining figure for Jodo-Shinshu Buddhism. It becomes clear that the basic metaphors and patterns with which Shinran worked were developed long before his time: they go back at least to Nagarjuna in the second century of the Common Era (128ff.). But of course Nagarjuna's work did not spring fully formed simply from his own mind either: it was grounded in traditions that had been taking shape for hundreds of years, from the time of the Buddha (500 B.C.E.) and even long before that. These Buddhist traditions did not develop in any simple linear way, as a kind of straightforward explanation and extrapolation of what was already clear in Sakyamuni's original teaching. Rather, they grew more like a gigantic historical tree, with new branches frequently appearing and moving off in quite different directions. The writings of a number of important figures, still much revered, mark some of the more significant of these branchings-off from the earlier Buddhist trunk as seen from the perspective of Shin Buddhism—

Nagarjuna, Vasubandhu, T'an-luan, Tao-ch'o and so on, finally down to Honen and Shinran. (Other forms of contemporary Buddhism, of course, with their own distinctive emphases and truth-claims, would trace their lineage in quite different ways than this. To them the Shin path, at least in its later developments, may well seem quite misleading, perhaps even completely false. Similarly, if one looks at the history of other religious traditions, for example, Christianity, Judaism, Hinduism, one also discovers many internal disagreements on central questions of meaning and truth.)

Some interesting things turn up as one examines this historical development of Pure Land Buddhism. In early Buddhism, for example, there was strict insistence that the only way to enlightenment is through strenuous disciplines and practices, possible for only a small minority of persons. With the emergence of Pure Land Buddhism, however, there gradually developed acceptance of an alternative way called "the path of easy practice" (128ff.). The only requirement made of persons on this path to Nirvana was that they entrust themselves without reservation to the power of Amida Buddha's vow to save all sentient beings: through "allowing oneself to be carried by the power of the Buddha's vow," as T'an-luan put it, "one quickly attains birth in the land of purity" (131). With Tao-ch'o the matter of salvation becomes further simplified: "If sentient beings, though they have committed evil all their lives, should say my Name [i.e., the name of Amida Buddha] at the time of death . . . ten times," they will be reborn in the Pure Land (135). And with Shinran it is finally insisted that this "true teaching, practice, and realization of the Pure Land way" is the "'One Vehicle,' . . . the single genuine path, the only way by which all beings may attain enlightenment" (140). Thus, the tradition of strict discipline (still maintained by most other forms of Buddhism) appears here to have turned completely upside down! Nevertheless, speaking from their perspective as Shin Buddhists, Ueda and Hirota do not hesitate to declare that here in "the works of Shinran, more than a millennium after the Pure Land sutras took written form, . . . the [true Buddhist] path stands most fully disclosed" (127).

The question we must ask ourselves now is how this sort of sharp disagreement in truth-claims among various branches of Buddhism, and in different stages of the historical development of Buddhism (as well as, for that matter, between Buddhism generally and other religious traditions) is to be interpreted. Religious truth emerges, as we have just been observing, through gradual historical processes; and there seems to be no obvious reason why the truth-claims of any one particular tradition, or one particular stage of its development, should be regarded as the normative standard for assessing all the others. Does this drive us, then, into a complete skepticism about all religious truth, or into a relativism that prevents us from making any judgments about it? I do not think so. What it does demand, however, is that we reconsider our conception of religious truth, and how it can best be understood.

I want to suggest that it is no longer reasonable to think of religious truth in monolithic terms, as if there were some single unified truth to which all religious truth-claims approximate and in terms of which all should be assessed. Rather, as modern historical understanding enables us to see, many quite diverse patterns of religious understanding and truth have emerged historically, each of them intelligible and persuasive in its own terms but standing in some tension—even contradiction—with others on some important issues. We are confronted here with a situation that is pluralized through and through. This requires us to develop a pluralistic conception of truth, or a conception of pluralistic truth, a notion that will be developed below in Chapter 12.[6]

Religious truth has, in fact, always been pluralistic in character, emergent from conversations among many different voices over many generations; and the efforts made, from time to time, to freeze it into authoritative, unchanging, monolithic forms have always failed. The several great religious traditions, I hope, can come to understand their deepest insights and truth in the historical and pluralistic way I am proposing here (and in Chapters 12 and 13), each seeing its own insights as contributions to the larger conversation of humankind on the deepest issues with which life confronts us all. If this occurs, we will be taking significant further steps toward finding a way to live together on our small planet as a single, though pluriform, humanity.

III

In this spirit of participating in the pluralistic search for religious truth, and inviting others to join me in that search, I would like now to pose a few questions about Shin Buddhism. I am deeply interested in Buddhist patterns of thought, and I believe the various Buddhist ways of understanding human life and the world have significant contributions to make in the larger conversation about religious truth in which we are all becoming increasingly engaged. If this conversation is to go forward, we must speak clearly and forthrightly with each other about what we understand and what we do not understand, about that with which we find ourselves in agreement and that which seems to us false or wrong. I have myself been engaged for most of my life not only in attempting to interpret in a positive way the meaning of Christian faith for life in the modern world; but also in seeking to identify, and call attention to, some of the deep problems in

Christian faith, in the Christian understanding of human existence, and above all in the Christian idea of God. In this spirit of commitment to pluralistic truth, and as one partner in this common enterprise, permit me now to pose some questions about aspects of Shin Buddhism that I do not understand, and which I find troubling.[7] I have four sets of questions.

First, some questions about the "Pure Land" of which Shin Buddhists speak. How is this Pure Land to be understood? The symbol itself suggests that it is a *place* of some sort, a kind of paradise of utmost beauty and purity. Obviously, however, it is a very different sort of place from this present world: its inhabitants, we are told, are perfectly happy, completely free of all suffering (122ff.). Apparently for most Pure Land Buddhists it has been taken for granted that this place could be entered only after death. Shinran, however, took the position that the Pure Land was accessible even in this life (126f., 169ff.).

How are we today to understand this Pure Land? Is there really some special *place* other than this world to which we may go after death, a Pure Land of joy and peace? Many religions have myths that speak this way. However, in the light of modern scientific cosmology and our modern knowledge of the grounding of human existence in the evolution of life and the earth's ecology, it is difficult to make sense of this kind of thinking. How do ordinary practicers of Shin Buddhism think about these kinds of questions? Do Buddhist teachers discuss these issues when instructing their students? Or do common folk, for the most part, believe that their faithful repetition of the *Nembutsu* will assure their entry into some sort of Pure Land—whatever that might be—after they die? Perhaps sophisticated Buddhists, following the lead of Shinran, understand that the Pure Land is not a real place at all, but basically a symbol for a different state of mind. But would such a notion be attractive and acceptable to ordinary practicers of Shin Buddhism? There are many such questions that one might ask about this central image of the Pure Land.

My second set of questions has to do with Amida's Vow. First, of course, one wonders who—or what—is Amida Buddha? Is Amida some sort of "cosmic person," a kind of god? If so, how are we to conceive this sort of being today? If Amida is not a person of some sort, how should we think of the "vows" that he is supposed to have made? Vows are made by personal beings, beings who can carry out purposes they have set for themselves: were Amida's vows made at some particular time and place (like ordinary vows), and then carried out later through his personal activity? How are we to understand the claim that Amida's vows bring about effects in *this world*, such as transferring women and men into the Pure Land? We are told that the making and carrying out of Amida's vows took many "kalpas" of time—apparently billions of years (117)—but how should this be understood? It is difficult to see what this kind of mythic thinking can mean if taken in anything like its literal sense. But if we do not take it in this way, what does it really signify?

Amida is said to be "the primordial Buddha who embodies the essence of all Buddhas" (121). This ultimate reality is taken to be utterly "formless," characterizable by such various terms as "emptiness, suchness, dharma-body, thusness, oneness" (176). If extremely abstract and vague terms of this sort are really the most adequate characterizations we can give of this "primordial Buddha," is it not seriously misleading to put such emphasis on the importance of a particular personal name ("Amida"), and to suggest that this "Amida" makes "vows" and then acts in certain quite specific ways to carry them out? These questions are not mere quibbles: they go to the heart of the claims of Shin Buddhism. For all salvation from the evils of this world, all movement into the Pure Land of fulfillment and bliss, is said to depend on the *activity* of Amida Buddha, the great "other-power" apart from which we wicked human beings could have no hope at all (131, 138ff., 219ff.). I am interested in learning more about how modern Shin Buddhists understand these central ideas connected with Amida Buddha.

My third set of questions focuses on the radical *dualism* suggested by the symbols of the Pure Land and Amida's Vow, a dualism that appears to run through all Shin Buddhist thinking. The entire understanding of human existence and its problems here rests on sharp contrasts like that between the Pure Land and this present world, other-power and self-power: everything right and good and true is concentrated on the one side of this contrast; everything evil and false and wrong is to be found on the other. However, further exploration reveals that Shin Buddhists are not in fact speaking (as I just have) about a simplistic or straightforward dualism between this world and some other reality. On the contrary, this very dualism, it is claimed, is itself delusion and confusion: entry into the Pure Land is nothing else than the discovery that this powerful dualism—experienced to deep levels by the self which lives in this world of *samsara*—is really false, an illusion. *Samsara* is really *nirvana*, and *nirvana* pervades all of *samsara*, as Nagarjuna long ago maintained. "The person of true *shinjin* [often translated 'faith']," as Shinran put it, "can be called equal to Tathagatas . . . even though he himself is always impure and creating karmic evil. . . . The heart of the person of shinjin already and always resides in the Buddha land."[8]

There is not opportunity here for us to explore the intricacies of this momentous turn, but we must take note of what it seems to imply about our humanness and the meaning of our human activities. For Shinran every thread of the human sense of a capability or power to *do* something on our own, to act in some meaningful or significant way, appears to be part of the illusion of *samsara*: we are not even able to say the name of Amida Buddha on our own. In the words of Ueda and Hirota:

> both the entrusting of oneself to the Vow and the saying of the Name are given . . . through and as the activity of the Buddha. . . . The person of shinjin . . . realizes that Amida's Primal Vow to liberate him has been fulfilled in the infinite past, and has always been working to grasp him (144, 180).

Thus everything of any importance that we might do or not do, indeed, everything about us that is of any significance, appears to have been caused by Amida Buddha long before our appearance on earth. We seem in this scheme to have no powers of any significance at all. Even our apparent power to do evil is undercut here: "Human judgments of good and evil," we are told, "hold no meaning from the deeper standpoint of the Primal Vow" (161).

This position seems to undermine all human sense of responsibility, on the one hand, and, on the other, to declare all apparent evil in this life—torture or murder, injustices of all sorts, poverty, disease, the suffering in war, polluting the environment, even the perpetration of a nuclear holocaust—to be our deluded interpretation of what is actually the beneficent outworking of Amida's Primal Vow. The distinctions necessary to maintain some sort of humaneness and decency in life all seem to dissolve away completely, as other-power becomes almighty, self-power disappears into nothingness, and the Buddha's mind and the mind of the practicer become one. The sharp dualism running through the stories and symbolism of Amida's Vow and the Pure Land has now become so decisively dissolved that all distinctions essential to ongoing human life—good and evil, right and wrong, truth and falsehood, reality and illusion—evaporate into nothingness. With them goes all human meaning, all discrimination of evils and problems in human existence, all human address of these problems and evils. Or is the undercutting of the radical initial dualism not this drastic? It is very difficult to tell. The paradoxes have become overwhelming, and one becomes dizzy, not knowing what to make of it all.[9]

This brings me to my fourth and final set of questions, and returns us to some of the main themes of this chapter: in what respects, and why, should outsiders like myself regard any or all of these Shin Buddhist claims to be *true*? As nearly as I can see, for Shin Buddhists themselves this judgment is made on the basis of three criteria of truth: First and foremost, virtually unquestioned *authority* is given to certain scriptural texts (particularly those dealing with Amida's Vow) and to a specific line of interpreters of those texts—the Pure Land line culminating in Shinran. Second, cogency of argumentation on specific points or positions in these texts is valued highly. Third, there appears to be a claim that the positions taken and points made in these texts and discussions make sense of (practicers') everyday experience of life and its problems, in a way that is totally convincing.

It is not difficult to understand why these three criteria might well appear adequate to persons living and thinking within the circle of Shin Buddhism, where the authority—that is, the ultimate truth—of these scriptural texts and this line of Pure Land interpretation is taken for granted; and where, therefore, human life, and the problems of life, are experienced, defined, and interpreted largely in Shin Buddhist terms. But it is not difficult, either, to see that arguments which invoke only these three criteria are completely *internalist* in character: they provide a self-confirming circle of interpretation and proof, in which nothing external to the perspective of Shin Buddhism—no ideas, evidence, or arguments—is drawn upon. It should not be surprising, then, if outsiders find it difficult to understand many of the specific pieces of this picture, or the picture as a whole. Nor should it be surprising if they regard it as but one more religious point of view, the expression of one voice among the many engaged in the ongoing conversation of humankind about ultimate questions—with no more claim to genuine truth than any of the others. Such "genuine truth," I want to claim here (and will argue in Chapter 12 below), does not actually exist, at least not in the way this phrase suggests. It can be approached only in the full conversation of all these many voices. The truth of the claims of Shin Buddhism, thus, will be discovered only through that wider conversation, not in the largely internalist dialogue that Shin writers—like those in most other religious communities and traditions (including Christian theologians)—ordinarily conduct.

My call to you today is to enter wholeheartedly into this wider conversation. There is no question that your voice is one that needs to be heard. As a Christian theologian, I have myself benefitted much in recent years from conversations and other exchanges with Shin Buddhist scholars. Each of our religious traditions has significant contributions to make to the others, and each has much to learn from the others, as we together discover the pluralistic and dialogical character of religious truth, and gradually come to perceive what that pluralism means for our own self-understandings and for the self-understandings of our traditions. Even more important than this, however, is the hope to which this pluralistic/dialogical consciousness can give rise: that through this deepening conversation we will come to see at last that we really are one human family, living together in one world. This should help motivate us to begin the long and painful process of acquiring the new attitudes and skills, practices and ideas and institutions, that are required if we are finally to find a way to live together in harmony, justice, and peace.

Chapter 9

God and Emptiness:
An Experimental Essay

The Christian view of 'ultimate reality'" was the topic assigned for the paper on which this chapter is based. This very general notion, therefore, defines the context within which the Christian symbol "God" and the Buddhist idea of *emptiness* are here brought into relation with each other. It is important to recognize from the outset that "ultimate reality" is not a common Christian technical phrase with a long tradition of meaning (though, due to Paul Tillich's influence, it has gained some currency in recent years). It is, rather, a term that our dialogue group agreed was open enough to allow for Christian and Buddhist comparisons of what is highest or most important or most central to each of these traditions. There is room for considerable argument, then, as to just what might be taken as "ultimate reality" in the Christian tradition. Some might wish to hold that it is the concept of *being* that should be explored here, since in western traditions all other realities are often said to presuppose being as the foundation on which they rest and in which they participate. Even God has been understood in certain main lines of the tradition as "pure being" or "being-itself." An argument could be made for such a move toward metaphysical issues, but I do not go that way here. Instead, I treat the symbol "God"—understood to refer to the "maker of heaven and earth," the "creator of all things visible and invisible"—as naming what western religious traditions regard as "ultimate reality." Reality of every sort (whether "visible" or "invisible") is said to have its origin and foundation in God—all value and meaning and truth as well as all being. In this respect, God is the

Originally published in *Buddhist-Christian Studies* 9 (1989): 175–87, along with formal responses by Rita Gross (189–96) and Takeda Ryusei (213–20), and further responses, questions, and remarks by myself and others in the Cobb-Abe Theological Encounter Group (196–212, 220–29). An excerpt from my responses is included here at the end of this chapter as "Further Remarks on the Concept of Trinity"; page numbers therein refer to locations in the above journal, except as explained in note 21, p. 223. Used with permission. Another, slightly different version of the original article can be found in *The Religious Philosophy of Nishitani Keiji*, ed. Taitetsu Unno (Berkeley: Asian Humanities Press, 1989), 82–97.

ultimate point of reference (as I often put it) for all reality, all reflection, all meditation, all devotion. It is surely legitimate to regard God as that (in the Christian scheme of symbols) to which the phrase "ultimate reality" can most properly refer. In any case, I proceed on that premise.

We shall be concerned here, then, with the Christian view of God. But once again, it is necessary to make qualifications immediately. For can one justifiably speak of *the* Christian view of God? I do not think so. There have been many different conceptions of God advocated in the course of Christian history—conceptions not completely consistent with each other. Even though there are usually "family resemblances" among these different views, their practical effects in religious life and practice may be quite diverse. One should, then, speak of a range of interpretations of God within Christian history, of an ever-present plurality of Christian theologies, rather than of *the* Christian view of God (though theologians have typically written and spoken as though they were presenting the single and only true conception of the Christian God, not one view among many). One kind of presentation, therefore, that would be quite useful would be of a typology of Christian conceptions of God, making clear the significance of the different views. However, I shall not follow that route here.

Instead, I will present an interpretation that I think has clear roots in certain central Christian claims, but which, to my knowledge, has not hitherto been set forth, at least not in this form. Our discussions together have enabled me to perceive certain possibilities in some features of traditional Christian views that have not been highlighted much in the tradition—possibilities of developing a conception of God that might bring Christian understandings into much closer proximity with Buddhist conceptions of "ultimate reality" than has usually been thought possible.[1] And it has seemed to me worthwhile for the purposes of our discussion, therefore, to take the liberty of experimenting here with a somewhat idiosyncratic Christian interpretation of God. The special peculiarities of this interpretation and the respects in which it departs from more traditional Christian views will become apparent, I think, as we proceed.

I

The symbol "God," like all religious symbols, has gained its complex and changing meaning(s) from the whole history and structure of practices, symbols, and languages within which it falls and has been used. To understand what Christians mean by "God"—involving a narrowing and qualifying of this wider historical complex—we have to see how this symbol has been employed within the broad developing context of Christian language and faith. These observations might seem to imply that it is necessary for us to consider in some detail the historically evolving Christian picture of the world and of human life within the world, along with the wider history within which these emerged. Undoubtedly, such a full contextualization would be desirable, but that is not possible in this chapter, and I do not think it is necessary.[2]

Any world-picture is given its full character and meaning by the whole complex of changing institutions and customs, words and symbols, liturgical practices and moral claims, stories and myths that are handed on from generation to generation and which shape and interpret the experience of all those living within that world. However, not all these expressions, patterns, and practices equally determine the basic structure and character of a worldview: a few fundamental categories give a world-picture its essential shape and order. These are connected and interrelated in various ways by the larger vocabulary of terms and symbols used in ritual and meditation, ideology and story, thus providing concreteness and filling in details of an overall picture or understanding, or of a developing complex of pictures and understandings, which accommodates and interprets the infinite variations and nuances of the experience of many generations. For our purposes here it will be sufficient to take note of the basic configuration of fundamental symbols—what I call the "categorial structure"—that gives Christian world-pictures their distinctive shape and character. Manifest in and expressing itself through the multiplicity of Christian institutions, practices, and liturgies, of Christian philosophies, theologies, and myths, is a historically enduring (but not utterly unchanging) categorial pattern. With this categorial pattern in mind, we can see something of what the symbol "God" means and how it functions in Christian faith.

In my view, as I indicated in Chapter 3 above, there are four principal symbols or categories that have given Christian world-pictures their basic structure and character: God, world, humanity, Christ.[3] I will not repeat that summary here, but I do need to call attention to certain features of three of these—God, humanity, and Christ. Any examination of Christian symbol-systems reveals immediately that the symbol "God" functions as the *ultimate point of reference* in Christian perspectives. Christian traditions have expressed this by speaking of God as the source of all that is, as the ultimate ground of all reality, as the creator of the world and the lord of history, as the Alpha and the Omega, as the one "from [whom] and through [whom] and to [whom] are all things" (Rom. 11:36), and in many other ways. In traditional Christian thought, God was conceived as a largely personal or agential reality. That is, this ultimate point of reference was conceived or constructed on the model of the human person. God was thought of and referred to as a king or lord, as a father or judge, as one who speaks and acts, who loves and hates, who creates and rules the world, and who will ultimately bring the world to its end. In ordinary piety God was thought of as a particular being—one who was the highest of all beings and the source of all other beings. However, this tendency to reify the conception of God has often been regarded as problematic by some (particularly certain mystics and theologians), and it has seemed increasingly difficult to defend, to many modern theologians. (We shall come back to this matter later.)

The category of "humanity" refers to those creatures here on Earth who are sufficiently self-conscious, creative, and free as to require symbolic orientation in the world in order to live. From the earliest period, humans were understood to be created "in the image of God" (Gen. 1:27). That is, they, like God, had powers of freedom and intelligence that enabled them to shape and determine their own lives and destinies in some respects and, above all, to enter into community and covenant with the source and ground of their being (God). There was a special kinship or connection between God and humanity that did not obtain between God and any other creatures. This feature of the traditional Christian categorial scheme raises special problems for many modern interpreters who are deeply conscious of the ecological interdependence and interconnection of all life. Some Buddhist notions seem in some respects to be more in accord with contemporary thinking on this matter than are these traditional Christian views.

The category of "Christ" has usually been understood to refer exclusively to Jesus of Nazareth, a historical figure believed by (many) Christians to reveal, on the one hand, who or what God really is and how God's will is to be understood, and, on the other hand, what true humanity consists in.[4] The historical figure of Jesus Christ has thus given concreteness and specificity to the understanding of both God and humanity. There has always been, therefore, a theological basis for taking the image of Jesus Christ to be decisively determinative of what is normatively human and truly divine. As we shall see below, this (potentially decisive) normativeness of the Christ-event makes it possible to open up a radical way of reconceiving the Christian notion of God, bringing it into closer proximity to certain Buddhist emphases. This position, developed in this chapter (and to some extent in Chapter 7 above), calls into question the often stated view that christology is a principal barrier to constructive dialogue between Christians and others. At least with respect to the interchange with Buddhists, I maintain, the symbol "Christ" can play a highly significant, positive role.

As long as a theologian continues to work within the basic fourfold Christian categorial scheme, it is proper (in my view) to regard his or her work as falling within the bounds of "Christian theology." In what follows I shall propose a radical reconception of the symbol "God" in light of an interpretation of the symbol "Christ"—one departing significantly from much that has commonly been held about God by Christians. If the criterion of the "Christianness" of a theological position were taken to be the specific images and concepts found in the so-called classical documents of Christianity—particularly the Bible—there might seem to be few grounds for claiming this reconception to be Christian. However, the conception that I develop here is both christocentric and trinitarian (as we shall see), and it is consonant with the fourfold Christian categorial scheme. I would hope that it is taken seriously in ongoing Christian reflection.

II

An important problem for all the Abrahamic religions has been a tendency toward reification of the notion of God. From within the mythic three-story universe in which these conceptions originally developed, it was not difficult to think of God as a kind of king in the heavens above who ruled the earth from on high. Despite the emergence of modern non-geocentric conceptions of the world, many Christians have continued to think of God as in some way a being "outside of" or "transcending" the mundane order in which we humans live, leading and guiding it providentially in various ways. To conceive of God as a particular being or person who created the world and continues to govern it has not, for much Christian piety, seemed significantly problematic.

However, this sort of thinking has become increasingly difficult for many theologians, and in modern times it has not been uncommon to deny that God can properly be thought of in this way, as similar in some respects to— or modeled on—the particular beings of ordinary experience. For example, Friedrich Schleiermacher regarded God as the "whence" of our sense of "absolute dependence," not to be regarded as in any sense a particular or individual being similar to individual beings in the world.[5] This notion of a "whence" is obviously very vague, and Schleiermacher is somewhat notorious for the care with which he avoids ascribing many of the traditional characterizations to God in any literal way. The notion of "absolute causality" (which obviously corresponds directly to "absolute dependence") seems to be the only concrete characterization that he is willing to use freely.[6] Paul Tillich, similarly, emphasized that "God does not exist" (i.e., God is not a particular being), but rather God should be thought of simply as "being-itself," or more metaphorically, as the "ground of being" or "the power of being."[7] This resistance to the objectification or reification of the concept of God has not been confined to modernity. It has a long history, particularly in the Christian mystical tradition beginning with Pseudo-Dionysius and the *via negativa*, and appearing again in such figures as Meister Eckhart, Angelus Silesius, and others.[8] Moreover, in Thomas Aquinas and many other mainline theologians it was taken for granted that God cannot be spoken of literally or univocally, but only analogically.[9] Thus, the reification or objectification of the concept of God in much traditional Christian piety has long been recognized as problematic. In recent times this issue has become severe enough to raise the question whether Christian God-talk can continue to be regarded as intelligible.

In my opinion this tendency toward reification of the Christian conception of ultimate reality arises from two sources that reinforce each other. Consider, for example, the fundamental metaphors out of which the idea of God was originally constructed—lord, king, father, and especially creator. All of these are based on, and ordinarily refer to, particular sorts of concrete human beings. How is one to think of a father or a king if not as a particular person with whom one can enter into familial and political relationships? The notion of king implies the conception of hierarchy, with concentration of power, reality, and being at the top. The image of father, with its highly personalistic overtones suggesting the possibility of "I-thou" relationships, implies a kind of over-againstness between the individual self and the divine reality, here conceived as another quasi-individual self.

Even if one wished to regard these particular notions as largely metaphorical anthropomorphisms, the conception of God as *creator* was bound to produce enormous logical and metaphysical pressures toward reification. Western thinking developed in such a way as to lead to an almost indestructible dualism between the creator and creation. On the one side, there is God-the-creator, the only reality with *aseity*—reality that comes from itself alone, that depends on nothing other then itself in order to exist, that is totally independent, underived, and autonomous. On the other side, there is created reality (everything else that exists, all of it dependent in all respects upon God)—derivative reality, contingent reality, reality of a totally different order than the divine. The creator and the created order are thus two qualitatively different modes of being, "wholly other" in their respective metaphysical characters. Human life (and everything else) gets its being and meaning from its relationship to God, but God's meaning and reality are grounded simply in God's own being; the relationship is thoroughly asymmetrical.[10] If the particular beings in the created order have reality and meaning, how much greater must be the meaning and reality of the source of them all, God. It should hardly be surprising that, when this kind of metaphysical dualism is combined with metaphors like king and lord and father (all of them suggesting a highly dynamic center of activity and creativity—a substantial agent-self), the conception of God that results is that of an absolutely real, particular, personal being, with totalistic powers over all other reality (omnipotence, omniscience, etc.). Thus, the personalistic metaphors that serve as models for constructing the conception of the divine being, combined with the dualistic conception of creator/creation, exert enormous pressure toward a reified notion of divine reality.

The other significant motif that played into this tendency toward reification of the divine came from the Greek philosophical tradition and language. From the time of Parmenides, there was an inclination to think of reality in terms of *being*, of what *is*. When this was combined with the Aristotelian logic of predication, which depends to some extent on the peculiarities of the copula in Greek grammar, it led to forms of philosophical reflection that emphasized the *substantiality* of things as the mark of their reality.[11] The real must exist, and it exists most fundamentally as *substance*. That is, reality was thought of in terms of a model based on the individual thing with its attributes and accidents.[12] Given this philosophical tradition, it would be very difficult not to think of God as some sort of *being*—if not a particular being, at least being-itself, substantiality as such.

When these two traditions come together—"God" thought of as *creator* (a person-like or agential being of enormous powers), and reality conceived of as fundamentally *being* or substance—it is hardly surprising that a highly substantialistic or reified notion of God should be produced. Indeed, as the so-called ontological argument of Anselm makes clear, in this tradition God is conceived as a reality that cannot be conceived not to exist. God is that "than which nothing greater can be conceived," and a reality of such an order necessarily must exist. Any other conclusion, as Anselm argues, would result in a *reductio ad absurdum*. So God is being, the highest mode of being that can be conceived, that than which nothing greater can be conceived, the necessarily existing being, the only reality that cannot be conceived not to exist.[13] Although it is clear to philosophers and theologians that the mode of God's being is of a qualitatively different order from the mode enjoyed by the particular finite and contingent beings which we ourselves are and which we regularly experience—and thus, that it would be a gross mistake to view God as simply one more particular being—it has seemed impossible to most western thinkers to conceive of God in any other way than as some highly intensified form or mode of being. Only in the mystical tradition was the idea seriously entertained that the difference between God and particular beings might be better expressed by moving in precisely the opposite direction. That is, by interpreting the divine as not-existing, as radical nonbeing, instead of interpreting it positively in terms of the notion of being.

I want to point out here that the characterization of the symbol "God" that I frequently employ, as designating the ultimate point of reference in terms of which all else must be understood, leaves open the question as to whether God should be thought of as being, as nonbeing, or in some other way. The phrase "ultimate point of reference" indicates the conceptual *function* of God-talk, not the content of the idea of God: the symbol or category "God" provides a unifying focus for attention, devotion, and service. In this way, life is given a center, enabling believers to hold all of its diversity together in some kind of unity, thus making it possible to avoid (or at least to counter tendencies toward) the disintegration of persons, societies, and indeed of the world as a whole. This unifying function, by whatever means it is carried out, is very important—perhaps indispensable—to human life. It might well be worth investigating whether every symbolical world does not have some ultimate point of reference that unifies it. In any case, this phrase points to a central function of western God-talk, and it does so without moving immediately into the reifying metaphors and images of the tradition.

III

Although this openness of the concept of ultimate point of reference is definitely a virtue, it is also a problem: for this phrase is almost completely abstract and empty until and unless it is given some kind of content; that is, until metaphors or models are supplied that give it specificity and concreteness. As we have seen, the models, metaphors, and metaphysical apparatus which the Abrahamic religions have usually employed made reification of their God-talk almost inevitable. It is difficult to employ the notion of, for example, creator—which so decisively concentrates all genuinely independent and autonomous reality on one side of the great divide in being—in a nonreifying way. Despite the claim made in Christian theology from the beginning that the definitive revelation of God is to be found in Jesus Christ,[14] Christians have in actual practice largely taken over the creator/lord/father metaphors of the tradition as the building blocks in terms of which they have constructed their conception of God. In consequence, Christian God-talk (as we have been noting) has always had to contend with the problem of reification.

From the vantage point we have been pursuing here, a somewhat different move appears to be open. What would happen if Jesus Christ, particularly Jesus' cross—his "weakness" (1 Cor. 1:25), his suffering and death—were made the central and defining image or metaphor in terms of which the ultimate point of reference for all of life and reality were conceived, instead of giving the dominant role to such metaphors as sovereign power and lordship? Although Christian theologians have often regarded themselves as radically christocentric, I am not aware that any have carried their christocentrism quite this far. Even Karl Barth, who thought of himself as developing all that he said about God directly out of the revelation in Christ, in fact uses the metaphor of lord as central and definitive when he works out his detailed view.[15] However, if we take the imagery of self-giving, suffering, and death (which the cross of Jesus signifies) as central and defining for our understanding of the ultimate point of reference for all of life, we will be driven in a significantly different direction. We will, in fact, find ourselves moving toward a conception suggestive of the view of some Buddhists, that everything must be understood in terms of *sunyata* ("emptiness").[16] That is, that which is utterly unsubstantial, that which does not maintain itself successfully through time and is thus not a "thing" or "substance," that which (as Tillich put it in his interpretation of Christ)[17] sacrifices itself completely to its context and to that beyond itself, is now to be seen as the ultimate point of reference in terms of which all else must be understood and grasped. If Jesus Christ—with his self-sacrificing stance and his emphasis on love, including even of enemies—were actually regarded as the *defining* revelation of what is meant by "God," Christian faith and Christian theology would move in emphasis and orientation toward those strands of Buddhism which interpret human life primarily in terms of such symbols as compassion and emptiness.* Moreover, such a movement would mean that the reification problems which have plagued traditional Christianity (along with the other Abrahamic religions) would now be left behind.

---

*I do not want to be understood as advocating in this book that Jesus by *himself* should be regarded as *the* "defining revelation" of God (though something like this seems suggested in this "experimental" essay). Such a position is too narrow and constricting, as I argue in chap. 7, above. There I set out a wider view of Christ that includes not only Jesus of Nazareth but also the new spirit and life experienced in the community that grew up in response to his ministry and death. Though this opens up a larger range of images and metaphors for constructing our conception of God, and makes our focus primarily *social* rather than individualistic (and male-gendered), it does not stand in significant contradiction with the essential point being made in the text of this chapter (written some years earlier), that a God constructed in *christic* terms would be of a strikingly different character than traditional Christian views of God usually suggest, and could make significant contact with Buddhist reflection on *sunyata*. (For further argument on some of these points, see *In Face of Mystery*, chaps. 25–26.)

It should be noted that an emphasis of this sort, on a kind of Christian "emptiness" and love as the ultimate point of reference for Christian faith, would not imply giving up Christianity's distinctiveness from Buddhism. Three points can be made in this connection: (1) The notion of God as the ultimate point of reference in terms of which all else is to be understood is retained here. (2) The importance of *history* for understanding reality, life, and the world also continues to be emphasized (in contrast to Buddhism), in that it is precisely a particular historical complex of events that is taken to be definitive of and revelatory of the ultimate reality. (3) The centrality of Christ for understanding both God and humanity is retained in this interpretation. Christianity thus maintains its own distinct integrity in this view, and it continues (and deepens) its emphases on the importance of historical action, on responsibility to the neighbor, on moral concern with the institutional structures of society, and the like. Moreover, with this line of interpretation, it becomes possible finally to conceive of God as love (1 John 4:7-12) in a very radical sense—even as "nonresistance" (as in Matt. 5:39-48) to all aggressive power—rather than (as in most strands of Christian tradition, and with the other Abrahamic religions) as fundamentally lordly power.[18] Hence, although Christianity in this interpretation remains formally (and in its historical pedigree) an Abrahamic religion—with God as the ultimate point of reference for understanding all else—materially it moves close to Buddhism in significant ways and distinguishes itself from Judaism and Islam.

IV

I will draw together this experimental sketch of a Christian conception of God with a few remarks on the doctrine of the trinity—a doctrine which has often been claimed to differentiate the Christian understanding of God from all others. The view set out here lends itself easily and directly to a trinitarian formulation. The doctrine of the trinity is intended (in my view) to express the claim that all Christian talk about God involves at least three quite distinct affirmations: (1) It must be clear that it is indeed God that we are speaking of—that is, that which is distinct from and in that sense transcends all other realities and modes of reality, that which can be characterized as the ultimate point of reference in terms of which all else must be understood. It is this that the notion of the "first person" of the trinity, that God is "the father almighty, maker of heaven and earth" is intended to express. (2) When Christians talk about God, it is emphasized that *Jesus Christ*, "God's only Son," is the definitive revelation or presentation of God's reality among human beings and in human history. He is the one through whom salvation is mediated to humankind. This is expressed in the "second person" of the trinitarian conception. (3) Any Christian understanding of God must also make clear that this God who has definitively revealed Godself in Christ *is always and everywhere present and active,* and is especially known and received in the church (the community of those aware of and responsive to God-in-Christ). The "third person" of the trinity articulates this point. As the doctrine of the trinity has been traditionally worked out, these three "persons" interpenetrate each other and are so interconnected with each other that they cannot properly be considered separate or distinct entities but are rather three indispensable modes or dimensions without which the one unitary God would not be God. That is, God—in order truly to be God in the Christian trinitarian understanding—must be at once (1) the transcendent or ultimate reality from which all else gains its being; (2) the reality manifest or revealed definitively in Jesus Christ; and (3) that reality which is everywhere and always present in and to all other realities or beings as their ultimate source, context, and destination. These three, inseparably together, are the one God. The one God is none other than precisely these three in their interdependence and interconnection with each other.[19]

This threefold or trinitarian claim provides a way to sum up and articulate precisely the conception of God as a kind of Christian "emptiness" and love (which I have just sketched). (1) God is that self-giving or self-emptying (Phil. 2:7) creativity and love which is the ultimate point of reference in terms of which every reality and every event must finally be understood. (2) This creativity and love is most dramatically and definitively incarnated and revealed in Jesus Christ, especially in his suffering and death.* (3) This self-emptying creativity and love is nevertheless always and everywhere present in such a way that it is correct to say that God is always and everywhere present. It is to be observed, now, that it is precisely this trinitarianism and christocentrism in my formulation of the Christian conception of ultimate reality that brings it into close proximity to Buddhist notions of the Buddha-nature, emptiness, and compassion. Paradoxically, thus, just those features of Christian faith and theology which have sometimes been regarded as barriers separating Christians from those belonging to other religious traditions, and which some have suggested should therefore be put into brackets by Christians or given up—namely trinitarianism and christocentrism—turn out to be the very vehicles through which Christian relatedness to at least some other traditions (such

---

*Were I writing this today, I would, of course, express this point in terms appropriate to the wider view of Christ which I now advocate. See preceding footnote.

as Buddhism) can be significantly articulated. For here God becomes understood in a truly nonreifying way—as the creativity and love that underlies and expresses itself throughout all reality, and which is particularly at work in human history, transforming human beings and human life into communities of faithfulness, love, justice, and peace (implied in the radical *christocentrism* of the position). And this nonreified God is, then, the ultimate point of reference in terms of which all human life and activity, indeed all of reality, is finally to be understood (implied in the *trinitarianism* of the position).

Such a view of God, of God's activity, and of the consequent human relationship to God, is summed up very compactly in a sentence found in Paul's second letter to the Corinthians: "In Christ God was reconciling the world to himself, not counting their trespasses against them, and entrusting the message of reconciliation to us" (2 Cor. 5:19)—although Paul was probably thinking of these matters in more reifying terms than I have been proposing here. Christian existence as understood here must be a continuous activity of reconciling love toward neighbor and toward enemy, toward "all sentient beings" (as Buddhists say), for such unceasing self-emptying creativity and self-giving love is the ultimate reality from which we all come, which daily sustains us, and to which we will ultimately return.

Further Remarks on the Concept of Trinity

Here I shall extend my remarks on the concept of the trinity as it bears on some of the issues brought up in the discussion of the dialogue group.[20] I begin by taking up a point made in a paper written independently of (and thus not in response to) mine, in which Francis Cook tells us that for Buddhists:

> the ultimate can be anything—my small grey cat, Leo, for instance, a splendid member of the species Felidae, and the ultimate. He is also absolute nothingness, the matrix of the Tathagata, and the limit of reality, appearing in grey tabby dress, with elegant ears and paws, splendid whiskers, and a penchant for being patted and petted. Therefore, I needn't look elsewhere in a vain search for another ultimate. This is It, if only I can see it (139).

Later in a summary sentence he draws this all together: "The true ultimate must be one which is exactly and literally identical with the nonultimate" (140).

In this last sentence, it seems to me, we have a lot of problems located in a very compact statement. Instead of suggesting that there is a kind of *dialectical* relation between Leo the cat and ultimacy, Cook says they are "exactly and literally identical." That's not an uncharacteristic statement for a Buddhist. If we go back to the earlier quote, however, you will note that Cook ended by saying: "This is It, *if only I can see it*" (my emphasis). It is evidently the case that when one looks at and experiences a cat, one sees immediately that this cat manifests the character of catness; but there is also some other dimension (Cook maintains) to our experience of the cat—a dimension which the word "ultimate" is here used to characterize. This is not the first thing most of us think of when confronted with a cat: *Ultimate!* That word is invoked here by Cook in order to call attention in a special way to something we might otherwise not see. And, in fact, he indicates that it is not easy to see this other dimension. What we all see when we look at Leo is the cat; what we do not all see is ultimacy. What I am suggesting is that there may indeed be some sense in which the cat is identical with the ultimate, but there is also a sense (a much more obvious one) in which the cat is not the ultimate. Precisely because of this ambiguity we need to understand the connection with ultimacy as a *dialectical* one rather than one of exact literalness (as suggested in Cook's remarks).

I can explain more precisely what I mean here by further comments on the concept of trinity. This concept was intended to help clarify matters of this sort: the sense in which—when we seek to speak of ultimacy—we must speak about the *identity* of two or three important things, while at the same time reserving a sense in which we must speak of *distinctness*, of differences among them. According to the concept of trinity, if we are to speak of God (or of ultimate reality), we must pay attention to three indispensable themes and the distinctive way in which they are interconnected. (I use the word "themes" here, rather than the traditional word "persons," because I want to focus attention on certain logical issues, and I do not want to deal now with all the baggage that the traditional word "persons" carries in our language.)

To explain this I shall take up some of the sentences in my paper, and then make some comments on how these are to be understood. The first theme emphasizes the importance of being "clear that it is indeed *God* that we are speaking of—that is, that which is distinct from and in that sense transcends all other realities and modes of reality, that which can be characterized as the ultimate point of reference in terms of which all else must be understood." Incidentally, I use the phrase "ultimate point of reference" here—not "external reference point" as Rita Gross states in her remarks (189–90)—because I do not want to get involved in the question of whether this "point of reference" is external or internal or somewhere else. It is the issue of *ultimacy* we are mainly interested in here, not externality. The traditional language about God as transcendent or mysterious—even the problematic language about God's "wholly otherness"—is intended to focus our attention on God's ultimacy or absoluteness. What is distinctive about these concepts in contrast to, for example, penultimacy, or relativity, or other conditioned states of affairs? How do we focus on the *ultimacy* of Leo the cat, and not simply on the catness of Leo? Even though these two aspects cannot be separated as though they were two different beings, or two different separable features of Leo, the question still arises: precisely what is it to focus attention on two such distinctly different themes with respect to Leo? One of the significant things about the name "God" (in contrast with the name "Leo"), according to the first theme of the concept of trinity, is that in uttering it we announce immediately that we are trying to focus our attention on ultimacy and not on anything else (such as cat-ness). It is God we want to speak about. It is ultimacy we want to attend to at this moment—not any number of other things.

The Christian tradition elaborated on this ultimacy of God by talking about God's *aseity*, about God as being-itself, and so forth. In the main body of this chapter I suggested that we try to express it by talking about God's "emptiness" (following some Buddhist writers). However, as all of the Buddhists here have been saying, it is not adequate to speak of empti-ness all by itself; this leads to a flat and thin conception (see below). We also have to speak of *pratitya-samutpada*, of *thusness*, of compassion, in order to understand what emptiness is. That is, other terms and other themes must be invoked in order to make clear what the theme of empti-ness is all about. Christians make a similar point. There are two other themes in addition to God's ultimacy that must also be emphasized, if we are to avoid serious misunderstanding when we speak of God.

In the text above, I express the second theme in this way: "When Chris-tians talk about God, it is emphasized that Jesus Christ, God's only Son, is the definitive revelation or presentation of God's reality among human beings and in human history." That is, *Jesus Christ* is the concrete image in terms of which we are to understand this ultimacy. Takeda Ryusei made a similar point about Buddhism in his remarks when he argued that *dhar-makaya* or emptiness apart from the compassion of a bodhisattva is extremely misleading. The theme of compassion is essential to understand-ing what dharmakaya and emptiness are all about (217–19). Christians have held that when we wish to speak of God, careful attention to the *christic* images and metaphors—which the name "Christ" signifies—is indispensable, in addition to emphasis on God's ultimacy or otherness (as signified by the first "person" of the trinity).

There is also a third theme in the doctrine of the trinity. "Any Christian understanding of God must also make clear that this God who has definitively revealed Godself in Christ is always and everywhere present and active." That is, God's "ultimate" reality is not something apart from, something totally separated from, all other reality—as dualistic talk of creator/creation may suggest, and as all reifying God-talk implies. (This point is somewhat similar to what Francis Cook seems to be maintaining about his cat.) Rather, the "ultimacy" of God must always be understood in connection with, as underlying, as present in, all other realities. (One could say that God is present in and giving reality to the very *thusness* of Cook's cat. Note that the formulation here is slightly, but significantly, different from Cook's claim that "the true ultimate . . . is exactly and literally *identical* with the nonultimate.") We could say that this is God as *pratityasamutpada*, perhaps—God as the interdependence, the interrelatedness, the connectedness of all things. This interconnectedness, clearly, is not the same as the particular *thusness* of each individual thing. Rather, it is what Yagi Seiichi called the "trans-individuality" of each individual (160–62). This third theme is also *God*; and it is just as indispensable as the other two, if we are to understand God rightly.

So there is a certain "threeness" that must be emphasized if it is indeed God (in the Christian sense) of which we are speaking: ultimacy, Boddhisattva-Christ, presence to and with and within all individual realities. And, if we are also rightly to understand the *thusness* of the many individuals in the world—including, of course, ourselves—we must see it in its relationship to this interconnectedness of God with all else. This means (to come back, once again, to Francis Cook's original point) that we have really been dealing with four themes in this discussion, all of them dialectically interconnected: the three that I've been principally focusing on are concerned with the *ultimacy* of the cat Leo and how that relates to what Christians have called *God*; the fourth has to do with the *thusness* of the cat.

As far as I can see, our Buddhist friends are also making all of these points. However, instead of carefully distinguishing these four themes from each other dialectically—so that we can understand the significance of each of them, can see what role it is playing in our discourse—they have tended to make highly paradoxical and undialectical statements that (to my mind) confuse the issue, such as the one in Cook's paper which I have been discussing: the true ultimate must be exactly and literally identical with the nonultimate. Many problems arise from this confusing, undialectical use of language. (Of course, there are a great many problems with Christian usage as well, for example the too-easy reification of Christian trinitarian language into three distinct persons.)

I want to mention one last problem that arises out of a failure to make these sorts of distinctions carefully. The problem came up most straightforwardly in Abe Masao's critique of John Cobb's paper.[21] Abe said that the solution to the problem of many perspectives is "a completely perspective-less-perspective . . . or a completely positionless-position" (71); and he claimed that Buddhism achieves this. Rita Gross made a similar point at the beginning of her remarks on my paper: "It is an awareness of things 'as they are'" (189) that Buddhists are after, she said, not some kind of perspective. Of course we are all after an awareness of things as they are! This assertion really does not move us very far. Cobb responded to Abe's point by saying that no such position is available to us humans: each of us always is at some relative point or other, some particular position. We are never at a "positionless-position" (75–77). What I want to suggest now, in conclusion, is that the symbol "God" (understood in trinitarian terms) can help us to understand just this contention.

The symbol "God" (as I have been arguing) constrains us to set out carefully what we mean by ultimacy—not that we should separate it out as a distinct *something*, but that we need to articulate carefully just what we mean by this term: how is "ultimacy" to be distinguished from the "contingency" and the "particularity" of the thusness of such individual realities as ourselves? The symbol "God" encourages us to note precisely what we are doing, or attempting to do, when we employ such words as "ultimacy." It functions as a kind of contrast-term to our particularity, reminding us that (in contrast with *God*) we, in our particularity, are always in some specific position, and thus we always have a relative perspective. We speak from our own religious, cultural, linguistic, ethnic, political, class, gender (and so on) points of view. We are never at an absolute or position-less point (whatever that might be), never can have a perspectiveless perspective. Our standpoint, therefore, may never be absolutized—that is, it may never be simply or literally *identified* with a God's-eye view. And what we see from our standpoint likewise may never be absolutized in a dogmatic claim, for example that precisely this—which we see and are articulating here—is how things really are. I am not inclined to quibble here about the relative superiority of the symbol "God" or the symbol "emptiness" (or the "emptiness of emptiness") as a vehicle for understanding this *parity* of us all in our relativity and our ultimate ignorance before the mysteries of life and death. But it seems to me obvious that without a deep consciousness of our parity on such matters, genuine dialogue is not really possible. The trinitarian conceptual apparatus has been devised specifically to call attention to these very special sorts of claims made when we attempt to speak about God—about ultimacy—and to enable us to see better what is at stake in them.

Chapter 10

Some Buddhist Metaphysical Presuppositions

Buddhism sometimes presents itself as basically practical and therapeutic in character, not interested in metaphysical or speculative questions, which may be regarded as misleading or misplaced. The Buddha himself seems to have taken such a position at times. This claim can, however, be quite misleading. Major questions which every therapist must face are: What is the disease that needs healing here? and how do we decide that precisely this is the *disease* (and not some symptom, perhaps, of some other malady)? One can answer such questions only on the basis of some conception of the nature of what is injured or sick, some knowledge of what has caused the difficulties that must be addressed, and some understanding of what will correct them. That is, we must know something about the sort of reality we humans are, the sort of environment or context we live in, the sort of ills beings like us are heir to, and the sort of medicines or disciplines that are available as cures. Fundamental *metaphysical* issues are thus raised here. Buddhism does, of course, take up positions on these questions, and some of these are doubtless profoundly insightful—but some may also be questionable or mistaken. In any comparative religions discussion such metaphysical-type questions should be brought directly to the fore because it is just here that we are likely to find profound differences among various traditions, differences that we need to inspect and assess.

In this chapter I present a response to Takeda Ryusei's clear, and very illuminating, discussion of the Pure Land Buddhist conception of *duhkha*, in which he distinguishes this central Buddhist notion carefully from the English-language concept of "suffering" (often used to translate it). I shall

Originally published in *Buddhist-Christian Studies* 5 (1985): 25–35, 48, as a response to a paper by Takeda Ryusei, "Pure Land Buddhist View of *Duhkha*," published in the same issue (7–24); page references in the text here refer to that publication. Discussion of the present paper (including Takeda's response to it) is also found in that same issue (35–48). Used with permission.

attempt to show that this Buddhist notion (as presented by Takeda) is grounded on a very unusual understanding of human life and the world, involving what seem to me to be some dubious ideas about human existence and, indeed, about reality in general. In short, it presupposes a quite particular metaphysical vision. There are, of course, arguments that can be given in favor of this metaphysics. But there are also some serious difficulties which raise doubts about it.

There are three principal topics I wish to examine here: (1) The Buddhist understanding of *duhkha* (*a*) as the fundamental evil in human life, and (*b*) as all-pervasive. (2) The claims made in Buddhism about what causes duhkha and how it can be and is overcome. (3) The position of Pure Land Buddhism that this overcoming is brought about preeminently (or perhaps exclusively?) through "other-power." These three topics do not, of course, exhaust the richness of Takeda's paper, but I shall have to pass by other important questions that could profitably be discussed.

I

Duhkha is presented by Takeda as at once the basic and all-pervasive character or quality of human life—even of all sentient life—and as a (or the) fundamental evil in life; that is, as something to be avoided or overcome or done away with. This is clearly a metaphysical claim about human existence (or about all of life), and we need to get clear why it is made. Though sometimes this claim is presented as straightforwardly empirical or phenomenological—life simply presents itself as continuous suffering—Takeda's paper shows that it is actually a metaphysical one, not simply a report about the character of experience. The all-pervasiveness of duhkha is not in fact self-evident (that is why it is necessary to give an argument for this claim). Since duhkha is initially defined simply as "the agony and distress caused by a situation which goes counter to one's wishes and perception" (7), it is clear that the concept itself presupposes a *variety* of situations and experiences in life, with duhkha being one sort of experience among many—namely, the experience of the frustration of desire. And we come to grasp this experience in its unique quality and its undesirability only in comparison and contrast with other experiences in which desire is satisfied, in which we do not feel "agony and distress," etc. Duhkha is, then, at the outset, simply one of the many qualities of human experience, albeit a not infrequent one and one that is complex and unpleasant.

Buddhism, however, does not leave the matter at this phenomenological level. Its intention is to make a metaphysical claim about duhkha: that it underlies and is present in *all* human experience, that it is in fact the "intrinsic mode of human existence" (7). This further claim rests on arguments which attempt to show that even experiences that appear to fulfill our desires and are thus pleasant are in fact also duhkha. The argument seems to be based essentially on claims about the temporality of all experience: every experience, even the most delightful, must come to an end. In that moment of perishing our experience goes counter to our desires and, since we would like happy experiences and the satisfaction of our desires to go on forever, thus gives rise to duhkha. All pleasant experience is thus bound up with "pain caused by perishing" (8) and must also, therefore, be accounted as fundamentally duhkha.

This movement to a metaphysical interpretation of duhkha is surely not self-evident, and some questions can be asked about the assumptions on which it rests. As in all moves toward particular metaphysical claims, one modality or quality of experience is chosen here as the *model* in terms of which all experience, or the basic structure of human existence, is understood. In making that choice, however, other qualities or modalities must be suppressed or ignored in favor of the one regarded as more revelatory or significant. In this case, experiences of pleasure and of happiness, of fulfillment of desire, of fundamental satisfaction or blessedness, are all discounted as simply superficial—present only on the surface of experience—and duhkha is taken as the real key or clue to the fundamental character of our existence. The arguments for this conclusion do not seem to me particularly persuasive. As we all know, other religious and philosophical positions affirm the fundamental *goodness* of life and the world, or the basic *diversity* and many-sidedness of experience with its sorrows and its joys. That is, they find the clue to the understanding of human existence in other features of life than duhkha and are prepared to give arguments for these positions. So the move toward the universality of duhkha is certainly a controversial and uncertain one. Yet it seems to be an absolute and unquestioned metaphysical foundation for Buddhism.

This move is itself made partly on the basis of another metaphysical presupposition, one common in the ancient world: an apparent belief that impermanence or change is fundamentally undesirable or evil; only the permanent or unchanging is truly good and ultimately to be desired. It appears to be taken for granted that since "nothing remains imperishable" (8), everything is duhkha, that is, ultimately counter to desire and thus evil. It seems to be assumed that whatever we desire, we desire to "endure everlastingly" (9). But surely these assumptions are questionable. However much I like the taste of lemon meringue pie, I have no desire that it linger in my mouth forever. Most of my desires, in fact, are temporally limited: I desire this for a time, and that for a time. I am not entirely clear about this, but I rather doubt that I desire that anything (of which I can form a fairly distinct idea) should last forever. I value change and variety in experience. I find the passage of time, the fact of "perishing," to be a positive value in life, not a negative one (though of course upon occasion it can be devastating to my happiness and sense of well-being). I do not dispute, therefore, that "perishing" is sometimes and in some situations a serious problem and perhaps a great evil. But I find myself unpersuaded to accept what seems to me the important metaphysical assumption (or claim) of Buddhism, that perishing is *as such* evil. Moreover (it seems to me), if this assumption is given up, the metaphysical claim about the universality of duhkha has been undermined.

There is a third presupposition about duhkha that also seems to me questionable. Duhkha appears to be defined entirely in anthropocentric, or even egocentric, terms: it is that which goes counter to one's wishes or desires, that which we humans do not want or do not like. But should such an anthropocentric modality as this be given such heavy metaphysical weight? Should relationship to human desire be made the basis of the model in terms of which the very structure of human existence and the ideas of evil and of good are developed?[1] One might even put the matter this way (giving the argument a quasi-Buddhist form): Does this sort of analysis and understanding not give the human *ego* and its *desires* much too central or fundamental a place in our attempt to grasp the nature of reality and the place of human life within that reality? Is it not important, indeed indispensable—as the Buddhist understanding of enlightenment suggests—to find a standpoint much less personally involved (a *disinterested* standpoint) if our goal is real insight into the *truth* about human life and the world? Buddhism's most fundamental claims about duhkha, it seems to me, rest on a basically anthropocentric analysis of experience and its frustrations. Whatever profound illumination they may throw on certain features of human existence, it is surely very questionable to make this the basis of one's overall understanding of the human predicament. Moreover, when one radicalizes this understanding even further, as Shinran appears to do (according to Takeda), the problematic character of the Buddhist position seems to become even more pronounced (as I shall argue below).

II

These questions about duhkha and its universality could be pursued further, but I must move on. Assuming, now, that duhkha is the fundamental structure of human existence, how is this problem to be addressed? What is to be done about it? The first thing necessary, of course, is to gain a clear understanding of what causes duhkha; only this will enable us to see how it might be alleviated. We are moved immediately thus, once again, to metaphysical issues: What is there about the structure of reality and of human existence, such that duhkha is the fundamental modality of human life and experience?

According to Takeda (as I understand him), duhkha arises because of a certain incongruity between the structure of human perception (that is, our perceptual apparatus) and the structure of the reality within which human life occurs. Duhkha is experience, it is a grasping or perceiving of things in a certain way. But it is in fact a misgrasping, a misperceiving. According to the Buddhist view, in human perception one grasps whatever one apprehends (1) as "permanent and immutable," and (2) "as one's own" (9). We become "attached" to what we perceive, and we thus desire to possess it "everlastingly." "'Possessiveness' is essential to ordinary perception in the sense that whatever is perceived is perceived as the perceiver's own. Hence, human perception is inherently blind to the perishing reality" (9).

There appear to be two fundamental claims here: (1) that all of reality is essentially flux, and (2) that in all our perceptions we misperceive this feature, taking what is perceived as something we can possess forever. What is required, then, is that our *avidya* (ignorance)—this innate blindness in our perception, which is so thoroughly bound up with specious attachments— be overcome through enlightenment or insight that enables us to apprehend reality in its true character as everlasting flux.

As might be expected, I have problems with both the metaphysical and the epistemological claims here. It is not at all clear to me on what grounds one could argue that reality is simply and purely continual flux, or whether that is even a meaningful claim. Certainly experience seems to give us realities that endure, at least for significant periods of time (the earth, the nearby mountain, the sun, the cycle of the seasons, the pattern of birth, growth, maturity and death in human and other forms of life, etc.). Some of these "endurances" are sufficiently lengthy and dependable that we can order our lives in terms of them with considerable confidence. To reduce everything to a kind of flat, metaphysical "flux" thus seems arbitrary and misleading, a one-sided picture of the human condition. Doubtless Buddhist traditions give careful accounts of the many nuances and subtleties of the changing and enduring dimensions of experience. Yet it seems that these subtleties somehow get lost in the oversimplified claims about the universal flux that reduces everything in which we live to "perishing," thus condemning us forever to duhkha as we grasp after this or that desired object. The negative bias against change and impermanence also seems to be

involved here. As already indicated, I see no reason to draw such negative
conclusions about the complex texture of our experience. This does not
mean that there are no negative or destructive elements in it. It means,
rather, that there is no obvious reason to reduce the richness of experience
completely to its negative elements, as the doctrines of the universality of
duhkha and of flux seem to do.

I also have difficulties with the understanding of perception that appears
to be enunciated here.[2] The "essence of human perception," we are told, is
"the intent of appropriating whatever is perceived as one's own" (9). This
seems to me flatly false. There appear to be at least four important components to perception, as it is described in Takeda's account. (1) There is an
awareness of *temporality*, of flowing, of the coming into being and the
passing away of whatever we are experiencing. (2) We bring to our perceiving a notion of *substantiality*, which we attribute to the object perceived. (In my view, this may be either a kind of "temporary" substantiality or a "permanent" substantiality. In most cases it is a *temporary*
substantiality that we attribute to the objects and artifacts roundabout us,
not the everlasting or permanent substantiality that Buddhist doctrine
seems to require.) (3) An awareness of *myself* as doing the perceiving is
involved in our perception. (In my view this may presuppose either a substantialistic or a processive notion of selfhood, but in neither case need it
involve the notion of absolute permanence, as Buddhist doctrine seems to
hold. Most of us seem to be aware on some occasions and at some level of
our being that we are going to die.) (4) For the Buddhist theory of perception there is also always present the component of *possessiveness*, a distinct
desire to possess whatever we are perceiving.

All four of these components or elements are present in every act of perception, if the theory that Takeda presents is true. But this seems to me
clearly false. Sometimes, for example, in a kind of dreamy consciousness,
there may be only the first element, the consciousness of flowing or temporality, with scarcely any sense of objects or of self, and consequently of the
desire to possess. At other times, in moments of concentrated attention, we
may be conscious only of the object being observed or contemplated, and
have little or no awareness—or perception—of the flow of time, of the self,
of desire to possess. Again, there are moments of sustained attention to
one's self, to one's own wishes, desires, needs, to one's pains and joys, and
so on, all apprehended as belonging to me, as my own, my possessions. In
such cases the third and fourth elements may completely overwhelm and
obliterate the first two. My point is that desire to possess is certainly present in some moments or dimensions of perception, but there seems to be
no good reason to regard it as present in all. To the extent, then, that the

Buddhist claim about the universality of duhkha is rooted in the analysis of perception as intrinsically involving possessiveness, it seems to be insufficiently supported (and largely dogmatic in character?). Moreover, if we grant that there are modes or forms of perception that do not involve grasping by the self, then there must be dimensions or modalities of experience that should not be characterized as duhkha. So the whole Buddhist analysis of the human condition seems put into question. A richer, more multivalent picture than classical Buddhism appears to offer (at least as presented in Takeda's paper) seems required.

There is one more metaphysical presupposition of the Buddhist position that I wish simply to mention here without going into much elaboration. It is what Takeda calls the "law of causality in which cause and effect are identical in nature" (13), and the application of this notion in doctrines of karma and reincarnation. According to these views the metaphysical structure of the universe guarantees that a kind of ultimate justice prevails in human affairs: in life we get what we deserve and we deserve what we get—provided we recognize that the condition of our existence can be understood only if we "take into account all that has occurred before birth and all that will result after death; its meaning cannot be known only by the span ranging from birth to death in this world" (13). Metaphysical claims of this sort are highly speculative—or at least so it seems to one reflecting on them from a modern western standpoint—and to the extent that they provide significant underpinning for the central Buddhist conceptions of duhkha and avidya, these latter become even more problematic.

It would seem, then (unless my analysis is completely wrongheaded), that some very important metaphysical and epistemological presuppositions which certainly are far from proved provide a principal basis for Buddhist interpretations of the human condition. With the breakdown—or at least the questionableness—of these presumptions, Buddhist claims about the significance of our avidya or ignorance of these matters also become problematic. Doubtless ignorance of many sorts contributes to human pain and suffering, and insight or enlightenment with regard to these matters is much to be desired. But ignorance of our metaphysical situation (as we have been considering it here) cannot itself be regarded as the sole or ultimate cause of our deepest ills. Enlightenment with regard to these matters should not, therefore, be regarded as a panacea for them.

As we can now see, Buddhist positions (to the extent Takeda has accurately represented them) are fundamentally *metaphysical* in character (as I suggested at the outset) and not simply practical forms of therapy. Moreover, it has become clear that it is important to examine carefully metaphysical issues of this sort—often involved in religious positions—even though the practitioners of those positions may regard such investigations as unimportant or even pernicious. Much more pernicious, it seems to me, is the advocacy of therapies based on false or highly questionable metaphysical and epistemological presuppositions assumed to be universally and unfailingly true. One of the problems in much traditional religion—Buddhist, Christian, and other—is that all too often it moves from highly significant and illuminating insights into the human condition, and valuable therapies for certain failings of humankind, to universalistic claims that this is *the* (single, ultimate, and universal) truth about the human condition, *the* fundamental problem with which humans must deal, *the* only and ultimate solution to that problem. Human life and human problems are much too diverse for any such monolithic or totalitarian claims to be appropriate. What is greatly needed in the religions, especially today as we are growing together into "one world," are more pluralistic approaches, open to quite varied insights and to illumination from diverse perspectives on human nature, its problems and its possibilities. How to conceive such pluralistic frames of orientation, and move toward them in our religious life and institutions, are problems to which women and men shall increasingly, I think, have to direct attention. (The next chapter, and also Part Four, present some proposals regarding these issues.)

III

Takeda Ryusei's paper is not confined to the Buddhist understanding of duhkha and the quest for that enlightenment which will overcome duhkha. Much the larger part of the paper deals with the distinctive approach of Pure Land Buddhism to these problems. There is a great deal here that is of interest and importance, and I cannot begin to do justice to it. I must, however, make a few comments, since the Pure Land position involves a radicalizing of the standard Buddhist position on duhkha and it thus "has fathomed the depth of human duhkha and carried the Buddhist doctrine of duhkha to its ultimate development" (8). All interpretations of Buddhism which hold that "self-power" is adequate to achieve enlightenment and thus salvation from duhkha (for example, Zen Buddhism; see 11) are ultimately optimistic about the human condition. They hold that given the correct discipline, or practices, or insight, humans are able to emancipate themselves from duhkha. Most forms of Buddhism have in fact made such claims. The Pure Land tradition, however, regards the human plight as so serious that no amount of merely human insight or effort can overcome it: the assistance of the Buddha, with his great compassion for the suffering of sentient beings—that is, "other-power"—is indispensable to release from duhkha.[3] In the reflection of people like Honen and Shinran it became increasingly evident that human enslavement to passions and to ignorance is so profound that there is simply no (human) way to become free of duhkha. Shinran concluded that he, and all other human beings, are in fact *icchantikas* (15, 19), "evil people, destined for hell, . . . [who] can never attain enlightenment by any means" (15). The human hope for salvation, thus, must rest entirely on other-power, on the Buddha's compassion. The concept of the *bodhisattva* (developed in the Mahayana traditions), who vows not to enter *nirvana* until he has succeeded in bringing all other sentient beings to salvation, provides a basis for hope that such other-power will be effective. Thus the balance in this type of Buddhism gets shifted radically from a religion based primarily on human insight and discipline to one expecting salvation from beyond the (present) human sphere.

I cannot take up here the interesting and intricate transformations which this works in the whole fabric of Buddhism (and which are nicely outlined by Takeda). Suffice it to note that Shinran moves from this point to the highly dialectical religious concept of the *Icchantika Bodhisattva* (15) who in his compassion shares the situation of icchantikas (those who cannot be saved) but who simultaneously is destined for salvation (as a bodhisattva), and who will be able therefore to bring all other icchantikas also into salvation (in fulfillment of his vow). Earlier Pure Land Buddhism had prepared the way for Shinran's position by holding that salvation is not in fact accomplished through particular difficult practices or insights or beliefs but is, rather, brought about entirely and exclusively through Amida Buddha's vow; all that is required of us, as Honen put it, is "so easy that it is possible for all people," simply the "recitation of Amida's Name" (20). Salvation here, thus, consists essentially in faith in Amida's vow and the recitation of the *nembutsu*.[4] This puts all sentient beings on an absolutely equal footing with regard to nirvana; and it now becomes clear that "nirvana can be attained without severing evil passion" (20).

Even reciting of the nembutsu, however, might be taken as a particular human practice or activity that must be carried out in a particular way in order to be effective. This would once more give an advantage to some humans over others, thus making salvation attainable by some but probably not by others; and this would in turn mean that the bodhisattva's vow was ineffective. So Shinran makes a move that will assure that absolutely every aspect of salvation will be the work of other-power: faith in the nembutsu and its recitation are themselves to be regarded as the gift of Amida Buddha, not our own work. The gift of faith involves a twofold awareness: "the awakening to the depth of evil passion ingrained in ignorance and the firm assurance of entering great nirvana. . . . The more awakened to evil passion one is, the more assured in the attainment of buddhahood" (21). Takeda concludes his paper with some remarkably paradoxical quotations from Shinran: "Hindrance of [by?] evil becomes the substance of virtue. . . . The greater the hindrance, the greater the virtue. . . . Evil passion and enlightenment are not two in essence. . . . Evil passions have become one in taste with enlightenment" (21–22).

This complex dialectic—approaching a position which even the highly dialectical St. Paul repudiated: Let us sin more that grace might abound more (Romans 6)—appears to have moved a great distance from the concern to overcome duhkha and avidya, with which we began. But it is, I think, as Takeda argues, in one sense simply a radicalization of that concern. For here duhkha has become so deep and evil, and avidya so all-pervasive and all-encompassing—because of the metaphysical structure of human existence and the epistemological structure of human perception and knowing—that there is no possibility that humans can extricate themselves from their plight. Hence there must be absolute and final dependence on other-power. And hence also, as with Martin Luther, there must be a highly dialectical notion of immersion in evil and simultaneously salvation from it: *simul iustus et peccator*.

It seems to me, however, that here—as also with Luther—we have in fact departed very far from the *experiences* of pain, frustration, desire, and enlightenment with which we began. Metaphysical dogma and deduction have almost completely taken over the religious consciousness. We earlier noted—in the transformation of the empirical notion of duhkha into a metaphysics of duhkha—the appearance of a kind of reductionism in Buddhist thinking combined with a movement into dogma, this being supported by a dubious theory of perception and a metaphysics of flux and transmigration. With Shinran all this seems to become hardened into absolutely unquestioned and unquestionable metaphysical truth. The inescapable dilemma in which it leaves humankind can thus be resolved only by further metaphysical postulations and claims having to do with realities like bodhisattvas, vows with cosmic impact, the special metaphysical efficacy of particular human words like the name "Amida," and the like. As in much Christian theology, here doctrine seems to be running wild. A series of increasingly dubious conclusions are reached, built on premises that (however significant were the partial insights they originally expressed) become arbitrary and one-sided when they are generalized into claims about the nature of things. Finally, these all are given an aura of unquestionable authority by declaring them to be articulations of divine revelation (in the Christian case) or expressions of profound enlightenment (in the case of Buddhism).

IV

Perhaps I have missed entirely the argument of Takeda Ryusei's paper. Perhaps I have read it much too metaphysically (in analogy with the way I read many Christian theological papers), whereas here the words are intended in a more practical or pragmatic way than I have taken them, or in some highly poetic sense. If I have badly misinterpreted or distorted what he is saying, I apologize and ask to be instructed. To assist us in coming to better understandings of each other, where we have seriously misunderstood, is (I take it) what Buddhist-Christian dialogue is all about. But such deepening of understanding can occur only if we are completely candid with each other—calling a strike a "strike," and a ball a "ball"—that is, trying to state as distinctly and as clearly as we can what we think we are finding in what we are hearing or reading, and then standing ready to be corrected in and through the response of others.

Much religious language seems to me very problematic (including much Christian theological language). I think it is often seriously misleading in many ways and sometimes becomes quite destructive. In our time—when, if certain fundamental human problems are not better addressed than they have been in the past, we will soon completely destroy all human life and culture—we must move as quickly and effectively as we can to cut through the vast undergrowth that has grown up in our several religious traditions, in order to uncover whatever truly salvific practices and truths lie concealed there. In our situation today it is imperative that we speak to each other with full candor; but also, of course, in generosity, love, compassion. I hope my comments in this paper will be taken in that spirit.

The major problem, perhaps, that I find with the Buddhism described in Takeda's paper, is that it raises in a very sharp way an issue about religious discourse generally that profoundly concerns me: the freedom with which hyperbole, highly exaggerated expression, is often employed without being clearly acknowledged as such—indeed, often being regarded as literally true, as dogma that must be believed. Certainly, duhkha is a powerful symbol or metaphor, quite useful in some contexts for some purposes. But when it is thought to be a kind of universal truth, we get into difficult problems. *Sunyata*, also, is a very significant idea, a concept that illuminates in marvelous ways certain kinds of issues. But when it is viewed as a universal that dissolves everything, and becomes an explanation or interpretation of everything, we go further than we should. In Christian theology the notion of human depravity has its uses. But when it becomes a kind of absolutistic claim (really a self-contradictory claim!), we have gone too far. The problems in Pure Land Buddhism that I have explored in this chapter appear to be expressions of this widespread religious tendency to turn metaphors, hyperboles, exaggerations—which doubtless make for powerful preaching—into dogmas. The Buddhist doctrine of suffering or duhkha, of turmoil and unrest, is an example of this. If we are going to understand each other as we attempt to converse together across religious lines, we will have to learn how to use our words more carefully than has often been done within our several traditions, refraining from extending their application beyond those contexts in which their meaning and use is clearly appropriate.[5]

Chapter 11

Christianity and Buddhism: Searching for Fruitful Dialogue

Significant dialogue between representatives of different religious traditions, such as Christianity and Buddhism, is extremely difficult. Not only are there quite distinct presuppositional patterns governing the language and thinking of these traditions as a whole. There is also great diversity of understanding within each tradition, as to just what these presuppositional patterns are and mean, what are the important claims or contentions of the tradition that need to be retained and emphasized today, which of the traditional standpoints and claims should be radically transformed or even discarded. In consequence, nobody can speak authoritatively for either Christianity or Buddhism. All of us in both traditions simply attempt as best we can to face the problems raised by contemporary life in light of those religious and philosophical understandings that are available to us and seem most appropriate. Each of us thus speaks from what must inevitably be at least a partially idiosyncratic stance, the peculiarities of which are perhaps completely unknown to our conversation partners (and even to ourselves). For this reason it is important, I think, that we attempt to identify ourselves in such a way that our hearers and readers can better understand where (at least some of) our comments and questions are coming from.

My own thinking is in many ways unrepresentative of traditional Christianity, and perhaps of much modern theology as well, and my comments here will reflect that fact. Nor am I a specialist in modern Buddhism, who is in a position to comment on the adequacy of interpretation

The major part of this chapter, not previously published and now edited and revised, was presented at the Third International Conference on Buddhism and Christianity in August 1987 in response to papers by Tanaka Yutaka ("Creativity and Absolute Nothingness") and Akizuki Ryomin ("'Inseparability, Unidentifiability, Irreversibility' Seen from the Standpoint of Zen"). Page references in the text are to those papers as presented. Section IV of this chapter was based on previously unpublished reflections written in January 1985.

of the work of philosophers like Hisamatsu Shin'ichi and Takizawa Katsumi. I will, therefore, use the papers by Tanaka Yutaka and Akizuki Ryomin essentially as a point of departure for posing certain issues that I hope will illuminate the problems discussed in them. I want to probe some of the (as it seems to me) unquestioned presuppositions underlying these papers, presuppositions which I myself do not accept, and the justifications for which I do not fully comprehend. I hope that by raising issues of this sort, I will be advancing our common effort to come to some understanding of each other across the boundaries of Christianity and Buddhism, and of contemporary American theological reflection and modern Japanese religious thinking.

I am a Christian theologian, but one who sees deep problems in traditional Christian theology and philosophy, and who is not, therefore, interested in attempting to defend traditional Christian principles or claims simply because these are the ones that have been handed down to us. There are, for example, severe difficulties in much Christian theological talk which are rooted in reification—of "God," "Christ," "man," and so on—and I have become interested in learning how other religious traditions, particularly Buddhism, with its sharp criticism of all forms of reification, deal with such issues. The kind of Christian theology I seek to develop is one open to the plurality of religious traditions of humankind, not one claiming dogmatic superiority for Christian "truth." Because of this interest in the diversity of human religiousness, I participate in dialogues like the present one, hoping to come to better understanding not only of religious diversity and its implications, but also of some of the other problems with which Christian theology must today come to terms.

I

Tanaka and Akizuki both take up Takizawa Katsumi's distinction between the primordial relationship of God and humanity that constitutes us as human, and the situation which arises when we awaken to this primordial relationship and respond to it. Takizawa held that there is "an irreversible order in the primordial divine-human relationship and . . . that the personal experience of enlightenment, however deep it may be, should not claim finality in the primordial sense" (Tanaka, 4). I do not wish to address here the interesting but exceedingly technical discussion of these matters presented by Akizuki and Tanaka, but instead would like to explore a presupposition of their arguments that seems to me to underlie many Buddhist (and other Japanese) discussions of this sort, but which itself remains unquestioned (as far as I know).

This kind of talk—as well as most Christian talk about the absolute distinction between God and the created order—seems to me to rest on a *dualistic* assumption, a dualism which I find highly problematical. In the case of traditional Christianity, as well as of Takizawa's thought, this dualism is expressed in the distinctly metaphysical terms of a primordial reality ("God") on the one side, and the everyday order of life (the "created order") within which we humans live on the other. In the case of Hisamatsu Shin'ichi, however (and apparently much Zen Buddhism), the dualism is expressed in more anthropological and soteriological terms, as obtaining between the unenlightened self of ordinary everyday life and the "Formless Self" with which one is said to be identical after (or in) enlightenment (Akizuki, 2). Since this Formless Self is an absolute or ultimate point of reference in terms of which all ordinary experience is interpreted, claims about it are in fact quasi-metaphysical ones. In both cases (Christian and Buddhist), then, there seem to be sharp distinctions between what is regarded as ultimately real, on the one hand, and the transient, relative, deceptive realities of everyday experience on the other. In the reified language of much Christianity this dualism is explicit and is claimed to be metaphysical truth: and on this metaphysical claim is based the supposed "irreversibility" of all God/human relationships. A similar dualism, it seems to me, is found in sophisticated forms of Zen Buddhist thought that speak about "the true man of no rank" or the Formless Self (Akizuki, 2), insofar as these terms designate some sort of True Reality distinct from, and not clearly visible to, ordinary self-consciousness, the ordinary "I."

In both Christianity and Buddhism, thus—even that form of Buddhism which denies dualism and irreversibility—there seems to be a deep dualistic presupposition, a presupposition that rests on certainty about what is ultimately real, on a fundamentally metaphysical claim. In both cases, moreover, it is this *certainty about what is ultimate (or "absolute")* that serves as the basis for distinguishing and interpreting the meaning of the transiency and deceitfulness of the realities of the everyday world. In these traditions most writers seem to feel qualified to express themselves quite categorically about the particular Absolute in terms of which they interpret the limitations and inadequacies of everyday experience. But, of course, they profoundly disagree with each other respecting the character of these putative Absolutes. Thus, that on which Buddhists and Christians seem here most nearly to *agree*—their affirmations that (much) everyday experience has an illusory or misleading character—is also that which (according to both of them) has least epistemic and metaphysical significance; and that on which they most sharply *disagree*—namely, the nature of that Absolute with reference to which these sorts of judgments are made—is that of which each is most certain.

What is going on here? It seems to me that this paradoxical situation arises (in both Christian and Buddhist thought) because certain *elitist* religious experiences or philosophical claims—which historically have come to impress themselves profoundly upon many persons in each of these traditions—are taken to be more valid or significant than the ordinary experiences of everyday life. In consequence, all else becomes judged in terms of those claims and experiences. I use the word "elitist" here because (it is widely agreed) not all Buddhists have the experience of "enlightenment," nor do all Christian believers have first-hand knowledge of God. In both traditions the understanding of these matters accepted by most devotees has come from special teachers or prophets or buddhas. As just noted, these religious elites, and the different traditions within which they worked and to which they contributed, have not been in agreement with each other on many important points. They emerged in different linguistic and sociocultural worlds and they developed quite different symbols and concepts to articulate—in strikingly different ways—their respective dualities between the religious certainty about what is ultimate, on the one hand, and the problems and distortions of ordinary experience, on the other. Contemporary Buddhism and Christianity are each products of these long histories of increasing refinement of distinctions in language, thought, and practices, histories that have led to very different overall religious stances. The problematic of "reversibility" and "irreversibility," to which I shall return later, is among these historically generated issues.

II

A number of ways to interpret diversity of this sort among religions and philosophies has been proposed. I shall briefly discuss two here. One holds that there is a common human core reality or core experience that underlies the different formulations. Each formulation, then, is to be regarded as an attempt to speak of that common core, but since these attempts are articulated in quite different languages and dialects they are often incomprehensible to each other. From this perspective, the problem in interreligious dialogue is to find bridging concepts which enable us to translate from one tradition to another, so that we can see the way in which each illumines our common human condition;[1] Buddhism and Christianity are here regarded as actually reaching for the same reality, the same understanding of the human situation in the world. We should seek, therefore, to formulate matters in such a way as to make clear that the "primordial fact which decrees the constitution of each religion" (Tanaka, 2) is this underlying metaphysical identity. This is their true essence "irrespective of the cultural and historical differences between Christianity and Buddhism" (1). For positions of this sort there is a *metaphysical ultimate* or *essence*, of which absolutely certain knowledge is available, and this dissolves or resolves the problem of religious and philosophical diversity.[2]

A second way to approach this set of problems (one to which I am more sympathetic) does not involve a metaphysical move of this sort, but instead sees the most common and ordinary features of everyday life— eating, playing, working, rejoicing, suffering, birth, death, sexuality, etc., found in everyday experience everywhere—as basic points of connection that all humans have with each other. Our religious institutions and traditions, beliefs and practices, then (like our political, economic, and social institutions, practices, and customs), gradually emerged historically—in the course of long histories of cultural creativity in different settings—in consequence of the growth, transformation, and extrapolation of various features of these underlying commonalities of human life. That is, our diverse religious ideas and practices—including our deepest and most firmly held convictions—are all products of the creativity of the human spirit, as it has developed symbolic articulations in terms of which it could understand itself, could orient itself in the world, and could find some ("ultimate"?) meaning for human life, in the many diverse historical and cultural settings in which humans have lived.[3] If we understand religious plurality in these more historical terms, we need not immediately accept without question the dualistic presuppositional patterns of reality and experience taken for granted by many (elite) religious teachers and thinkers (whether Buddhist or Christian) and then proceed to a search for ways to mediate these to each other through bridging notions. Rather, we will seek to assess each of these various religious and metaphysical proposals in terms of their success in providing orientation and meaning for common everyday human life (not just the life of religious elites) in diverse cultural settings. That is, we will seek to learn from each whatever we can about the problems human beings have in getting along in the everyday world, but we will not take over too quickly the exaggerated claims about Ultimate Reality or Ultimate Truth (the exaggerated metaphysical claims) which these traditions have bequeathed to us. Religious traditions generally, it seems to me, claim to know too much—claim to know more, and to know it with more certainty—than is actually possible for us finite human beings: we should be more suspicious than we often are of all such dogmatic metaphysical certitudes.[4]

III

Let us turn briefly now to the debate about the ultimate "reversibility" or "irreversibility" of the divine-human relation that supposedly obtains between the "primordial reality" and the finite order of which we are part. I do not think any of us is in a position to address that issue as just stated; therefore, this whole discussion should be defused. If religious plurality shows us anything, it shows us (in my opinion) that human beings simply do not have unmediated access to the "primordial" or "ultimately" Real or True—whether through "divine revelation" or through "enlightenment": we have many different sorts of experience, and many different sorts of interpretations of experience, and our various religious traditions highlight diverse possibilities that have seemed important to them. Instead of assuming that there is some authoritative or finally valid answer to these questions about the ultimate or the primordial or the divine, or some authoritative or definitive standpoint or experience where such answers become available—and then trying to reconcile the diversity of proposals made to us in different traditions on the basis of this standpoint—I want to suggest a different way to look at these matters. The issues arising in the reversibility/irreversibility debate suggest to me two quite distinct approaches to understanding the world, and the human situation within the world. Neither of these (in my opinion) should be seen as the ultimate truth (as each tends to claim itself to be). Each is, rather, a *proposal* for human self-understanding and orientation in life—a proposal based on a particular illuminating *metaphor*—and each should be assessed in terms of the respects in which this metaphor can in fact provide significant orientation.

Those who take the "irreversibility" position (preeminently theists) seem to be using (perhaps unbeknownst to them) the metaphor of *foundation* to understand human existence and its situation in life.[5] For "foundationalists" the most important question for humans concerns the ultimate ground or foundation on which human reality supposedly rests, that in relationship to which it gains its being and its well-being, that without which it would wither away and die. The metaphor of foundation-and-superstructure—in which it is understood that without the foundation there could be no superstructure—implies an underlying relationship that is necessarily unidirectional, irreversible.[6] When Christians, then, develop the doctrine of creation in a unidirectional way—or when Takizawa talks about the "primordial divine-human relationship" that underlies all human reality—we are simply being presented with the implications of this underlying "root metaphor,"[7] now being worked out systematically. In all such views human reality is understood to be in relationship to a foundation or ground on which it depends absolutely. The essence of human wisdom, thus, is to become aware of that relationship and to live accordingly.

Another metaphor with quite different implications is based on the idea of an organic whole.[8] "Holism" emphasizes the mutual interconnectedness and interdependence of all things, rather than the necessity that all (finite) things rest on some ultimate foundation. Arguments supporting an ultimate *reversibility* in all relationships are generated by thinking shaped by this metaphor. When one thinks of human life as essentially part of such an overarching environing whole, it will be seen to be in interconnection with everything else, affecting all other realities in its own way and being affected by them in turn (in "dependent co-origination," as Buddhists say). The metaphysical argument about reversibility vs. irreversibility, thus, is really a disguised discussion about the virtues of a holistic approach to the understanding of human life in the world vs. a foundational approach.

Each of these metaphors can be elaborated in ways that will assist humans to understand major features of their situation and some of the problems they must face; and they each suggest ways to address these problems. However, these two metaphors (when thus elaborated) also contradict each other in important respects: hence the debates. As long as we proponents of these diverse positions fail to discern that our arguments are often actually about the virtues and the shortcomings of two quite distinct metaphors that can be used to interpret the human situation in life—and that what we should be doing, therefore, is attempting to find ways to assess and appropriate what can be learned from each of these metaphors—our discussions will remain on a dogmatic metaphysical level and will continue without end. They will be focused upon what are actually derivative abstract issues like reversibility vs. irreversibility, and these issues will be argued dogmatically because their real source and meaning has not come clear. Instead of trying to find ever more nuanced ways of expressing the respects in which our relationship to some supposed primordial reality is reversible or is irreversible, we should be examining directly the metaphors of holism and foundationalism themselves, seeking to ascertain the respective strengths and weaknesses of each, and how and when each can be most appropriately applied to the interpretation of human existence. If we understand our most profound religious and philosophical conceptions to be the product of the human spirit's attempt, over many generations in many different geographical and historical contexts, to come to terms with the problems of life through developing systems of symbols and concepts that can illuminate our situation in the world and thus provide us with practical orientation—instead of thinking of them as metaphysical absolutes, become known through some fundamental immediate experiences of reality that produce "enlightenment" or through direct "revelations" from God on high—we will be in a better position to clear up some of our misunderstandings and disagreements.

One can ask, now, about the standpoint from which my remarks here about holism and foundationalism have been made. There is apparently some third position, not to be identified with either of these, in terms of which and by means of which the character of each can be perceived and interpreted. This third standpoint is nothing else than the biohistorical one (outlined at various points in this book, especially Chapter 4), with its understanding that all of our religious claims and standpoints have themselves developed in history, as the human spirit has tried to find its way in our problematical and mysterious world. In some respects this biohistorical standpoint has a foundationalist (and thus "irreversible") side to it. In other respects it expresses something akin to holism (and thus "reversibility"). For example, according to it all our present experiencing and thinking is grounded ("irreversibly") upon a history and biology that have shaped us, our institutions, languages, religious practices, and traditions, in certain specific ways; and it is only in relationship to this biohistorical foundation (this social karma, we might say) from which these all spring, that they can be properly understood. But our biohistorical perspective has holistic (and "reversible") characteristics as well, in its awareness that we are not only *products* of these ongoing historical and biological processes but we also continuously react upon them, transforming and reshaping them in new and distinctive ways. So there is mutual interdependence and interconnection, as well as irreversibility and unidirectionality, in the processes that situate human existence in the world. Both holistic insights and foundational insights must be drawn upon, if we are to understand ourselves in biohistorical terms.

In proposing this understanding of the human as a basis for interpreting and mediating the disputes about reversibility and irreversibility, I am not claiming that we now have an *absolute* standpoint from which to survey and relativize all other positions—the kind of move in traditional religious thinking that I have just been criticizing. On the contrary, our biohistorical perspective understands that it is itself based on metaphors—the metaphors of evolution and particularly (with respect to this matter) *history*—metaphors which, moreover, can be extrapolated and developed (as the holist and foundational metaphors have been in the past) in order to see how well they can in fact orient human life.[9] Since our biohistorical perspective keeps us aware that such extrapolation is our *own doing*—situated in the world as we are today, with a strong consciousness of the historical and biological shaping and origins of our selves and our cultures—

we can see that it is not appropriate to make absolutistic claims for it. A biohistorical standpoint, rightly conceived, understands that it is itself historical (a parallel, perhaps, to the insight that emptiness must be understood as itself empty). We are simply seeking in this approach to understand better our situation in the everyday world. It was the failure to acknowledge this point that led the advocates of both holism and foundationalism to mistake the symbolic schemes (which they themselves had constructed in the course of history) for direct insight into or experience of ultimate reality, or direct revelations from God on high. Once moves of that sort were made, and it was supposed that absolute Reality or Truth had been found, religious imperialisms, wars, and other monstrous inhumanities could all too easily be legitimated. The position I am proposing here, in its willingness simply to begin in, and to remain within, the human biohistorical order (what some Buddhists may call the "conventional" order)—making no claims to absolute certitude, or to any forms of absolutistic authorization—has the virtue of keeping us humble about our every conviction and insight, as we face a world within which the confrontations of fanatical certitudes with each other can easily explode into utterly destructive conflagrations.

IV

The distinction between elitist religious truth-claims and commonsense everyday knowledge that I have sketched here can be illuminated further by some reflections on the Buddhist conceptions of "two truths" and "emptiness."[10] The "two truths" doctrine (as Nagarjuna appears to elaborate it) need not be interpreted either as highly paradoxical or as dependent on mystical experience of some "other world" that exists beyond and corrects what is learned in this one. Its significance can be understood as consisting largely in its pointing out clearly an important distinction between two "levels" of knowledge or truth: (1) ordinary ("conventional") knowledge or understanding of everyday experience and the world (including scientific knowledges of these matters)—what we can call, for our purposes here, "first-order knowledge"; and (2) whatever knowledge and understanding we may come to have of the character and limits of this ordinary knowledge—"second-order knowledge." This metaknowledge involves awareness that all our first-order knowledges are at best approximate but useful for guiding everyday life. That is, they have pragmatic utility but cannot claim metaphysical validity, they do not tell us "how things really are" in the world. Not that "metaphysical" knowledge going beyond, and more valid than, our "ordinary" knowledges is available to us anywhere else (such as in certain elite circles): all so-called metaphysical knowledge itself stands under the same fundamental limitations as (other) first-order knowledge, and should be regarded as simply an extension of the latter. Rather, it is because of limitations intrinsic to our very language and logic that certainty is unattainable in any of these knowledges, limitations inherent in the human activity of constituting experience and "representing" it to ourselves symbolically.

All signs (or names) presuppose (as Plato long ago argued) a certain fixity of meaning, an apparent self-identity through time that is requisite if they are to function as vehicles of communication. If the meanings of our words continually slipped around in various directions, we could neither think nor speak. (We can, of course, be seriously misled by this supposed fixity and definiteness of meaning, as Plato perhaps was with his doctrine of Forms.) Signs gain their meanings in part by the linguistic context in which they are being used. These meanings thus inevitably exhibit some variability and indefiniteness,[11] and in some cases they can vary over such broad ranges of signification that we distinguish a number of meanings of a particular word, meanings that must not be confused with each other. Because of the abstractness of every sign (accentuated by its supposed fixity of meaning) it is inappropriate to think of it as capable of *representing exactly* anything in the continuous flux of experience. Moreover, since every symbol has its own distinctive richness and fullness that is different from what it symbolizes (derived from its interconnections with other signs), and since what we regard it as signifying is itself always in process of change, rapid or slow, into something else (it never "stays put" as the sign suggests it does, it is never in fact *identical* with itself), in the nature of the case all our symbolizations always *mis*represent. If we do not realize this and in consequence reify our symbols—that is, use them as if they in fact adequately represented what they purport to represent, as if there were *things* that directly or precisely "corresponded" to them—our supposed knowledges will actually get in the way of our living fittingly and well, instead of helping us "get along in life." We will understand aright neither ourselves nor the context in which we find ourselves, and we will thus be out of rapport or attunement with "reality." Reification of our words and concepts (whether commonsense, scientific, religious, or metaphysical) is a continuous temptation encouraged not only by our languages, but also by our desires (and assumed need) to *know* "how things are." We must be continuously on guard against it, lest we be seriously misled by our speaking and thinking, rather than aided by them in the business of living.

The doctrine of the "emptiness" of all things and ideas, that they are not what our speech and knowledge represent them to be, is intended (as I understand it) to alert us to this "natural" misuse of our language, by warning us of these insurmountable limitations of our speaking, thinking, and writing. It expresses an important (second-order) insight into our various knowledges: they provide us with valuable "approximations" that have pragmatic utility in everyday life, but we should never suppose they give us more than that. Even "emptiness" is only an approximation of this sort that can easily mislead or be misused, so we should remember that it too is "empty."[12] This second-order understanding of our ordinary language and knowledge is not a kind of *rival* knowledge that, in "enlightened" persons, displaces ordinary knowledge. It is, rather, a sophisticated understanding of the status and limits of our human thinking and knowing, an understanding that can enable us to lead our everyday lives more effectively and thus with greater satisfaction and fulfillment. Our second-order knowledge, thus, does not move us out of the world of everyday life. Rather, it gives that life back to us again with cautions about the distortions introduced by our reifications.

In my view, this understanding implies neither a metaphysical claim that our everyday world is itself "ultimate reality," nor an epistemological claim that commonsense knowledge is "ultimately" more valid than, say, scientific theories about atomic structure or "black holes," or, for that matter, metaphysical theories about "actual occasions" or "being-itself." These various constructs, and their relationships to each other, are all to be assessed in whatever ways commend themselves to us as we employ them and reflect on them. Each is connected with (one or another species of) what I have here called first-order knowledge. Each of these sorts of knowledge, or knowledge-claims, continues to perform important functions in human affairs today (in one or more regions of everyday life), and each therefore has its proper place, usefulness, and justification. But it should not be supposed that any of these modalities of language and knowledge give us Ultimate Truth: that is simply not available to us humans, whose understanding and knowledge is intrinsically limited (as suggested above) in ways that we cannot overcome. In this respect the doctrines of emptiness and of two truths, as I am interpreting them here, fit well with the theological view that all human knowledge is intrinsically finite (and sinful), Ultimate Truth being reserved to God alone. Christian and Buddhist understandings of knowledge can be interpreted as converging here—provided we grant that all doctrinal claims in both traditions, whether metaphysical, revelational, intuitive, or common-sense are to be understood as limited in the ways prescribed by the second-order conception I am sketching.

This "two truths" conception throws light, I believe, on my own attempt—in Chapters 1, 3, and 4 above (and also in Parts I and II of *In*

Face of Mystery)—to work out an anthropology appropriate for theological understanding and construction today. Since these anthropological proposals are all admittedly corrigible (certainly not to be regarded as a "secure foundation" on which all further theological work should be based), "foundationalism" of the vicious sort so widely criticized today is not involved here. What I am trying to do in these texts is sketch a way of understanding human existence—that is, human communities and individuals of various commitments and faiths—that will enable us to see both (1) why we develop religious and other mythologies to orient ourselves in life, and (2) the usefulness and meaning that frames of orientation focused by the symbols "God" and "Christ" might have. This biohistorical anthropology, like any other (pragmatic) human attempt at knowledge, has value for us only to the extent that it contributes significantly to our human self-understanding and to our understanding of the world in which we live, thus assisting us in living our lives. We need to see that and how we are related to the rest of the living creatures on planet Earth, what it is to be culture-creating beings, why politics and morality are so central to human life, and so on. It is these matters—taken together with the significance and place of our religious symbolisms and practices in human affairs—that I attempt to work through in these theoretical reflections. No finality, obviously, can be claimed for any of this: our second-order understanding of the limitations of human cognitive claims underlines precisely that point.

I do not confine myself, however, to working out an *anthropological* interpretation of these matters. I am also centrally engaged in constructing a concept of God, in doing *theo*logy. That is, I attempt to set out a wider and deeper (pragmatic) framework for understanding human life and the world, a framework developed in Christian theological terms. And this theology addresses itself to and interprets (for instance, through the concept of mystery) the finitude and sinfulness of our common human situation, expressing in its own way, thus, the second-order understanding of human language and knowledge that we have just been considering. To the extent that this theology makes proposals or claims about "how things really are," it is, of course, subject to the strictures of our second-order understanding of such truth-claims. (Theologies have virtually always, I think, made such metaphysical-type claims.) In the respects, however, that our theological formulations themselves relativize our first-order truth-claims—including, of course, those made in these theological expressions themselves, and the languages or symbolisms in which they are formulated—they should be understood to be expressing second-order insights. (This second-order knowledge also, in that it involves *knowledge*-claims about our first-order knowledge, must itself be regarded as falling under its own strictures: "emptiness" is itself "empty." But in this case these strictures have their effects a full remove from our actual living and experiencing, our day-to-day negotiating life in the world, so they affect our living less directly.) It would, I think, be interesting to see what changes would occur in Christian theological conversations if Christian doctrines became more widely understood as in significant respects symbolical forms of second-order truth, and thus to be interpreted largely as a kind of metaknowledge rather than (as has usually been the case) of the same order as metaphysical knowledge.[13]

This interpretation—modeled in certain respects on Nagarjuna's "two truths" doctrine—can provide us with a fairly precise understanding of the dialectical relation of my biohistorical anthropology to my constructivist understanding of theological as well as all other sorts of knowledge. Just as the theory of two truths was held by Nagarjuna to be itself first-order or "conventional" knowledge, so for me the theory of "theology as imaginative construction" is a part of first-order anthropology, the understanding of human nature. But also—just as second-order ("absolute") knowledge put all conventional knowledge into question for Nagarjuna—so for me theological understanding (in its second-order functions), including the understanding of theology as imaginative construction, puts all human claims (including theological claims!) into question. Any fully critical view of human existence and knowledge must be developed simultaneously on both levels, the material level of actual knowledge-claims and the second-order critical level that continually assesses and reassesses the status and limitations of those claims. Theology has always been working on both these levels. Unfortunately through much of its history this was not clearly recognized, and it was supposed that (all) theological claims were themselves essentially material metaphysical-type claims, rather than (in part) a kind of meta-understanding that provided critical leverage on our material understandings of human life and the world roundabout.

V

I have argued here, first, that in Buddhist-Christian dialogue it is more important that we attempt to gain some common understanding of our human diversity and its significance—of the reasons for the plurality of our religious and cultural traditions—than to find ways simply to adjust the basic concepts and symbols of two or three major traditions to each other. Second, I have suggested that a biohistorical interpretation of human life in the world (of the sort outlined here and in other chapters of this book) provides us with a standpoint that can illuminate this diversity of human religions, and leads us to ask how effectively each has functioned in orienting human life. It thus puts us into a position to assess these various interpretive frameworks in relationship to each other. Third, I have sought to show that when this approach is applied to the reversibility/irreversibility arguments, we begin to see that what is really going on in them is a debate about the usefulness and significance of two distinctive ways of seeing our human situatedness in the world—holism and foundationalism—each being grounded in an imaginative extrapolation and development of a metaphor capable of interpreting wide ranges of human experience and meaning. These ways of seeing the world and the human (the one more emphasized by Buddhism, the other by Christianity—a matter to be taken up in the next chapter) can illuminate much for us; and we may wish to commit ourselves—in faith, as Christians would say—to one or the other of these, along with its implications for orienting life. Fourth, I have suggested that in fact no one is in a position to know that one or the other of these two patterns of understanding—or, for that matter, to know that the biohistorical understanding with which I work, and in terms of which this whole analysis has been developed—is the special key that can unlock the ultimate mysteries of life. Therefore, none of these should be thought of as leading us to some sort of final or absolute wisdom or truth: all should be regarded as under the strictures that our second-order understanding of the "emptiness" of all our human truth-claims imposes on us. In today's world of unprecedented human problems, whatever we can learn from these various approaches to human understanding will be needed—as well as whatever we can learn through other metaphors whose illuminating power is still untapped.

Part Four

Religious Truth as Pluralistic

P art Four brings this book to a conclusion by continuing our move beyond the concerns of Christian theology as such to some of the broader questions that our reflections in the preceding chapters have raised.

Chapter 12 explores further one of the most contested questions posed by the new consciousness of the significance of religious pluralism: how should the enormous variety of religious *truth-claims* be understood today? In connection with fuller metaphor analysis of the significantly different symbolic patterns of Buddhism and Christianity, it is proposed that in place of the somewhat monolithic conceptions of truth that have usually been taken for granted in reflective studies in the philosophy of religion—as well as in the major religious traditions themselves—we begin to develop an idea of religious truth as itself essentially pluralistic and dialogical in character.

Chapter 13, reflecting on the issues that religious and cultural diversity pose for academia, suggests that these concerns may (and probably should) lead to the emergence of a new kind of "critical theology" in which comparative investigations of a variety of faith-stances—from Buddhism, Judaism, and Christianity to humanism and positivism, Americanism and feminism—are undertaken in a dialogical way. Such studies—presupposing and likely eventuating in further elaboration of the pluralistic conception of truth proposed in Chapter 12—should lead to the development of more adequate criteria for comparing and assessing diverse faith-orientations; and might ultimately lead to constructive proposals about how persons and communities with significantly different commitments could live together more peacefully, in our increasingly pluralized societies and our rapidly shrinking world.

Chapter 12

Religious Diversity and Religious Truth

It never occurs to most of us . . . that the question "what is *the* truth?" is no real question (being irrelative to all conditions) and that the whole notion of *the* truth is an abstraction from the fact of truths in the plural, a mere useful summarizing phrase like *the* Latin Language or *the* Law. . . . Truth grafts itself on previous truth, modifying it in the process, just as idiom grafts itself on previous idiom, and law on previous law. . . . Far from being antecedent principles that animate the process, law, language, truth are but abstract names for its results.

—William James[1]

Anyone who works as a Christian theologian today increasingly comes up against the problem of the enormous diversity in religious claims about truth, as one moves from one religious tradition to another. John Hick has done more than any other individual, perhaps, to push theologians to acknowledge the significance of this fact for their work. As will become clear in this chapter, I am not in agreement with Hick's way of addressing the problems raised by religious diversity, but I do want to express my deep appreciation for all that he has done to lead many of us to see its importance for theology today.

Unlike historical or scientific truth-claims—which can be examined and assessed in the light of public criteria that are widely accepted even in what are otherwise very different political, social, and cultural situations—there is little agreement on questions of religious truth, or on how disagreements in this field should be adjudicated among Buddhists and Moslems, Hindus and Christians. Each tradition seems to have worked out what it will regard as "true," and by what criteria these "truths" can be validated. If other traditions disagree with these judgments, so much the worse for them. Most

The original version of this chapter appeared in *God, Truth and Reality: Essays in Honour of John Hick,* ed. Arvind Sharma (London: Macmillan, 1993). Used with permission.

religious thinkers seem satisfied to live out of, and hold themselves responsible to, only the resources of their own tradition, paying little attention to the fact that other equally thoughtful and sincere folk in other traditions hold quite different views. If dialogue is pursued, it is largely more for purposes of gaining information about another way of life, or perhaps with the intention of converting those who differ from one's own way of thinking, rather than addressing the broader question of what this enormous diversity and disagreement implies for our understanding of the phrase "religious truth." What does it really mean to speak of religious *truth* (or truths)?

In this chapter, although I write as a Christian theologian, I am not interested in attempting to set out an argument for specifically Christian truth: rather I want to examine some aspects of this broader and more general question of the peculiar character and status of religious truth and religious truth-claims. This is a question that needs to be more directly faced, in my opinion, by those aware of the religious diversity of humankind. Should—or can—we regard the various claims made in the different religious traditions as somehow all true? Or are they all false—religious claims about truth being in fact a sham? Or is each such claim a partial and inadequate version of some ultimate truth toward which it reaches but which no religious tradition has succeeded in articulating adequately? Or should we each say (as most often happens in our actual practice, I suspect) that it is really only in my own tradition that the ultimate truth which brings salvation and fulfillment to human beings is to be found?—where others agree with the way my group thinks, they are basically on the right track; where they disagree decisively, they must be in the wrong. I do not think any of these (all too common) answers to our questions about religious truth is very satisfactory. What I would like to do in this chapter is propose a somewhat different way of thinking about this whole nest of problems.

I recognize, of course, that the question of religious truth(s) can be approached from many different angles—from the point of view of the needs of religious proclamation or catechetical instruction, or the necessity for prophetic criticism of political oppression or social injustice, or the conditions that facilitate quiet meditation to nourish the soul, or the tendencies of religious piety too easily to deceive itself. All of these perspectives—and more—on the nature and problems of religious truth are valid and important, and would need to be considered in any full treatment of this subject. I cannot even begin to undertake that here. The most that I can do in this chapter is to take up some of the special problems which the fact of religious diversity poses for our attempts to conceptualize religious truth today, and then propose a model which can, I think, help (those of us interested in these issues) address them more fruitfully. The important questions about how this model bears on the other concerns just mentioned—and how they must be made to bear on it—will have to be left for other occasions.

I

We are, of course, not faced here with completely novel issues. Wherever dissimilar communities and traditions have confronted each other with different religious claims, men and women have become aware of the possibility and the reality of strong disagreements on religious questions, disagreements with the potential of exploding into bitter wars and leading to brutal oppression. Consciousness of what we today would call religious differences (and of the importance of these) has been widespread among human beings for thousands of years. In some civilizations, for example in India, religious diversity has been recognized as a problem that itself called for religious interpretation and understanding. The approach that was developed in India—that there are many roads leading to the top of the mountain, and different individuals and communities should follow the road they find most accessible and helpful—seems attractive to many persons around the globe. This position appears to take for granted that all (or nearly all) religions are concerned with essentially the same basic human questions, and they each offer answers that, in one way or another, meet the deepest religious needs of humans. Despite all appearances of diversity, then, humankind is actually one at its core. The various religions are all concerned with addressing these needs of women and men to break through the illusions and partialities and evils of life, thus coming into touch with Reality. On this view it is a mistake to suppose that there is real disagreement among the religions on questions of truth. Though they frame their interpretations of religious need and religious meaning in quite different ways, they all are concerned with the one ultimate Truth and ultimate Reality which answers to our deepest human problems.[2]

This is a very ancient, and at the same time quite modern, answer to the question we are exploring here: essentially it denies that religious diversity cuts as deeply as I claim in this book, and asserts instead that at bottom all religions are one. Clearly, this is one way to handle the problem, but I do not think it is satisfactory. It requires us—in the name of a deeper and more profound knowledge, available only, perhaps, to a few philosophers—to turn away from and largely ignore what seems on its face to be so obviously true: that the various religions really do make different sorts of claims; that they understand what human life is all about in quite dissimilar ways; and that, in the various parts of the world where they have been able to shape human living and acting, they have each brought into being (over many generations) significantly different forms of human existence. As nearly as we can see today, there are many quite distinct ways of being religious and of being human—human existence is pluralized through and through—and although it is, of course, possible to deny this obvious fact in the name of some allegedly special insight or knowledge, there is no more reason to accept *that* particular religious claim as true than there is to accept any of the other particular religious claims with which the world today confronts us. What is needed instead, in my opinion, is an approach to human religiousness that begins in and with this enormous diversity and difference itself, and—instead of playing down its significance—seeks to show its import for our understanding of human existence and religious truth.

What does this mean, to begin "in and with this . . . diversity . . . itself"? How do we do this? Let us call to mind how and why we moderns have become so conscious of this question. Two points should be noted in this connection. (1) The immense increase in contacts between persons and communities with very different cultural and religious backgrounds and forms of life—made possible by modern methods of communication and transportation—has impressed upon many today the fact that human beings are capable of living and thinking, feeling and acting, in enormously dissimilar ways. There appear to be, thus, many ways of being human. (2) In connection with these increasing cross-cultural contacts in the modern world, there has emerged the attempt to understand these matters *historically*, that is, in terms of the processes—the successions of historical events—through which these diverse patterns have each developed. Historical consciousness—together with historical, anthropological, linguistic, ethnic, and other studies—has helped to create our modern awareness of the significance of religious and cultural pluralism. And it will be (I shall argue here) through further exercise of our historical consciousness, and reflection on what it means for our understanding of human religiousness, that we will become able to develop a more adequate understanding for today of the significance of religious pluralism.

Wilfred Cantwell Smith has pointed out that our growing awareness of the history of human religiousness—made available by modern studies in the history of religions—provides us with an overall framework within which each of the known religious traditions can be given a significant place and be meaningfully interpreted, without in any way compromising its integrity. Every religious community/tradition grew up within a historical context provided by other communities and traditions. From this context it acquired many of its beliefs and practices. And in relationship to this context it defined and understood itself, developed its own distinctive institutions and ways of living, worked out its particular conception of the world and the place of human beings within that world. It is now possible to see, Smith contends, that the wide religious history of humankind is actually a single interconnected whole, and that only this whole can today rightly be regarded as the proper context for understanding and interpreting the myriad particular expressions of human religiousness.[3] Although culturally and economically we are increasingly aware of our interdependence as well as our diversity, the meaning of this for our religious institutions and traditions, and for our religious self-understandings, has barely begun to dawn upon us. Today fundamentalistic reifications of religious positions appear around the globe with increasing frequency, offering religious legitimation for dangerously parochial social and ethnic movements and practices that, in their divisiveness and destructiveness, are a threat to all humanity. We need a way to understand our religiousness that can honor the integrity and meaning of each religious tradition and yet open it to appreciation of and reconciliation with others. Historical understanding and interpretation of human religiousness can help make that possible.[4] In the remainder of this chapter I will attempt to show how such historical understanding can lead to a new approach to the problem of the diversity of religious truth-claims.

II

Human beings have been confronted, in their varying circumstances of time and place, with quite different contingencies and problems. In their attempts to address these they have drawn, of course, upon the resources of knowledge and wisdom and skill made available to them through traditions and practices passed on by earlier generations. But they have also used their own inventiveness and ingenuity, as they sought to deal with new and unexpected issues and difficulties. Each new generation added to the traditions it had inherited, deepening and enriching and refining them in response to the new circumstances that it confronted. What ultimately became regarded as valuable and important in a tradition—indeed, as true—emerged in connection with the attempts of women and men to address the concrete problems with which life confronted them. Over the course of time certain modes of thinking and acting, of meditation and practice, proved increasingly helpful in defining and diagnosing some of the more difficult problems and ills faced by the society, thus making available treatments and remedies that were healing and in other ways effective. These modes of understanding and practice became honored and respected and preferred to others—regarded as good and right and true, to be followed if humans were to find some way to survive the terrors and evils of life in a threatening world. In the various religious and cultural traditions developing around the globe there emerged quite naturally, thus, diverse ways of picturing and understanding human life and the world—that is, significantly different conceptions of what is true about human existence and the context within which it falls.

It is important that we do not confuse the conception of truth which developed in premodern (and prephilosophical) religious traditions with our modern highly reflective notions. Religious truth in these early stages was not essentially a piece of information about what is the case, a statement of "fact" in our modern sense (heavily influenced, as it is, by scientific ideas). Nor was it a highly reflective, carefully argued metaphysical claim about "ultimate reality." Truth was, rather, a symbolization or articulation of what was "useful," as the Buddha put it, to bring the fullness of life to human beings, "salvation" or "enlightenment" or "liberation" from the various sorts of bondage to which humankind is heir. "I have taught a doctrine similar to a raft," the Buddha said; "it is for crossing over" to the other side, not something to be grasped or clung to.[5] For the Jesus depicted in the Fourth Gospel, also, religious truth was an eminently practical matter: "If you continue in my word, . . . you will know the truth, and the truth will make you free" (John 8:31f.). Here truth is understood as what makes possible "abundant life" (10:10). Indeed, Jesus declares himself to be "the truth" (14:6). For these great religious teachers (as they have been remembered in the traditions that grew up around them) truth appears to have been essentially practical insight or wisdom into what was believed indispensable for proper human living and dying, not a collection of metaphysical dogmas or other speculative beliefs. In time, of course, this practical wisdom often became formulated in terms of quite specific truths, maxims, and practices to be passed on from generation to generation. And in some cases these truths became formally fixed as bodies of belief (creeds or confessions) to which all the faithful were expected to subscribe. Other traditions remained more informal, though they nonetheless came to have great authority in ordering the lives of women and men. But in all these cases "truth" and "truths" were largely matters of practical commitment and belief.[6]

Since religious truth came into being this way in connection with quite specific practical problems and difficulties and emergencies in human living, it should not surprise us to discover profound disagreements emerging, among the religious traditions of humankind, when these insights were interpreted as liberating or saving truth for all human life. In each case the understanding of truth(s) and practice(s) was defined and shaped largely by the particular problems being addressed as well as the previous experience of the society. Meditation and reflection on the problems of life were guided by the issues taken to be important and by the ways those issues were articulated and framed in the particular cultures involved. Thus, what came to be regarded as "true" in the different religious traditions was a function of the way in which each had come to picture or conceive human life in its environment. This symbolic conception or picture was itself defined and shaped in many respects by the metaphors and images, and even the grammar and syntax, of the language in and through which it was articulated.[7] Religious traditions structured by significantly distinct symbolical patterns came to have profoundly different understandings of reality and truth.

As an example of this point, consider the basic symbolical patterns that came to structure Buddhist life and reflection on the one hand, and Christian on the other. Buddhist patterns of religious symbolism appear to be essentially holistic in character; Christian patterns, in contrast, are dominantly foundationalist. And the differences between these two patterns of experiencing and thinking explain a great deal about the differences between these two religious orientations.[8]

It is not difficult to understand why Christian symbolism can be characterized as essentially "foundationalist." Christian faith is a form of monotheism, the idea that there is a single reality—God—that underlies and gives rise to all other realities without exception. God is "the creator of all things visible and invisible," as the creeds put it; and that means that everything that exists depends absolutely on God for its existence. God alone has *aseity*, is self-existent. God is the ultimate ground or foundation on which all else rests. Thus, at their deepest level Christian faith and understanding begin with grasping a distinction, the distinction between creator and creation. Until and unless we understand that there is a single *ultimate* reality with which we humans have to do, and that we ourselves—as well as all other realities in our world—are derivative, transitory, and contingent, are finite beings and thus not ultimately reliable, we will not be able to grasp what this faith is all about. For at its very heart Christian faith is a claim about our alienation from this God on which we depend in all respects, and about the healing of this alienation through God's own reconciling work—a healing which also restores our proper relations to the rest of the created order. I call this underlying creator/creation pattern—with its radical asymmetrical dualism—*foundationalist*: the central structural features of this symbolism are nicely caught up in the metaphor of foundation-and-superstructure (for without the foundation

the superstructure could not be at all). For those who see all human problems through foundationalist eyes, the really important religious questions
are about the ultimate ground or foundation on which all human life rests,
and about our relationship to that ultimate ground.[9]

The human situation in life may, however, be significantly illuminated
by other metaphors with quite different implications; for example, the idea
of an organic whole. Our experience of our own bodies—made up, as they
are, of hands and feet, stomach and brain, skin and bones, each distin-
guishable from the others and yet all interconnected and interdependent
parts of a unified living organism—may well be the originary source of
this second metaphor. In any case, *holistic* symbolic patterns are those
based on metaphors that emphasize the mutual interconnectedness and
interdependence of all things, rather than the "absolute dependence"
(Friedrich Schleiermacher) of all finite beings on some ultimate foundation. I am no authority on these matters but, as nearly as I can see, the
basic Buddhist symbolic pattern is essentially holistic in character. On the
one hand, Buddhists resist the reification of anything and everything that
women and men can directly identify and name—anything of which they
can speak and know—in their insistence that all things are "empty"
(*sunya*). The frequent use of the symbol of emptiness (at least in
Mahayana Buddhism) thus tends to weaken foundationalist tendencies in
this tradition, since it undermines every symbolic claim about some
absolute or utterly independent reality. Even emptiness, we are told, must
be understood to be empty.[10] On the other hand, the idea of "dependent
co-origination" (*pratitya-samutpada*) emphasizes the mutual interdependence and interconnectedness of all things with each other, as in an organic whole, an organism. In this vision of the world, then, human lives are
seen as essentially integral moments or passing phases of this interdependent network of transient realities always coming into being and passing
away. It is the realization of this that both makes possible and constitutes
human release from the evils of life. This is a very different picture of the
human, and of human problems and prospects in the world, than that con-
veyed by Christianity's foundational pattern.

Each of these metaphors (holism and foundationalism), through providing an illuminating way to grasp the ultimate structure of things, has its
own distinctive plausibility; and there appear to be no independent criteria
on the basis of which a rational choice between them might be made. (The
historicist approach to questions of this sort, developed in this book,
enables us, however, to see some of the respects in which the virtues of
these perspectives may be complementary to each other, as suggested in
chapter 11.) Each metaphor can be expanded and developed into a power-

ful framework within which human beings gain significant understanding of important features of their situation and of major problems with which life confronts them. And they each suggest ways to address these problems. As we can readily see, however, these metaphors and implications—when worked out, as in Buddhism and Christianity, into detailed symbolic pictures or conceptions of human existence in the world—will necessarily contradict each other at important points. It is not germane to our purposes here to examine these contradictions. But we do need to take note of certain implications of this profound difference between the symbolic patterns of Buddhism and Christianity for our understanding of the problem of religious truth. How should we interpret the fact that these two religious traditions understand the deepest truth about reality, and about human life in the world, in such diverse, even contradictory, ways? Should we take it for granted that only one of these positions (at most) can be right and true, the other thus being false? Or is there some other way to interpret differences as fundamental as this?

The existence of such striking differences in the basic symbolic patterns that give world religions like Christianity and Buddhism their underlying structure and meaning suggests that it may be a mistake to regard either of these understandings of human life in the world—and their religious truth-claims—as a straightforward expression of direct insight into, or knowledge about, the nature of the world and the human place within it. Rather, each of these frames of orientation appears to have been built up in the course of a long history of refinement and development of the potential of a particular "root metaphor" (Stephen Pepper)[11] that is capable of providing illuminating ways of grasping and holding together wide reaches of human experience and knowledge. It takes many generations (as we have noted) for overall pictures of the world and the human to be constructed. And it is only as well-articulated symbolic frameworks of this sort are developed that the kind of (religious) experiencing and reflecting, meditating and knowing, capable of uncovering and addressing the deepest problems and evils in life, can occur. The appearance of profound insights and understandings—one thinks, for instance, of the conceptions of sin and salvation in Christianity, and of *duhkha* (suffering) and enlightenment in Buddhism—is in fact essentially a nuancing and deepening (and perhaps further unifying) of these symbolic resources made available by each tradition's root metaphor. All such developments, of course, amplify and extend the tradition in significant ways. Thus, the momentums of the central metaphors and symbols of each tradition become reinforced and deepened as history rolls on and a symbolic pattern of increasing refinement emerges, enabling humans to come to terms with their problems more

effectively. In this way the great religious traditions have grown and developed historically into vehicles of enormous insight, meaning, and truth for
human life. But in each case what they have to recommend as "true" is
grounded, ultimately, on the metaphorical and symbolical resources they
have acquired in the course of their diverse histories.

This analysis suggests that it may no longer be feasible to think of religious truth in largely monolithic terms, as if there were some single unified pattern of truth to which all religious truth-claims approximate and
in terms of which all should be assessed. Rather, as modern comparative
studies enable us to see, there are a number of (quite dissimilar) patterns
of religious understanding and religious truth, each of them intelligible
and persuasive in its own terms but, on certain fundamental issues, standing in tension (or even contradiction) with others. Through most of
human history men and women—in provincial fashion—seem to have
taken for granted the finality and normativity of the truth(s) and prac-
tice(s) available in their own local tradition(s), judging all others by these
standards. It should be apparent, however, that such parochial religiousness does not—and cannot in principle—address the issues which religious pluralism poses for us today, since it does not come to terms with
the implications of our awareness that the symbolic and linguistic patterns
underlying our own criteria of judgment may well be as provincial as
those others we are seeking to assess.[12]

What moves, then, are open to us? Are we driven into a complete skepticism about all religious truth(s), or into a relativism that prevents our
making any judgments at all? I do not think so. What is demanded is that
we reconsider our conception of religious truth in light of (1) the way it
develops historically, and (2) the large disagreements with respect to it that
we find in history. A *pluralistic* conception of truth, I want to suggest now,
or a conception of pluralistic truth, can provide us with a way to address
the issues we face here.

III

In recent years there has been growing interest in religious dialogue, that is,
wide-ranging conversations among representatives of various religious traditions about matters of belief and practice, about values and meanings,
questions of morality and justice and human well-being, about institutional arrangements and patterns of symbolism, about religious truth-claims.
Often in such dialogues the conversation is confined to imparting and
acquiring information and knowledge about the several religious traditions
represented, with special care being taken not to call into question impor-

tant beliefs of any of the participants. Were this to occur, it is feared, the spirit of open interchange might be undermined. The presence of such protective constraints means that although various truth-claims of different traditions may be presented, serious examination of issues of religious *truth*—that is, of what is to be taken with religious seriousness *across the lines* that distinguish the traditions—seldom occurs. Our parochial, somewhat monolithic, ways of thinking about religious truth divide us against each other in ways that make such discussion difficult.

In place of the absolutistic conceptions of truth which we have inherited in our several religious traditions, I suggest that we attempt to think in terms of a dialogical and thus pluralistic conception. The experience of everyday conversation, particularly the free and spontaneous conversation that can occur among equals such as friends, can provide us with a model for developing such a notion.[13] Traditional conceptions of religious truth and its dissemination appear to be connected with fundamentally *authoritarian* models, such as teacher/student or guru/disciple, in which truth is something *known* to one of the parties—it is a *possession* of one of the parties—and is then communicated to, passed over to, the other party who receives and accepts it. A unidirectional relationship or movement of this sort characterizes much traditional religious thinking and practice with respect to truth—consider the special authority given to sacred texts by readers and interpreters, and especially by religious communities; the religious importance of prophets to whom God is believed to have revealed divine truth, or otherwise "enlightened" persons whose insight into the truth is thought to go far beyond that of ordinary folk; the authority of most religious teachers in relation to their disciples; the importance in many religions of the activity of preaching to audiences (large or small) who remain basically hearers, recipients of the word; the authority given to traditional doctrine or teaching by most religious groups. In all these instances truth appears to be understood on the model of *property*, something that is owned by one party, and thus is not directly available to others, but which can be passed on or given over to others if the owner so chooses. If we move away from this property model of truth, however, to a model based on the experience of free and open conversation, a quite different conception comes into view.

In sharp contrast to many formal religious "dialogues," in which all of the participants have specific agendas in mind which they wish to pursue in representing properly their respective communities and traditions, a typical conversation among friends often proceeds quite spontaneously. Though in each remark the speaker is attempting to say something that is fitting at that moment—and in that respect has something "true" in mind—the truth that may emerge in the course of the conversation cannot be understood simply by taking up these individual speeches one by one, as though each stood on its own feet. For the interchange may have developed a life of its own, and it may have moved in directions no one anticipated and led to new insights and ideas which none of the participants had previously considered. (Here the difference between our conversation model and most interreligious dialogues—where formal papers are prepared ahead of time and then published afterwards, often without significant alteration of the text—is obviously quite marked.) Thus, conversation is itself sometimes the matrix of significant creativity in human life. Let us see if we can unpack a bit the way in which this creativity in conversation occurs. Then I want to point out the significance of this model for our understanding of religious truth.

Some light can be thrown on this creativity if we take note of the mixture of determinateness and indeterminacy that is characteristic of every word used and every speech made in a conversation.[14] Each word in a language has, of course, certain fairly definite meanings and uses; but these shade off into each other, and into a rather indefinite penumbra of meaning that surrounds the word. The various participants in a conversation understand each other because of the relative determinacy of meaning of each word spoken—a meaning made even more definite by the particular context (in the sentence, in the ongoing conversation, in the private and the common experience of the participants) in which the word is used at this particular moment. But the penumbra of connotations and indeterminacy surrounding each word's relative determinateness of meaning, taken together with the diverse kinds of experience and history undergone by the participants in the conversation, make it inevitable that each hearer will grasp and attend to something slightly different from the others and from the speaker. Thus different responses are called forth from the different hearers, and the conversation proceeds down pathways not expected by the original speaker or by anyone else. (This may be an exciting and happy development on some occasions; on others it may be tragic, ending in the bitter enmity of hitherto friends.) An intervention by speaker B moves the conversation in a way that A had not intended. A succeeding intervention by C moves it on a slightly different tack, not anticipated by either A or B, so that when A responds again, it will be with a comment not directly continuous with his or her earlier remark, but one that takes into account what B and C have unexpectedly said. And thus the path of the conversation as a whole, though continuous, is not a direct working-out of the original intention which A (or anyone else) was attempting to express.

If this pattern of conversation is allowed to proceed for a while, it may depart radically from the apparent subject matter of A's original remark, going down quite unexpected pathways that none of the participants have followed before. Sometimes, in an exciting conversation of this sort, the participants are "carried away" by the flow of the conversation itself, which has come to have a seeming intention of its own. These can be moments of high spirit for human beings, even of ecstasy. They are moments in which the creativity of the social process is being directly experienced. It is important to note that this social experience, in which a spirit of the group comes alive and takes over, does not mean that the individuals cease to act as free agents in their own right: they each contribute to the conversation out of their own freedom, not under some external compulsion. And yet that freedom is led beyond anything any of them could have independently decided to think or say. It is a moment of creativity that only the group process makes possible. In the course of this sort of conversation, new insights or meanings appear that, though not directly intended by any of the speakers, are of great interest to them. Indeed, these may become of greater interest than what they themselves had originally intended in their own contributions. The freedom and creativity of the participants, far from being in any way diminished by their participation in the social process, have actually been expanded and extended by it; and the conversation proves to be the matrix in which new truth emerges for them, truth that goes beyond anything they had known before. It is truth grounded in what each had to contribute to that conversation, but truth that could not have been either discerned or formulated from the standpoint of any one of the participants.

This model, by leading us to focus on the way truth comes into being rather than on its existence as a possession that belongs to someone, can assist us in our reflection on religious truth. In this model it does not seem particularly illuminating to regard truth as a possession at all, even a possession belonging in common to a community (for example, to the group of friends who are conversing together). Rather, truth is perceived as a process of becoming, a reality that emerges (quite unexpectedly) in the course of conversation—a reality that, if the conversation continues, may (or may not) continue to break in upon the participants. This truth will harden and die away, moreover, if the participants in the conversation attempt to reify it into legalistic definitions and formulas that are regarded thereafter as authoritative bits of knowledge, to be respected and revered and learned but not to be criticized and creatively transformed in further conversation. I call this a pluralistic or dialogical conception of truth, because here—instead of taking truth to be a property of particular words or propositions or texts that can be learned and passed on (more or less unchanged) to others—it is identified as a living reality that emerges within and is a function of ongoing, living conversation among a number of different voices.

We can see better what is involved here by contrasting a conversation with a lecture. In its very form a lecture expresses an essentially monolithic and finitistic conception of truth: it suggests that truth is the sort of thing that can be presented quite adequately by a single voice in continuous ongoing monologue and that can be brought to a satisfactory conclusion at a particular point in time. The model of conversation suggests, in rather sharp contrast, that many voices, representing quite different sorts of experience and points of view, are required even to begin articulating truth. Beyond that, it implies that truth demands a kind of open-endedness into an indefinite future (conversations are often simply broken off for extraneous reasons without being brought to any conclusion)—even a plurality of voices is not fully adequate to it. In conversation every voice knows that it is not complete in itself, that its contribution is in response to, and therefore depends upon, the voice(s) that came before, and that other voices coming after will develop further, modify, criticize, qualify what has just been said. Free-flowing conversation presupposes a consciousness of being but one participant in a larger, developing yet open-ended, pattern of a number of voices, each having its own integrity, none being reducible to any of the others. And it presupposes a willingness to be but one voice in this developing flow of words and ideas, with no desire to control the entire movement (as in a lecture or other monologue). When truth is conceived in these pluralistic and dialogical terms, no single voice can lay claim to it, for each understands that only in the ongoing conversation as a whole is it brought into being. Moreover, in this model, truth is never final or complete or unchanging: it develops and is transformed in unpredictable ways as the conversation proceeds.[15]

It would be foolish to argue that this notion of dialogical truth can answer all questions or should displace all other conceptions. Truth manifests itself in many different forms—scientific and historical knowledge, mathematical formulae and logical proofs, religious teaching and poetic insight, the surprising intuitions of persons of unusual sensibility, ordinary common sense, and many more—and these will continue to play important roles in ongoing human life and to require diverse modes of conception. I do want to suggest, however, that a pluralistic understanding of *religious* truth, based on the model of what can occur in serious conversation, is much better fitted to the needs of contemporary interreligious dialogue than the ordinary monolithic conceptions taken for granted by most participants. One may hope, perhaps, that it will come to be seen as fitting for religious life generally, as we find ourselves increasingly forced to grow into a single interdependent humanity. For this is a model which demands that all participants in the dialogue—that is, each of the different religious traditions represented—enter into conversation with the others on (formally) equal terms: all are there to participate with the others in the search for truth; none claims exclusive possession of final religious insight or understanding; each wishes to contribute whatever it can from the riches of its own tradition to the ongoing conversation, and will be listened to respectfully and attentively; all expect to learn from the others, through appropriating with appreciation what they have to offer, and through opening themselves willingly to probing questions and sharp criticism. Each participant in the conversation posits the others as substantive contributors in this collective pursuit of (religious) truth, and thus is open in principle to collaboration with those others—instead of these several voices each presuming it is capable of expressing (by itself) what needs to be said. Through such a process of free and open conversation on the most profound religious issues—a conversation intended to continue for years, even generations—it may be hoped that deeper religious truth than that presently known in any of our traditions will in due course emerge.

Historically, all too often, religious knowledge has taken authoritarian forms, with truth believed to be accessible only to special elite groups who could interpret sacred texts and explain obscure ideas. Under these circumstances, the path to knowledge and truth was a more or less direct movement toward those (texts and personages) regarded as ultimate *authorities* in these matters, with little open discussion and criticism along the way. This fostered hierarchical social patterns easily subject to abuse: religious knowledge and power were in the hands of the few, and the masses of ordinary people were expected simply to believe what they were told and to obey. The conversational model of truth which I am proposing here, in contrast, is not hierarchical and linear but is instead essentially dialectical. It is democratic, open and public —a model which encourages criticism from new voices, and insights from points of view previously not taken seriously. This conception avoids the nihilistic tendencies of an unqualified relativism, for it is *truth*—with its unique and undeniable claims upon each voice in the conversation—with which we are here concerned. But simultaneously, in its acknowledgment that this truth is *pluralistic*—that no single voice or formulation can possess or adequately express it—this conception undercuts the tendencies, so prominent in traditional views, to become absolutistic, dogmatic, imperialistic.[16]

Modern historical studies have shown that it was often through internal dialogue and external exchange that what was regarded as "truth" in fact grew and developed in the great religious traditions (although this has not been well understood and is an idea that has often been resisted). Religious truth has always been pluralistic in character, emergent from conversations among many different voices over many generations; and the efforts made, from time to time, to freeze it into authoritative monolithic forms have always (ultimately) failed. If the great religious traditions could come to understand their deepest insights and truth in the historical and pluralistic way that I am proposing in this chapter—that is, as contributions to the ongoing larger conversation of humankind on the deepest issues with which life confronts us humans—we would move a step further toward finding a way to live together on our small planet as a single, though pluriform, humanity.

IV

In Chapter 8 I suggested that if we understand religious symbols, practices, and claims in historical terms, we will be able to appreciate and honor all aspects of their meaning. It is important now to admit that the pluralistic conception of truth that I am proposing does not quite fulfill that promise. For the *authoritarian* and *absolutistic* characteristics of traditional religious truth-claims are not, in fact, given full respect in this more democratic, open, dialogical understanding. What I am suggesting here is that in the modern world, at least those parts of the modern world that emphasize democratic values and the necessarily public character of knowledge and truth, hierarchical patterns of the traditional sort no longer are appropriate or justifiable. On this point modernity (and postmodernity) strongly clash with most traditional religions: we are forced to choose between the older religious models and this newer one, which is consonant with our historical knowledge about the development of human religiousness and is demanded by our democratic values. It should be forthrightly acknowledged that if we move to a conception of religious truth as essentially pluralistic in character, we will in fact be modifying in significant respects more traditional understandings of religious insight and knowledge.

This openness to some of the values of modernity and postmodernity does not mean, however, that this pluralistic conception of religious truth is basicly *secular*, one completely unconnected with important traditional moral and religious insights. For it expresses well—better, in fact, than any monolithic notion can—religious understandings of human finitude; and it incorporates moral insights appropriate to those understandings. This pluralistic/dialogical conception is based on the recognition that truth-claims are always made by *particular finite human beings*, with their idiosyncratic limitations of vision, insight, and understanding, and their propensities to prejudice and self-interested falsification. Precisely for these (religio-moral) reasons, no human claims to incorrigibility or absoluteness are justifiable. In entering into conversation with others on religious questions, therefore, a proper humility about one's own position, and a respect for the other, is always called for. This requires willingness to listen to the other who sees things differently, accepting criticism and correction from the other when appropriate. Moreover, it demands that we open ourselves to conversation with any and all who care to participate with us on free and equal terms.

Through most of human history our epistemic traditions—religious, philosophical, scientific—have been elitist and thus esoteric. In contrast, a pluralistic/dialogical conception of truth can help break down all forms of exclusion and domination—whether based on authoritarianism, elitism, or any other form of unfair discrimination—while encouraging in their stead the practice of truly democratic interaction when matters of ultimate import and concern are under consideration.

Chapter 13

Critical Theology as a University Discipline

> A very popular error: having the courage of one's convictions; rather it is a matter of having the courage for an *attack* on one's convictions!
>
> —Friedrich Nietzsche

The emergence of modern critical thinking—symbolized most vividly, perhaps, in the "radical doubt" of René Descartes, and carried through most systematically in the critical philosophy of Immanuel Kant—not surprisingly made the place of Christian theology precarious in the university. Theological reflection, for much of its history in the West, had been grounded on a principle of *authority* derived from the Christian belief that God had decisively revealed Godself to humanity in the history of Israel and especially in and through the ministry, death, and "resurrection" of Jesus Christ. Theological truth, therefore, was not thought of as something that humans discover (or create) in their work. It was, rather, something made available in the traditions of the church, especially in the Bible, which was commonly regarded as the very "word of God." Theology's task was to extract this truth from the traditional writings in which it was contained and to interpret it in such a way that its significance (for each new generation) was clearly expressed. What the truth is was already determined (who could call into question what God had revealed?): we humans were simply to believe and seek to understand. Christian theology, thus, took itself to be working out of authoritative tradition, and its task was to interpret and pass on that tradition, certainly not to sit in critical judgment upon it.[1]

The rise of critical consciousness in modern intellectual life threatened this self-understanding of theology and, indeed, its very being. Because

This chapter first appeared in *Theology and the University: Essays in Honor of John B. Cobb, Jr.*, ed. David Ray Griffin and Joseph S. Hough (Albany: State University of New York Press, 1991). Used with permission.

modern universities have increasingly come to see themselves as engaged essentially in critical thinking—about philosophical and scientific ideas; about religion and culture; about history, literature, and the arts; about legal, political, economic, and social institutions and ideologies; in short, about the whole range of human ideas and practices—the place of Christian theology in the university became, and has subsequently remained, somewhat precarious. Many, especially from F. D. E. Schleiermacher on, have sought to address this problem by rethinking the responsibilities of theology in the modern world. John Cobb has provided significant leadership in this task for the last thirty years. It is especially fitting, therefore, that appreciation for his work be expressed with a volume of essays on theology and the university; and I am happy to have been given the opportunity to contribute some of my thoughts on this topic in honor of him.

I argue in this chapter that, although it may quite properly be questioned whether *authoritarian* Christian theologies have any rightful claim to a significant role in modern university life, what I shall call "critical theology" does have important contributions to make to university studies. Critical theology should, therefore, be recognized as a legitimate discipline even in entirely secular institutions, and it would be desirable for persons practicing this discipline to be appointed to full-time positions in departments of religious studies or in independent departments of theology. It is important that we Christian (and other) theologians address ourselves more self-consciously than has often been done in the past to the cultivation and development of the critical potential of theological symbols and modes of reflection. This redirection would prepare us to take up more directly some of the major intellectual issues with which modern universities concern themselves. To the extent that theologians fail or refuse to take up the critical opportunities and responsibilities that are peculiarly ours, we can expect to continue to lack credibility in much contemporary university life.

I

A large topic such as "theology and the university" involves many complex issues that cannot be elaborated upon in a brief chapter. It is important, however, to set the stage for my central concerns here in at least a few broad strokes.

What theology is, what its objectives are, and to whom or what it is responsible, are matters on which there is little agreement among theologians. There are, consequently, many different types and kinds of theology. The situation with regard to the university is no simpler: there is no agreement either within modern universities themselves or outside of them as to what the university is, what its purposes are or should be, and to whom or what it should be held accountable (or whether it is accountable to anything beyond itself); and there are, in fact, a good many different kinds of universities, that is, institutions that claim this title. In view of this complexity and ambiguity in the two central terms of our topic, how should we proceed? With respect to the university, I shall make a stipulation. With respect to theology, more preliminary discussion will be necessary.

I mean by *university* to refer to the whole wide compass of higher learning in America. In this chapter, however, I shall confine myself to matters of especial interest to the humanities and the social sciences, those sectors of the university that concern themselves with human existence in the extraordinary complexity of its many features, dimensions, and relations. Most institutions of higher learning in this country today would probably be considered "secular," but there are also many colleges and universities that are sponsored by churches and that describe themselves as "Christian." For the most part I will not be addressing myself to this latter segment of American higher education. In these institutions the presence of (some form of) theological reflection is often regarded as appropriate for, or possibly even indispensable to, intellectual life. Here I shall be arguing, however, the importance of theology to modern secular universities and colleges, institutions with no explicit religious commitments.

How then, for the purposes of this discussion, is theology to be understood? It should be clear that we cannot proceed with a completely open conception, according to which whatever is claimed by someone or some group to be theology is included under that title. No institutions of higher learning define chemistry or economics or English literature or medicine or architecture in this utterly open way—such a completely normless approach would make it impossible to determine what is to count as education in a field—and there is no more reason to follow a procedure of that sort with theology than with other disciplines. Our question thus becomes: what criterion can be formulated to help us identify and define the sort of theology that would be appropriate as a regular university discipline?

One might suppose that, because of the disagreements about what theology is and ought to be, it is not possible to specify such a criterion. I do not, however, think that is the case. Many claimants to the title of theology can be immediately ruled out of consideration for our purposes because of the importance given to critical consciousness in modern university life. For example, the theologies of religious groups that refuse to take a critical stance toward their own religious beliefs—holding them, on dogmatic grounds, to be beyond questioning—can play only a very limited role in the life of a modern (secular) university. We need not, therefore, take these theologies directly into account in formulating our criterion for determining the sort of theology appropriate for university disciplinary status. Some who think theology is inherently dogmatic and uncritical in character may suppose that this move eliminates all possible candidates from further consideration. This is not the case, however, although it is obvious that it significantly limits the field—and makes it, therefore, more manageable.

In narrowing the field in this way, I have already been implicitly invoking a criterion. To help us define more precisely the sort of theology with which we will here be concerned, I want now to make this criterion explicit. Theology that takes critical consciousness fully into account (and is, thus, itself an expression of such consciousness) is what we are looking for: theology that opens itself willingly to severe criticism from outside perspectives (as well as from within). Such theology, formulated in connection with the exercise of critical judgment with respect to all pertinent evidence and arguments—what we can quite properly call *critical theology*—has an important and distinctive role to play in university life today.

This characterization of critical theology is quite abstract and formal. How can we make it more concrete? It is helpful here to distinguish two different ways in which theological work may be of importance to the tasks and responsibilities of the university. The first is well known and widely acknowledged: theological writings of all sorts are nearly always products of the intellectual activity of religious communities attempting to further their own self-understanding and the goals to which they are committed. Such writings present careful articulations and interpretations of the symbols and meanings, the values and purposes, the activities, practices, and institutions of significance to their authors and the communities to which they make themselves accountable. Texts of this sort from earlier periods of history have always been studied in universities by historians and others attempting to understand and interpret various features of human life in the past. Similarly, many different kinds of contemporary theological texts are of importance (in the study of current religious life and culture) to sociologists and others seeking to understand modern worldviews, cultural values, and complexes of meaning; to philosophers examining value-orientations and patterns of thinking about the meaning and problems of human life; to literary critics interested in exploring various types and styles of writing; to psychologists studying human motivation and self-interpretation; to scholars attempting to understand contemporary human religiousness and its various expressions; and so on. Virtually every kind of theology may quite properly find a place in university studies addressed to the examination, interpretation, and assessment of the many sides of human life and culture. Theological study of this sort, however, can be accomplished without appointing theologians to university faculty positions, although scholars with sufficient theological understanding to provide intelligent interpretation of these materials are, of course, required.

In my view contemporary theological reflection has more to offer the university than mere documentation for various sorts of (nontheological) explorations and studies. In contemporary critical theological reflection analytic tools, conceptual schemes, and ways of thinking are being developed that make possible grasping and interpreting features of human life and its meaning that nearly always escape the attention of other university disciplines. Such theological work can make available important resources for the university's proper tasks. It should, therefore, be given its own place within the intellectual life of the university. My reasons for making this claim should become clear in the remainder of this chapter.[2]

II

Theology has often been characterized, following Anselm, as "faith seeking understanding." This has usually been taken to mean that the task of theologians is to examine the *content* of (some particular) faith, with a view to understanding what it means and how it is to be interpreted to the community of faith and to others. There is another way in which Anselm's phrase can be understood, however. This way opens up a rather different conception of the theological task; or at least it leads to focusing attention on another dimension of theological inquiry that is of especial importance for our concerns here. Theology, as faith seeking understanding, may be seen as an inquiry into the role of faith-commitments in human existence, an inquiry into the meaning in human life of believing (or "faithing"). In this interpretation, "faith" is taken in a generic sense (rather than the particularistic sense just mentioned), as pointing to some fundamental features of human existence: that men and women live out of and on the basis of their trust in and loyalty to what they take to be most meaningful, precious, important in life; that human lives are always (often?) oriented by some (perhaps implicit) "center[s] of value" (H. R. Niebuhr); and that it is out of underlying faith-commitments such as these that (all?) humans act and live in face of the unknown future into which they must inexorably move. The exploration of the role and significance of faith in human life (including such closely related dispositions as trust, loyalty, and commitment), and of the symbols that structure the various forms of faith, is by no means something of importance only to those with specifically religious interests. It is a matter central to the understanding of human being and well-being.[3] Theology as "faith seeking understanding" in this sense, providing it is critical theology, quite properly belongs among university studies.[4]

From the time of the Enlightenment onwards an increasingly self-critical strand of Christian theological reflection evolved (nourished by the works of such writers as Descartes, Benedict Spinoza, John Locke, Kant, Friedrich Schleiermacher, G. W. F. Hegel). This development in the theological tradition can provide the basis, I believe, for a new and distinctive conception of theology as essentially a critical discipline. It would be a discipline in which participating theologians carefully scrutinized their own faith-commitments in the context of similar examinations within a range of (competing) frames of orientation. A critical Christian theology of the sort I am envisioning here would, in contrast with more traditional "dogmatic" theologies, entertain—indeed pursue—the most radical sort of questioning of its own commitments. It would do so, however, as a contribution to a conversation in which similar radical exploration and questioning of other living orientations of life—humanism, Buddhism, secularism, Judaism, Marxism, feminism, positivism, Islam, Americanism, hedonism, and so on—was also being carried on. Attempting to examine and assess the major dimensions of one's own commitments as openly and critically as possible does not mean that one does not consider them to be a serious matter; on the contrary, precisely because of their import and consequence they deserve the most penetrating scrutiny we can bring to them. Critical theology, as an umbrella discipline within which the investigation of many (religious and secular) faiths was pursued, could provide the sort of context that would facilitate this kind of examination and assessment of diverse living frames of orientation today. Such examination could in turn lead to the development of proposals for significant reconstruction of some (or all) of these perspectives.

As envisioned here, critical theology would be a discipline that attempts to uncover and explore the major meaning-complexes that provide orientation within the cultures of modernity and postmodernity (including within the university itself), developing appropriate concepts and theoretical frameworks for articulating these studies sharply and clearly. In connection with this exploration, it would seek to develop criteria for comparing and assessing these frames of orientation and commitments to them, so that it would become possible to make responsible critical judgments with respect to them. This, in turn, would lead (we can hope) to the construction of proposals for transformations and improvements in these orientations that seemed appropriate and important. Theological reflection of this sort would address itself to some of the most important cultural problems faced by pluralistic societies such as our own: How should the diverse frames of orientation in these societies be understood? How is their fundamental human significance to be ascertained and assessed? Can these differing perspectives be encouraged to accommodate themselves to each other in ways that would be more beneficial to society as a whole? Moreover, it would be preparing intellectual tools and methods for helping to address humanity's major worldwide problem of finding ways to persuade the great diversity of human groups around the globe to live together more peacefully on our rapidly shrinking planet. It would be a "public theology,"[5] working at a very important public task.

The university is the best location for carrying on investigations of this sort, for at least three reasons. (1) The research resources that universities can make available for such studies are unparalleled. (2) The traditions of academic freedom, which developed in the universities and continue to be cherished there, provide an indispensable context and support for the sorts of sensitive (and possibly unpopular) proposals and investigations that might be pursued. (3) The ongoing conversations in universities about questions of knowledge and value, morality and meaning; about the arts, the sciences, and history in their complex interrelations with each other; and about the broad social and cultural issues of the day, provide a setting indispensable for such critical theological reflection. Many of the issues to which such reflection must address itself have been posed in their sharpest form in the universities; and it seems likely that the most direct and significant contribution of critical theology to culture at large could best be made, therefore, from within these institutions. It should not be forgotten, of course, that the cultures of universities themselves include important faith-assumptions, many of which become clearly perceptible only from social locations outside them. It would be essential to make certain that persons capable of discerning and articulating such meaning-complexes (and their potentially corrupting effects) participated fully and freely in university critical theology studies.[6]

Critical theology, as I am envisioning it here, is not a kind of *generic* theological reflection, unencumbered by any specific loyalties or faith-commitments. This sort of intellectual work can be carried on effectively only by persons who are well aware of what commitment to a specific way of life means, and what it may cost—that is, who know from within what a faith-commitment is, and what it demands of individuals and communities. I do not mean, of course, to suggest by this that only avowedly religious persons can reflect upon such matters: let me emphasize again that we are concerned here with a broadly human quality or dimension, one evident in Marxists and positivists as well as in Methodists and Muslims. Commitment is an *act* or *attitude*, a posture of selves and communities that is taken up deliberately (in some sense) and is maintained deliberately (in loyalty and through reaffirmation). To the extent that this is the case, important dimensions of commitment can be known and understood only in connection with and through the active participation of the one who seeks to know and interpret. If the objective of critical theological reflection is to gain some understanding of, and to assess the human significance of, this dimension of human life—our unavoidable involvement in (our faith in and commitment to) broad but specific patterns of living and doing, of thinking and being, of value and meaning—that reflection will have to be carried on by persons both self-conscious about such matters and trained to discern and to articulate them.

Critical theology, then, is not to be understood as a discipline that attempts to *transcend* all particular commitments and perspectives through developing a universal or generic theological stance (an impossible project, in my view). It is to be seen, rather, as a pluralistic discipline that attempts to investigate and understand, and to find ways of assessing and reconstructing, the actual orientational commitments to which women and men today give themselves. In a fully staffed university program of critical theology there would ordinarily be persons with, for example, Roman Catholic, Afro-American, Jewish, Buddhist, Protestant, feminist, humanist, and other commitments, all actively engaged in examination of the orientations characteristic of the communities with which they identify themselves. Moreover, these would be in ongoing conversation with each other and with others in the university, critically examining the whole spectrum of positions they were collectively exploring.

III

When I speak of a discipline of critical theology here, or a department of theology, I am, of course, using the term "theology" in a broad sense, as referring to a range of studies exploring matters of "ultimate concern" (Paul Tillich), foundational values, frames of orientation, ultimate points of reference, and the like; and I am suggesting that we need secularist and Marxist theologians as much as Christian and Muslim ones, and that it is important that all of these together should explore these problematics. This conception stretches the term "theology" a good bit beyond its ordinary use. I recognize, of course, that this term is most frequently employed in reference to specifically Christian thinking, and in addition that it is etymologically loaded in ways that may make it repugnant to thoughtful persons committed to other (religious or nonreligious) perspectives on life. "Critical theology," therefore, may not be the most apt name for the academic discipline I am proposing. Nevertheless, because the kind of intellectual inquiry with which we are here concerned is clearly an extension and generalization of major themes of traditional theological reflection, and since no more appropriate title appears to be readily available, it seems to me justifiable to use this characterization, at least for the present.

A significant transition or transformation in the self-understandings and faith-commitments of most theologians would be required if they were to take part in the sort of critical reflection here being contemplated. Instead of undeviating attention to the claims of their own faith, and unequivocal commitment to the truth of those claims, theologians here would find it necessary to take up a pluralistic stance from the outset, giving serious consideration to the claims of other perspectives and engaging in radical criticism and reconstruction of their own views, when this seemed appropriate and necessary. They would need to distance themselves in certain respects from the traditions that nourished them, taking a step back from simple unmediated commitment to them.

To many theologians (though they may not always admit this in their public pronouncements) this sort of move is not entirely new. All inquiries into faith-stances require consideration of questions of many different sorts. Some of these are potentially quite threatening, for one cannot really understand what is at stake in them without carefully examining the issues they pose for the faith under consideration; that is, without seriously exploring the alternatives they suggest. Theologians, thus, have always had to give some attention to ways of thinking that were significantly different from those endorsed by their own faith-community. Indeed, it has been precisely through taking into account such differing perspectives that they have, on occasion, been led to creative transformations of the traditions to which they were committed. In the work of critical theology, however, this concern with and interest in new ideas, questions, and criticisms would not be motivated primarily (as often in the past) by the necessity to protect one's tradition against enemies from without; it would, rather, be understood as constitutive of the theologian's proper task, a principal means of acquiring the critical insights and perspectives essential to the assessment and reconstruction of his or her own faith-orientation. Theologians have always, of course, appropriated insights and understandings from the likes of Plato and Aristotle, Kant and Hegel, Karl Marx and Sigmund Freud. In critical theological work such appropriation would not be regarded as peripheral to the main theological task, as optional and possibly somewhat questionable. Rather, it would be central to what the theologian was attempting to do: contribute to the critical examination and constructive transformation of the frame of orientation to which he or she was committed.

In the past, most Christian theological reflection (as noted above) took for granted a principle of authority. It was assumed that saving truth was present and available in the received tradition (especially the Bible) and that the theologian's task, therefore, was essentially a hermeneutical one: interpreting the essentials of that tradition as faithfully, cogently, and clearly as possible. In an approach of that sort, religious truth seems to be understood in certain respects on the model of property (as suggested in Chapter 12 above): it is a possession of the tradition (and not available elsewhere), and it can be passed on from one generation to the next. With such a view it is especially important that theologians interpreting the tradition be wary of distorting or diluting its truth with contaminants from without. Significant theological conversation under such circumstances becomes (for the most part) a matter internal to the faith-orientation itself, an essentially defensive activity concerned with protecting and preserving the truth that the tradition already possesses.[7]

The critical theology outlined here as an appropriate university discipline stands in sharp contrast with this somewhat provincial conception of theological work. Here the theological conversation is not conceived as largely internalistic, confined to persons with closely allied faith-commitments. It is, rather, essentially open, with persons of other commitments welcomed as indispensable partners. This sort of conversation is premised upon and encourages a notion of (religious) truth rather different from the traditional one just mentioned, a "pluralistic" or "dialogical" conception, as elaborated in Chapter 12. In this view, religious truth is not so much a possession owned by a particular tradition as it is something expected to emerge in the conversations among persons of differing faith-commitments—as they work together seriously in their collaborative effort to understand and assess their diverse frames of orientation. Instead of taking truth to be a property of particular words, symbols, propositions, or texts, which can be learned and passed on (more or less unchanged) from one generation to the next, it is here regarded as a living reality that emerges from within and is a function of ongoing conversation among a number of different voices. In this model, religious truth is something that develops and is transformed in unpredictable ways as the conversation proceeds. It is not to be expected, then, that some final, complete, or unchanging truth will ever be reached.

Although the recent increase in interreligious dialogue seems to suggest some movement toward a pluralistic and dialogical model of religious truth, I am not aware that a conception of this sort has been explicitly articulated elsewhere.[8] Even John Cobb, despite his emphasis on going "beyond dialogue" to "mutual transformation" of our several religious traditions,[9] appears to think of some central Christian truth-claims as virtually certain, as providing foundations for human life so secure that it is unlikely they will need to be critically reconsidered: "When the Christian witnesses to Christ in the dialogue, the hope must be to do more than provide minor insights. Christ is understood only when Christ becomes the center around which life is lived." Although Cobb holds that "our present need is to learn through dialogue . . . to rethink our beliefs," and that the "Christian purpose in the dialogue with Jews must be to change Christianity,"[10] it seems clear (at least in *Beyond Dialogue*) that he does not expect the reality made available through such fundamental symbols as "God" and "Christ" to be put into serious question. Moreover, Cobb apparently looks forward to a time when the present diversity of religious truth-claims can be grasped (to use the words with which he characterizes Alfred North Whitehead's goal) in a single "conceptuality through which every type of human experience could be understood"; and he continues to think of Whitehead's work as a large step in this direction.[11] It seems unlikely, then, despite his remarkable openness to insights and image/concepts from religious and cultural traditions other than his own, that Cobb would be willing to regard religious truth as pluralistic through and through, to be conceived in principle as a dialogical reality.

In my view only such a radically pluralist understanding of truth permits and encourages unrestricted openness in discussion of the most fundamental religious and human questions. Such a conception can be particularly helpful, therefore, in a situation in which persons of diverse religious and ideological commitments are attempting to understand and learn from each other's perspectives. Perhaps, as we increasingly move toward becoming a single interdependent humanity, this way of thinking about truth may come to be seen as appropriate for human religio-cultural life generally. In any case such a conception would greatly facilitate the sort of university theological conversation that I am proposing here, for with a pluralistic and dialogical understanding, all who participate in the conversation are accepted on (formally) equal terms. Thinking in this way would, accordingly, encourage just the kind of critical and constructive reflection that is appropriate in a nonsectarian university and is much needed today in our pluralized society. Religious truth has always emerged from conversations among many different voices over many generations. In advocating the establishment of a dialogical setting within the university to explore, evaluate, and reconstruct various religious (and secular) insights into and understandings of human life and its meaning, I am proposing that we attempt to carry out more systematically, deliberately, and constructively what has been going on throughout history in the rivalries and interchanges among persons and groups with different faith-orientations.

IV

I hope this essay will not be understood as simply an advocacy piece for the kind of theology to which I am myself committed; for it could then be dismissed by treating it as just one more sectarian view, in this case sectarian academicism. The discipline of critical theology as conceived here is intended to provide a context within which a *variety* of living religious and nonreligious faith-orientations could be openly and responsibly explored and assessed. I am not proposing either an elitist academic supertheology that seeks to swallow up all other positions or a metatheology that stands above or beyond the others. Critical theology, as I have sketched it here, is not one more particular theological *position* at all. It is, rather, an ongoing *conversation* about fundamental issues of life and death, conducted by persons representing diverse living faith-commitments (diverse theological positions) and having different methodological concerns. This dialogical structure, and this alone, can ensure its thoroughly critical character.

An ongoing conversation of this sort, devoted to exploration of deep-lying questions about our human ultimate loyalties and frames of orientation, would gradually (one could hope) move our great universities more fully to recognize, and address themselves to, the weighty role that human religiousness plays in the massive social and cultural problems with which we all today must come to terms.

Notes

Preface

1. Philadelphia: Westminster Press, 1981.
2. Cambridge, Mass.: Harvard University Press, 1993.
3. Ibid., xii.

Introduction: The Vocation of Theology

1. Edward Farley has published a very illuminating study of the history of theology in *Theologia: The Fragmentation and Unity of Theological Education* (Philadelphia: Fortress Press, 1983).

2. See esp. *Radical Monotheism and Western Culture* (New York: Harper and Bros., 1960).

3. For some discussion of both the possibilities opened up by monotheistic orientations, and the limitations of such orientations in comparison with polytheisms, see my recent book *In Face of Mystery: A Constructive Theology* (Cambridge, Mass.: Harvard University Press, 1993), chap. 6.

4. For further spelling out of this point, see *The Theological Imagination: Constructing the Concept of God* (Philadelphia: Westminster Press, 1981), chap. 3. For some reflections on the notion of critical theology itself, see chaps. 2 and 13 of this book.

5. In chap. 7, below, I will sketch in more detail my way of dealing with these issues.

Chapter 1. Christian Theology and the Modernization of the Religions

1. Such a view of human existence—as a "biohistorical" reality—is presented below in chap. 4.

2. Such reconstruction can be found below in chap. 6.

3. For further radicalization of this way of thinking of God, in light of the Buddhist notion of "emptiness" (*sunyata*), see chap. 9 below.

4. Further, more recent, reflection on this set of problems is to be found in chaps. 11–12, below.

5. This contention is fundamental to the understanding of Christian faith and theology worked out in detail in my book *In Face of Mystery*; and a much fuller argument for it will be found there.

6. Since this essay was originally written (1976), a number of other writers have also suggested moral/humanistic criteria as appropriate for assessing the claims of various religious traditions; see, e.g., the articles by Rosemary Radford Ruether, Marjorie Hewitt Suchocki, and Paul Knitter in *The Myth of Christian Uniqueness: Toward a Pluralistic Theology of Religions*, ed. John Hick and Paul Knitter (Maryknoll, N.Y: Orbis Books, 1987).

Chapter 2. Theology: Critical, Constructive, and Contextualized

1. Further (more recent) elaboration of my conception of trinity will be found below in chap. 9, and also in chap. 27 of *In Face of Mystery*.

Chapter 3. Religious Diversity, Historical Consciousness, and Christian Theology

1. Living and thinking out of a received tradition in this way is characteristic not only of Christians. It is in fact the common practice of most individuals and groups, including those who regard their commitments as fundamentally secular—e.g., Marxists, Freudians, nationalistic patriots, humanists. Men and women ordinarily orient themselves in life more or less unquestioningly in terms of the values and truths they have inherited from the community or communities with which they are most closely associated. Christian beliefs about God's revelation, however, deepen and harden this allegiance to tradition by giving it seemingly divine authorization and making it a matter of religious faithfulness and obedience.

2. I am, of course, not arguing here that there are no dimensions of Christian faith that motivate and sustain interaction with and sympathy for non-Christian persons and communities. The central Christian moral imperative that we love both our neighbors and our enemies as impartially as does God, who "makes [the] sun rise on the evil and on the good, and sends rain on the righteous and on the unrighteous" (Matt. 5:45), requires Christians to concern themselves directly and wholeheartedly with human suffering and need, wherever it is found. This imperative has in the past initiated not only worldwide missionary activity; it has also motivated efforts to alleviate physical suffering through the establishment of medical centers, through engaging in relief and rehabilitation work around the world, through providing agricultural assistance of many sorts, etc. But, however helpful these activities have been in breaking down barriers between Christians and others, they have not, for the most part, affected the Christian sense of *religious superiority*—they may even have enhanced it!—a sense grounded in the conviction that Christians have a unique and universally valid gospel needed by all peoples. It is a gospel whose ultimate truth is believed to be grounded in God's own special revelation in and through Jesus Christ. This is taken to set Christian faith apart from all other religious orientations in a special way. The barriers to genuine interreligious dialogue and community raised by these sorts of special truth-claims are what I am trying to overcome in the theological reflections presented in this book.

3. For further elaboration of my conception of the Christian categorial scheme and its reconstruction, see *In Face of Mystery*, esp. chaps. 6–7 and pp. 393–95, 423f.

4. The complications introduced by trinitarian thinking are briefly discussed in ibid., 423f.

5. For a discussion of the continuing positive usefulness of the concept of revelation, see *In Face of Mystery*, esp. 352–54.

6. In chap. 11 this point is developed comparatively with attention to the "root metaphors" governing, respectively, Buddhist and Christian orientations in life.

Chapter 4. A Biohistorical Understanding of the Human

1. Clifford Geertz, *The Interpretation of Cultures* (New York: Basic Books, 1973), 67, 49. The sociobiologists C. J. Lumsden and E. O. Wilson, with their concept of "gene-culture coevolution," appear to concur with this judgment; see their *Promethean Fire: Reflections on the Origin of Mind* (Cambridge, Mass.: Harvard University Press, 1983).

2. These five points are discussed more fully in *In Face of Mystery*, 127f. The subsequent pages of chap. 10 of that book provide qualifications and nuancing of these points; and the full ethic implied in them is sketched in chaps. 11–15.

Chapter 5. A Note on Evil, Salvation, and the Criterion of Humanization

1. Benedict Spinoza long ago noted that our concepts of good and evil were fundamentally anthropocentric (see his *Ethics*, Pt. IV).

2. Somewhat fuller discussion of some of these matters, but still much too brief, can be found in chaps. 8–10 of *In Face of Mystery*.

3. For a fuller elaboration of these matters, and an attempt to outline an ethics that accords with the criterion of humanization, see *In Face of Mystery*, chaps. 10–14.

Chapter 6. Mystery, God, and Human Diversity

1. *Foundations of Christian Faith* (New York: Seabury Press, 1978), 22 (trans. slightly altered).

2. The Bible is not entirely consistent in this emphasis; some "theophanies," for example, are reported in the Bible, but these seem to be more manifestations of God's *power* than of God in Godself. However, Enoch "walked with God" (Gen. 5:22, 24), we are told; God "appeared" to Abraham (Gen. 17:1; 18:1) and spoke to him; Jacob wrestled with "a man" all night long (Gen. 32:24), and then later said he had "seen God face to face" (32:30); and the book of Job ends with a powerful theophany after which Job declares, "Now my eye sees thee" (42:5). It is not evident, however, that these passages should be treated theologically as more than metaphorical, especially if one takes into account the explicit statements that humans cannot "see" God.

3. See, e.g., Sallie McFague, "Cosmology and Christianity: Implications of the Common Creation Story for Theology," in *Theology at the End of Modernity: Essays in Honor of Gordon D. Kaufman,* ed. Sheila G. Davaney (Philadelphia: Trinity Press International, 1991), chap. 1; see also her *The Body of God: An Ecological Theology* (Minneapolis: Fortress Press, 1993).

4. The concept of "steps of faith" is developed and elaborated in *In Face of Mystery*; see esp. 63f. and chaps. 17 and 29.

5. *Toward a New Philosophy of Biology* (Cambridge: Harvard University Press, 1988), 435.

6. "New Concepts in the Evolution of Complexity: Stratified Stability and Unbounded Plans," *Zygon* 5 (1970): 34.

7. Even so resolutely anti-teleological a writer as Ernst Mayr cannot avoid acknowledging that looking backwards from where we stand, an almost teleological movement comes into view: "Who can deny that overall there is an *advance* from the prokaryotes that dominated the living world more than three billion years ago to the eukaryotes with their well organized nucleus and chromosomes as well as cytoplasmic organelles; from the single-celled eukaryotes to metaphytes and metazoans with a strict division of labor among their highly specialized organ systems; within the metazoans from ectotherms that are at the mercy of climate to the warmblooded endotherms, and within the endotherms from types with a small brain and low social organization to those with a very large central nervous system, highly developed parental care, and the capacity to transmit information from generation to generation?" (*Toward a New Philosophy of Biology,* 251f.; emphasis mine).

8. It has recently begun to appear possible, even likely, that the continuous increase in entropy over time in the universe may itself, in the natural course of events, give rise—through the development of so-called dissipative systems—to complex forms of organization, eventually including living systems. "The picture that is emerging in . . . recent thermodynamic analyses . . . [suggests that] the movement of the [entropic] stream *itself* inevitably generates, as it were, very large eddies *within* itself in which, far from there being a decrease of order, there is an increase first in complexity and then in something more subtle—functional organization, . . . There could be no self-consciousness and human creativity without living organization, and there could be no such living dissipative systems unless the entropic stream followed its general, irreversible course in time. Thus does the apparently decaying, randomizing tendency of the universe provide the necessary and essential matrix (*mot juste!*) for the birth of new forms—new life through death and decay of the old" (Arthur Peacocke, "Thermodynamics and Life," *Zygon* 19 [1984]: 430).

9. In this chapter I am concerned almost entirely with bringing the symbol "God" into significant relation with contemporary cosmological and historical patterns of thinking, and the significance this has for our response to human diversity. Hence, I have not engaged here in critical deconstruction of the imagery (e.g., "creator/lord/father") constituting the traditional concept of God. In view of what we now know of the consequences of the employment of this traditional concept—its oppressiveness to women, its promotion of religious imperialism, its encouragement of various sorts of infantilism and immaturity, etc.—such deconstruction is indispensable today. This chapter, thus, does not present a full-blown reconstruction of the conception of God for today. My attempt to provide this can be found in chaps. 21–27 of *In Face of Mystery*.

Chapter 7. The Meaning of Christ in Our Pluralistic Age

1. Other potential implications of this symbol for theology—cutting much deeper than those taken up here—will be suggested below in chap. 9.

2. For brief examination of some of these New Testament texts, see *In Face of Mystery*, 382–85.

3. Peter C. Hodgson also works with what I call a "wider christology": "God was 'incarnate,' not in the physical nature of Jesus as such, but in the gestalt that coalesced both in and around his person—with which his person did in some sense become identical, and by which, after his death, he took on a new, communal identity. . . . For Christians the person of Jesus of Nazareth played and continues to play a normative role in mediating the shape of God in history, which is the shape of love in freedom. Jesus' personal identity merged into this shape insofar as he simply *was* what he proclaimed and practiced. But Jesus' personal identity did not exhaust this shape, which is intrinsically a communal, not an individual shape. . . . the *communal* shape of spirit is the true and final gestalt of God in history" (*God in History: Shapes of Freedom* [Nashville: Abingdon Press, 1989], 209f.)

4. In chaps. 25–27 of *In Face of Mystery* I work out a notion of incarnation in terms appropriate to the wider christology sketched here.

5. *Early Latin Theology*, ed. S. L. Greenslade, Library of Christian Classics, vol. 5 (Philadelphia: Westminster Press, 1956), 169.

6. Cf. Augustine: "I desire to know God and the soul. . . . Nothing more." "The Soliloquies" in *Augustine: Earlier Writings*, trans. J. H. S. Burleigh, Library of Christian Classics, vol. 6 (Philadelphia: Westminster Press, 1953), 26f.

Chapter 8. Shin Buddhism and Religious Truth

1. In chap. 12 I will sketch a pluralistic conception of religious truth (briefly mentioned in this chapter) as a way to address these issues more directly.

2. See "Thick Description: Toward an Interpretative Theory of Culture," in *The Interpretation of Culture* (New York: Basic Books, 1973).

3. *Towards a World Theology* (Philadelphia: Westminster Press, 1981), 15f., 20.

4. Ibid., 44.

5. *Shinran: An Introduction to His Thought* (Kyoto, Japan: Hongwanji International Center, 1989). All page references in the text of this chapter are to this volume.

6. The section of the original lecture (on which this chapter is based), in which a pluralistic conception of truth was sketched, has been dropped here, since this idea is more fully developed in chap. 12.

7. Additional discusssion of some of these matters and related issues will be found in chap. 10, below.

8. *Letters of Shinran*, ed. Ueda Yoshifumi (Kyoto: Japan: Hongwanji International Center, 1978), 26f.

9. Further discussion of some of these features of Pure Land Buddhism will be found below in the latter part of chap. 10.

Chapter 9. God and Emptiness

1. Others have also considered this problem. Cf., e.g., John B. Cobb, Jr., "Buddhist Emptiness and the Christian God," *Journal of the American Academy of Religion* 45 (1977): 11–25, and his *Beyond Dialogue* (Philadelphia: Fortress Press, 1982), esp. 110ff. See also the discussion of Cobb's position by David W. Chappell, "Comparing Dharmakaya Buddha and God," in *Spirit within Structure: Essays in Honor of George Johnston*, ed. E. J. Furche (Allison Park, Penn.: Pickwick Publications, 1983).

2. For some further discussion relevant to this matter, see the Introduction, Part One, and chap. 6, above, and chap. 11, below.

3. A full elaboration of the Christian categorial scheme can be found in chaps. 6–7 of *In Face of Mystery*.

4. For a wider view of Christ, see chap. 7, above.

5. See F. D. E. Schleiermacher, *The Christian Faith*, trans. H. R. Mackintosh and J. S. Stewart (Edinburgh: T. & T. Clark, 1928), §4.

6. Ibid., §§50–54.

7. See, e.g., Paul Tillich, *Systematic Theology*, vol. 1 (Chicago: University of Chicago Press, 1951), 204–10, 235–39. My own discomfort with such reification is indicated in chap. 6, above, and is a recurrent theme in *In Face of Mystery*.

8. The concerns of the mystical "negative theology," however, appear to be somewhat different from modern worries about the reification of God-talk. In modern writers, this problem is grounded principally in the epistemological consciousness of (1) the limits of human knowledge, and (2) the illegitimacy of humans making claims about any being which is beyond the world of human experience and knowledge; i.e., it is grounded in a certain agnosticism. In contrast, in the mystical tradition's *via negativa*, the rejection of reifying God-talk appears to be grounded in a powerful positive experience and consciousness of God's "super-reality." In this tradition, *agnosia* "does not mean a failure of the intellect, but its coalescence with God" (I. P. Sheldon-Williams, "The Pseudo-Dionysius," in *The Cambridge History of Later Greek and Early Medieval Philosophy*, ed. A. H. Armstrong [London: Cambridge University Press, 1970], 470). The early history of the notion of the *via negativa* can be conveniently traced by references to that term listed in the index of Frederick Copleston, *A History of Philosophy*, vols. 2, 3 (London: Burns, Oates & Washbourne, 1950, 1953).

9. *Summa Theologiae* I, Q. 13; *Summa contra Gentiles*, I, chaps. 30–36.

10. Reflection on some presuppositions of (as well as further implications of) this asymmetrical dualism will be found below in chap. 11.

11. For some discussion of the grammatical basis of the interest of western thought in *being*, see Edward O. Sisson, "The Copula in Aristotle and Afterwards," *Philosophical Review* 48 (1939): 57–64; Charles H. Kahn, "On the Theory of the Verb 'To Be,'" in *Logic and Ontology*, ed. M. K. Munitz (New York: New York University Press, 1973); and Hiroshi Obayashi, *Agape and History* (Washington, D.C.: University Press of America, 1981). For the first two of these references, I am indebted to the Th.D. dissertation of Abe Nobuhiko, "Semiotics of Self in Theology: A Comparative Study of James and Nishida" (Harvard University, 1992). Helmut Fischer, *Glaubensaussage und Sprachstruktur* (Hamburg: Furche Verlag, 1972) presents the fullest discussion (of which I am aware) of the thoroughgoing depen-

dence of a wide range of theological concepts (and problems) on basic characteristics of Indo-European grammar and syntax.

12. Cf. Nishitani Keiji: "Throughout the history of Western thought, from the days of ancient Greece right up to the present, being or existence has, by and large, been thought of in terms of either the category of 'substance' or that of 'the subject.' Whether animate or inanimate, man or even God, insofar as an entity is considered to exist in itself, to be on its own ground, it has been conceived of as substance. The concept of substance points to that which makes a thing to be what it is and makes it preserve its self-identity in spite of the incessant changes that occur in its various 'accidental' properties. Now *being* is looked upon as substance because, from the very outset, *beings* are looked upon as objects" (*Religion and Nothingness* [Berkeley: University of California Press, 1982], 110). See also Fischer, *Glaubensaussage*, 185–205.

13. See *Proslogium*, esp. chaps. 2–4. For a very illuminating discussion of Anselm's subtleties in these matters, see Karl Barth, *Anselm: Fides Quarens Intellectum*, trans. I. W. Robertson (London: SCM Press, 1960).

14. Cf.: "No one has ever seen God. It is God the only Son, who is close to the Father's heart, who has made him known" (John 1:18); "He is the image of the invisible God" (Col. 1:15).

15. Any reading of the *Church Dogmatics*, vol. 2: *The Doctrine of God*, with attention to the metaphors used to construct Barth's conception of God, will quickly make clear the overwhelming dominance of "lord" in his thinking.

16. For a general discussion of "emptiness," see Frederick J. Streng's *Emptiness: A Study in Religious Meaning* (Nashville: Abingdon Press, 1967). Not all Buddhist writers hold this all-encompassing view of *sunyata*, but some who do have themselves noted the possibility of connecting this concept with certain Christian notions; see, e.g., the reflections on the *kenosis* of Christ by Abe Masao: "The problem of the kenosis of Christ inevitably leads us to face the problem of the kenosis of God. . . . God's self-emptying [like Christ's] must be understood not as partial but as total to the extent that God's infinite unrelatedness has no priority over relatedness with the other and that God's self-emptying is dynamically identical with God's abiding and infinite fullness. . . . only through this total kenosis and God's self-sacrificial identification with everything in the world is God truly God. Here we fully realize the reality and actuality of God, which is entirely beyond conception and objectification. . . . This means that kenosis or emptying is not an *attribute* (however important it may be) of God, but the fundamental *nature* of God. God is God . . . because God is a suffering God, a self-sacrificial God through total kenosis. . . . everything, including the unjust and sinner, natural and moral evil, [is] forgiven, redeemed and satisfied, and the love of God completely fulfilled. The notion of the kenotic God . . . opens up for Christianity a common ground with Buddhism by overcoming Christianity's monotheistic character, the absolute oneness of God, and by sharing with Buddhism the realization of absolute nothingness as the essential basis for the ultimate" ("Kenotic God and Dynamic *Sunyata*," in *The Emptying God*, ed. John B. Cobb, Jr. and Christopher Ives (Maryknoll, N.Y.: Orbis Books, 1990), 13, 16–17; see also his "God, Emptiness, and the True Self," in *The Buddha Eye*, ed. Frederick Franck [New York: Crossroad, 1982]).

Cf. also the observations of Nishitani Keiji: "What is it like, this nondifferentiating love, this *agape*, that loves even enemies? In a word, it is 'making oneself empty.' In the case of Christ, it meant taking the form of man and becoming a servant, in accordance with the will of God, who is the origin of the *ekkenosis* or 'making himself empty' of Christ. God's love is such that it shows itself willing to forgive even the sinner who has turned against him, and this forgiving love is an expression of the 'perfection' of God who embraces without distinction the evil as well as the good. Accordingly, the meaning of self-emptying may be said to be contained within God himself. In Christ, *ekkenosis* is realized in the fact that one who was in the shape of God took on the shape of a servant; with God, it is implied already in his original perfection. That is to say, the very fact itself of God's being God essentially entails the characteristic of 'having made himself empty.'. . . Hating one's enemies and loving one's friends are sentiments typical of human love. They belong to the field of the ego. Indifferent love belongs rather to the realm of non-ego. And it is this characteristic of non-ego that is contained by nature in the perfection of God" (Nishitani, *Religion and Nothingness*, 58–59).

17. "Jesus of Nazareth is the medium of the final revelation because he sacrifices himself completely to Jesus as the Christ. He not only sacrifices his life, as many martyrs and many ordinary people have done, but he also sacrifices everything in him and of him which could bring people to him as an 'overwhelming personality' instead of bringing them to that in him which is greater than he and they" (Tillich, *Systematic Theology*, vol. 1, 136).

18. In my early *Systematic Theology: A Historicist Perspective* (New York: Scribners, 1968), I proposed the "nonresistance of God" as an attribute in counterpoint with the "power of God" (see 219–22; cf. 151–60).

19. For further elaboration of this general approach to the doctrine of the trinity, see *In Face of Mystery*, 296f. and chap. 27. See also chap. 2 above, theses 3–5.

20. The following paragraphs are an edited and abridged version of my extended response to the puzzlement of Rita Gross ("Response to Gordon Kaufman: 'This Is It: Nothing Happens Next,'" *Buddhist-Christian Studies* 9 (1989): 189–96) about my remarks on the trinity. The full discussion from which these remarks have been excerpted is in 196–201. Page references in the text and in this note refer to locations in this volume of the journal.

21. These two papers, "Ultimate Reality: A Christian View" (Cobb) and "Response to John Cobb" (Abe), were published in *Buddhist-Christian Studies* 8 (1988): 51–74. Citations for these writers' remarks refer to this volume.

Chapter 10. Some Buddhist Metaphysical Presuppositions

1. Monotheistic perspectives generally answer "no" to these questions (see chap. 5, above).

2. In discussion Takeda has said that it is really our attachments to *concepts* not *percepts* that is intended in his analysis. If so, my problems may be partially dissolved, though I am uncertain of this. In any case his paper uses the term "perception." Perhaps the problems I find in the paper arise in part out of difficulties in translating Japanese into English.

3. For a brief historical sketch of Pure Land Buddhism and its antecedents, including some discussion of other-power, see chap. 8, above.

4. For brief discussion of Amida's vow, and problems connected with this notion, see chap. 8 above.

5. This final paragraph was not part of my original paper. It has been adapted

from a comment of mine in the discussion that followed the presentation of the paper, and that was published along with it.

Chapter 11. Christianity and Buddhism: Searching for Fruitful Dialogue

1. This sort of notion, I think, underlies Takizawa's idea of "the primordial divine-human relationship" (Tanaka, 1), and also Akizuki's claim "that both Christians and Buddhists have common understanding as far as [the] inseparability and unidentifiability" of the "Transindividual and the individual" are concerned (Akizuki, 5). It also is presupposed in Tanaka's suggestion that it would be illuminating to bring the Buddhist notion of nothingness into relationship with the Whiteheadian notion of creativity, since both of these are "convertible transcendentals in terms of which we can conceive the God-World relationship" (Tanaka, 9).

2. Perhaps the best known proponent today of this way of addressing the problems posed by religious pluralism is John Hick. For brief discussion of his views, see chap. 12, below.

3. Such *historical* understanding of human religiousness is elaborated more fully above in chaps. 1, 3, 4, and 8.

4. This point is developed more theologically in chap. 6.

5. Use of the foundational metaphor specifically in Christian faith and thinking is elaborated more fully below in chap. 12. (See also the discussion of the creator/creation complex in chap. 9.) Recent emphasis on "irreversibility" (and thus foundational thinking) by some Buddhists would seem to be due to the impact of Christian patterns of reflection on their ideas.

6. It should be clear that this "religious foundationalism" is not to be confused in any way with the "epistemological foundationalism" so widely criticized today.

7. Stephen Pepper's term; see his *World Hypotheses* (Berkeley: University of California Press, 1942).

8. The predominance of this "holistic" metaphor in most Buddhist reflection and experience will be discussed further in chap. 12.

9. The construction of conceptions of the world and of God sketched in chap. 6 could be considered an example of such an "extrapolation and development" from our human biohistorical situation as today understood.

10. For this section of the chapter I draw on some previously unpublished reflections written in January 1985, after reading Robert Magliola's stimulating book, *Derrida on the Mend* (West Lafayette, Ind.: Purdue University Press, 1984). I am not (it should be said) qualified to vouch for the historical accuracy or adequacy of my interpretation here of Nagarjuna and the Buddhist "two truths" doctrine (though I hope, of course, that it is not entirely off the mark). Magliola, certainly, should not be held responsible in any way for the position I set out. I am including these reflections not because of their historical value but rather because they elaborate further, and seem to me to illuminate more fully, the interest that both Buddhists and Christians have in taking seriously the humanly finite character (emphasized throughout this book) of all our religious activities and theological work.

11. For observations about the significance of this point for human creativity, see chap. 12, below.

12. Further discussion of the concept of emptiness will be found (above) in chap. 9; see also Frederick J. Streng's *Emptiness: A Study in Religious Meaning*

(Nashville: Abingdon Press, 1967); and Abe Masao's "Kenotic God and Dynamic Sunyata," in *The Emptying God*, ed. John B. Cobb, Jr. and Christoper Ives (Maryknoll, N.Y.: Orbis Books, 1990), 27–36.

13. In *The Nature of Doctrine* (Philadelphia: Westminster Press, 1984), George Lindbeck seems to make a somewhat similar suggestion, but he appears to be unwilling to follow through consistently its implications for religio-metaphysical truth-claims (see esp. 63–69, 79–84).

Chapter 12. Religious Diversity and Religious Truth

1. *Pragmatism* (New York: Longmans, Green and Co., 1910), 240–42.

2. John Hick in particular (in recent years) has been developing a full philosophical articulation of this approach. An early statement of his emerging views is to be found in *God and the Universe of Faiths* (London: Macmillan, 1973); his most recent—and most thoroughly worked out—statement is in his Gifford Lectures, *An Interpretation of Religion: Human Responses to the Transcendent* (London: Macmillan, 1989). Here he concludes that the variety of doctrinal and other claims made in various religious traditions actually reflect "experiences that . . . constitute different ways in which the same ultimate Reality has impinged upon human life." He argues that the "important ideas within different traditions which on the surface present incompatible alternatives . . . can be seen on deeper analysis to be different expressions of the same more fundamental idea." For instance, where there are "rival conceptions of the Real as personal and as non-personal . . . the Real in itself is the noumenal ground of both of these ranges of phenomena." The various "mythic pictures [in the different traditions] are true in so far as the responses which they tend to elicit are in soteriological alignment with the Real. . . . [They] may each mediate the Real to different groups of human beings; and . . . in fact do so, as far as we are able to judge, to about the same extent" (pp. 373–75). Hick regards the position he has worked out as "pluralistic." In my opinion, however, it is utterly monolithic, for according to him there is a single universal philosophical framework—one known to John Hick and articulated by him quite straightforwardly—that takes up into itself *all* religious conceptions, however diverse, and explains that, as far as truth is concerned, they all come down to *essentially the same thing*. (The quotations just given make precisely this point.) Although this position resolves the problems of diversity by moving to a very abstract ultimate unity, there is much to be said for it. But I cannot go into that here. It obviously differs sharply from the "pluralistic" conception that I seek to articulate in this chapter (and this book as a whole)—a conception which goes so far as to attempt to conceive even what we call "truth" in thoroughly pluralistic terms. (Related discussions of the kind of interpretation of pluralism represented by Hick, and my objections to it, can be found in chaps. 8 and 11, above.)

3. For direct quotations from Smith that bear on these points, see chap. 8, above.

4. Further elaboration of this claim can be found above in chaps. 3, 8, and 11.

5. See Walpola Rahula, *What the Buddha Taught* (London: Gordon Fraser, 1967), 12–14.

6. See W. C. Smith, *Belief and History* (Charlottesville: University Press of Virginia, 1977); and *Faith and Belief* (Princeton: Princeton University Press, 1979).

7. For further discussion and some references bearing on this point, see chap. 9 above, esp. section II and nn. 11, 12.

8. Another, somewhat briefer, discussion of holism and foundationalism will be found in chap. 11, above.

9. It is important that this *religious* or *ontological* "foundationalism" not be confused with the *epistemological* foundationalism widely under attack today.

10. For a full discussion of the notion of emptiness, see Frederick J. Streng, *Emptiness: A Study in Religious Meaning* (Nashville: Abingdon Press, 1967). For a brief but pointed discussion, see Abe Masao, "Kenotic God and Dynamic Sunyata," in *The Emptying God*, ed. John B. Cobb, Jr. and Christopher Ives (Maryknoll, N.Y.: Orbis Books, 1990), esp. 27–36.

11. See Stephen Pepper, *World Hypotheses* (Berkeley: University of California Press, 1942).

12. Different sorts of elaboration of this point are to be found in chaps. 3, 6, 11, and 13.

13. In actual human life there are, of course, many different sorts of situations within which conversations occur, most of them shaped in important ways by differences in status, roles, class, gender, levels of education, and other factors that generate domination/submission power differentials of many sorts. These all affect the flow, content, freedom, and spontaneity of conversations in diverse (often hidden) ways. I bring up this truism to make clear that the model of conversation which I will be discussing in the next pages—the "free and spontaneous conversation that can occur among equals such as friends"—is very specific and doubtless somewhat idealized, and my observations with respect to it (about creativity, for example) obviously may not be applicable to other quite different conversational situations. I want to emphasize that this brief examination of certain features of some conversations should not, therefore, be interpreted as implying some sort of claim that *all* conversations satisfactorily model what human interaction should be: that, of course, would be quite false. (For some discussion of the problematic character of conversation as a model of ideal human interaction, see Sharon D. Welch, *A Feminist Ethic of Risk* [Minneapolis: Fortress Press, 1990], esp. chap. 7).

14. Cf. Wolfhart Pannenberg, *Anthropology in Theological Perspective* (Philadelphia: Westminster Press, 1985), 370–76.

15. I am aligning myself here with the recent increasing interest among philosophers and theologians in conversation or dialogue as a proper goal for intellectual activity, instead of the more traditional pursuit of truth. Cf., e.g., Richard Rorty, *Philosophy and the Mirror of Nature* (Princeton: Princeton University Press, 1979) and *Consequences of Pragmatism* (Minneapolis: University of Minnesota Press, 1982); Jürgen Habermas, *Theory of Communicative Action*, 2 vols. (Boston: Beacon Press, 1984, 1987); Richard S. Bernstein, *Beyond Objectivism and Relativism* (Philadelphia: University of Pennsylvania Press, 1985); Helmut Peukert, *Science, Action and Fundamental Theology: Toward a Theology of Communicative Action* (Cambridge: M.I.T. Press, 1984); David Tracy, *Plurality and Ambiguity* (San Francisco: Harper and Row, 1987).

16. It will be obvious to the readers of this chapter, I am sure, that many of the most difficult questions about (religious) truth are not touched on here: at most I have proposed a new model for thinking about such truth. I have presented no carefully wrought definition of truth, nor have I suggested criteria for judging what is true, or tests that truth-claims must meet. Obviously the question of how emerg-

ing new insights are to be evaluated would need to be taken up in any such further elaboration, and the importance of the pragmatic criterion of "fruitfulness" (in stimulating further dialogue and new moral and religious reflection, in suggesting new modes of action, etc.) would have to be carefully considered. These questions and many others need attention, but they cannot be addressed here. (Further discussion of the idea of pluralistic truth, and some of its implications for academic institutional arrangements, will be found in chap. 13.)

Chapter 13. Critical Theology as a University Discipline

1. For a thorough historical analysis and deconstruction of this traditional authoritarian approach to theology, see Edward Farley, *Ecclesial Reflection* (Philadelphia: Fortress Press, 1982). A somewhat earlier but very influential analysis of many of the issues raised by the authoritarian dimension in theological work is to be found in Van A. Harvey, *The Historian and the Believer* (New York: Macmillan, 1966). For my own brief analysis of, and reasons for rejecting, an authoritarian approach in Christian theology, see *Theology for a Nuclear Age* (Manchester: Manchester University Press, and Philadelphia: Westminster Press, 1985), chap. 2; *An Essay on Theological Method* (Atlanta: Scholars Press, 1975, third ed., 1995); and *In Face of Mystery*, Part I.

2. I will not in this essay illustrate my argument by taking up specific theological symbols and modes of analysis and showing how they can contribute directly to the critical reflective work of the university; such examples can be found scattered through my writings over the years. See, for example, "Metaphysical Assumptions and the Task of Theology," chap. 10 of *Relativism, Knowledge and Faith* (Chicago: University of Chicago Press, 1960); "The Secular Utility of 'God–Talk,'" chap. 11 of *God the Problem* (Cambridge: Harvard University Press, 1972); "The Idea of Relativity and the Idea of God" and "Metaphysics and Theology," chaps. 3 and 9 of *The Theological Imagination* (Philadelphia: Westminster Press, 1981); and virtually the entirety of *In Face of Mystery* (1993).

3. It must be granted, of course, that a focus of this sort on the importance of such dispositions as "faith" and "commitment" has a distinctly Christian (indeed Protestant) ring to it; and that utilizing this language *exclusively* to define the problematic with which we are here concerned, might well seriously bias the investigation of such orientations as, e.g., Buddhism or Judaism. The language in which I am seeking to call attention to the issues on which critical theology would focus—arising out of study of the basic forms of orientation in terms of which women and men today order and organize their lives—is indeed drawn from a particular tradition that has attended closely to these questions. And it would be important, therefore, in developing the program of critical theology proposed in this chapter, to make the limitations of this language—and the availability of alternatives to it emphasized in other traditions—itself an object of critical analysis and assessment.

4. In recent years Wilfred Cantwell Smith in particular has emphasized the usefulness (for religious and anthropological studies) of thinking of faith as a generic human quality; see especially his *Faith and Belief* (Princeton: Princeton University Press, 1979); *Belief and History* (Charlottesville: University of Virginia Press, 1977); and *Towards a World Theology* (Philadelphia: Westminster, 1981). But he is by no means alone in this emphasis: contemporary theologians such as H. Richard

Niebuhr, from *The Meaning of Revelation* (New York: Macmillan, 1946) to *Radical Monotheism and Western Culture* (New York: Harper and Bros., 1960) and the recently published *Faith on Earth* (New Haven: Yale University Press, 1989); Paul Tillich, *Dynamics of Faith* (New York: Harper and Bros., 1957); Bernard Meland, *Faith and Culture* (London: G. Allen and Unwin, 1955); and Schubert Ogden, *The Reality of God* (New York: Harper and Row, 1966), have all presented interpretations of faith as a generic human quality. They have been dependent on earlier writers such as William James, see especially *The Will to Believe and Other Essays* (New York: Longmans, Green and Co., 1897); Josiah Royce, *The Philosophy of Loyalty* (New York: Macmillan, 1908) and *The Problem of Christianity* (New York: Macmillan, 1914); and George Santayana (*Skepticism and Animal Faith* (New York: Dover, 1955). Recently James W. Fowler (along with some others) has utilized the generic notion of faith as a basic concept in the psychological study of human development; see, for example, *Stages of Faith: The Psychology of Human Development and the Quest for Meaning* (San Francisco: Harper and Row, 1981).

5. For recent discussion of the idea of "public theology," see Linell E. Cady, "A Model for a Public Theology," *Harvard Theological Review* 80 (1987): 193–212; and idem., *Religion, Theology, and American Public Life* (Albany: SUNY Press, 1993).

6. An interesting discussion of the many ways in which the university context that shapes much theological work today itself biases and obscures much Christian theological reflection (as seen especially from liberation theology perspectives) will be found in Mary McClintock Fulkerson, *Changing the Subject: Women's Discourses and Feminist Theology* (Minneapolis: Fortress Press, 1994), esp. chaps. 6–7; see also her article, "*Theologia* as a Liberation *Habitus*: Thoughts toward Christian Formation for Resistance," in *Theology and the Interhuman: Essays in Honor of Edward Farley*, ed. Robert Williams (Valley Forge, Penn.: Trinity Press International, 1995).

7. For brief discussion of such "internalist" practices by Pure Land Buddhists, see the concluding paragraphs of chap. 8 above.

8. There has been, however, increasing interest among philosophers and theologians in conversation or dialogue as a proper goal for intellectual activity, at least partially replacing the more traditional pursuit of truth. For references, see chap. 12, above, n. 15.

9. Dialogue "that does not intend to go beyond itself stagnates," he writes. "In a successful dialogue both partners are engaged in fresh thinking. . . . *Beyond* dialogue, I suggest, lies the aim of mutual transformation" (*Beyond Dialogue: Toward a Mutual Transformation of Christianity and Buddhism* [Philadelphia: Fortress Press, 1982], viii, xi, 48).

10. Ibid., viii, 51, 49.

11. Ibid., 147.

Index of Names

Index of Subjects